SCENARIOS OF
THE IMAGINARY

SCENARIOS OF THE IMAGINARY

Theorizing the French Enlightenment

Josué V. Harari

CORNELL UNIVERSITY PRESS

ITHACA AND LONDON

Cornell University Press gratefully acknowledges
a grant from the Andrew W. Mellon Foundation
that aided in bringing this book to publication.

First published 1987 by Cornell University Press.

International Standard Book Number 0-8014-1842-9
Library of Congress Catalog Card Number 86-24247
Printed in the United States of America
Librarians: Library of Congress cataloging information
appears on the last page of the book.

The paper in this book is acid-free and meets the guidelines for
permanence and durability of the Committee on Production Guidelines
for Book Longevity of the Council on Library Resources.

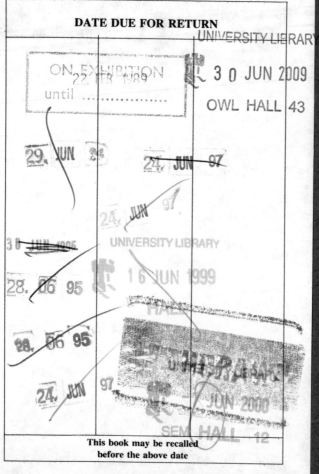

For Jack G. Goellner

Contents

Acknowledgments

I have benefited over the years from the advice and generosity of the two colleagues who first introduced me to eighteenth-century literature and critical theory: the late J. Robert Loy and the late Eugenio Donato. In many ways, this book is a testimonial to their enduring intellectual presence.

Three persons contributed an inestimable amount to this book. Wilda Anderson has been a constructive and untiring reader and a uniquely supportive companion during its long gestation. Susan Willey-Blood's opinion has been my chief test of the soundness of many a chapter. Anne Vila shared her insights and advice, as well as her translating and editorial talents, in more ways than I can hope to return: to her my debt is most profound. I was also privileged to have as close readers of the manuscript friends who were both sharp and generous critics: Homer O. Brown, Vincent Descombes, Marie Hélène Huet, François Roustang, and Edward Saïd. In addition, the expert readings of Thomas Kavanagh, Charles Porter, and Aram Vartanian provided me with valuable criticism.

This book was written in trying professional circumstances, and how much I have appreciated the amicable support of Carlos Alonso, David Bell, Suzanne Guerlac, David Hult, Michèle Richman, Marilyn Rugg, David Sachs, Pierre St Amand, Tobin Siebers, Richard Stamelman, and George Wilson (to name a few) cannot be overemphasized. I am also indebted to Eric Halpern and William P. Sisler for their active interest in this book. My editor at

Cornell, Bernhard Kendler, was his usual self: efficient, generous, and unstinting in his support.

Finally, I thank Lois Krieger and Kay Scheuer for their editorial improvements and Kitty Letsch for typing several versions of the manuscript, always cheerfully, if not always approving of certain Sadian passages.

An earlier version of Chapter 4 and substantially shorter versions of Chapters 5 and 6 have appeared in *Modern Language Notes*. I am grateful to The Johns Hopkins University Press for permission to make use of this material.

JOSUÉ HARARI

Baltimore, Maryland

SCENARIOS OF
THE IMAGINARY

Knowledge consists not in correct vision, but rather in the effective production of simulacra. In other words, knowledge is that which makes it possible to produce a *scenario*, that is, simulated situations; for knowledge is all the more true—"trustworthy"—if, by virtue of this deploying of theoretical fictions, it grants a greater control over the processes at hand.

Fiction stands for both "simulation" and "convention." It is a simulation sanctioned by a consensus: an agreement is made in order to substitute the reality of the referent with a discursive construct, and to reason about this eminently manipulable "model" as if it could represent in every respect what is still called the real.

Vincent Descombes, "La vérité du vrai"

today we have reached the point at which the excitement over the initial effects of theory is in the process of turning into its opposite: the ennui that comes from repetition. Our critical discourse reflects this "theory fatigue," and the multiplication of adherents has but one consequence: theory has become institutionalized as an academic discipline taught in universities and consequently subject to repetition. The result is a kind of theoretical monotony which is being acclaimed, noblesse oblige, as a mark of intellectual snobbery.

One caveat is in order. It is not my intention to advocate either a complete return to "old-fashioned" criticism or a rejection of theory, but rather to attempt to rediscover the early moments of theory—those moments when we are not bored, when we are under the spell of the surprise and excitement that come with first discovery. One might well ask whether such an enterprise is still possible after all the theoretical excesses to which we have been exposed in the last decade. The question becomes even more pertinent if one believes, as I do, that it is the very "advances" of theory (and the supersophisticated concepts it has yielded) which are blurring our present attempts to understand what theory is. Indeed, the theoretical presuppositions with which we work have built up a store of knowledge at the very heart of theory which is completely out of proportion to the texts that theory claims to clarify; in consequence, theory has become essentially a repeated commentary on its own discourse. Breaking up the "monopoly" held by theoretical discourse on itself would require a general remodeling of our theoretical configuration. Montesquieu used the surprised eyes of two supposedly naive Persian travelers to establish the distance necessary to make his commentary on French society. Based on this model, a supposedly naive return to the "beginnings" of theory might produce an effect of surprise, that is, a *series of divergences* vis-à-vis the strict exigencies of today's theoretical discourse—divergences that could help us understand the constitution and function of (a) theory from its moment of inception. Let me illustrate this suggestion by way of an example.

The modern controversy that has taken place between Claude Lévi-Strauss and Jacques Derrida concerning the question of writing is well known. The reader certainly recalls the famous "Writing Lesson" in which Lévi-Strauss relates the scene of the

Nambikwara Indian chief who acts out the "comedy" of writing in order to appropriate power.[3] Lévi-Strauss's analysis of this episode leads him to conclude that deviousness and violence accompany the "advent" of writing among Nambikwara Indians.[4] On the basis of this conclusion, he develops his thesis of the exploitation of man by man through writing. In turn, Derrida takes this same Nambikwara episode as a point of departure in *Of Grammatology* in order to demonstrate that Lévi-Strauss's ethnological discourse is produced according to concepts and values integral to occidental metaphysics, a metaphysics that invokes the fall into evil after the primordial innocence of the Verb.[5] According to Derrida, if writing can be said to embody the ethical instance of violence, it is not, as Lévi-Strauss would like us to believe, the result of an outside violence that imposes itself upon an inherent natural goodness characteristic of a people without writing. Derrida's brilliant theoretical development rests upon two interrelated points: (1) the Nambikwara writing lesson does not represent a scene of the "birth" of writing, but is only an instance of its mimetic importation; and (2) corruption existed among the Nambikwara Indians long before writing's advent, hence violence is not an exclusive quality of writing (as opposed to the innocence of speech).

Let me stop for a moment here and, in counterpoint to the Lévi-Strauss/Derrida theoretical debate, recount a fictional version of the advent of writing. It appears in the *Abrégé de toutes les sciences à l'usage des enfants*, dating back to 1790. In response to the question "Who invented writing?" asked in the chapter "Languages," the child is told an Indian myth that I quote here in its entirety:

> The *Hebrews*, struck by the wonder of the art, called it *Dikduk*, that is, subtle invention. The *Americans*, upon seeing someone read from a book, at first believed that paper could speak.
>
> There is a story told about an Indian slave who, having been entrusted by his master with a basket of figs and a letter to be sent to

[3] *Tristes Tropiques*, trans. John and Doreen Weightman (New York: Atheneum, 1974), 294–304.

[4] "Writing and deceit had penetrated simultaneously in their midst" (*Tristes Tropiques*, 300).

[5] "The Violence of the Letter: From Lévi-Strauss to Rousseau," in *Of Grammatology*, trans. G. Spivak (Baltimore: Johns Hopkins University Press, 1976).

an acquaintance, ate a portion of the figs along the way, and gave the rest along with the letter to his master's friend. When he read the letter and discovered that it promised a greater quantity of figs than he had actually received, the master's friend accused the slave of having eaten the missing figs and read to him the contents of the letter. Yet the Indian swore that it was not so, cursed the letter, and accused it of bearing false witness.

A few days later, the slave was charged with a similar task, with a letter that indicated the precise number of figs that he was to transport. As he was walking, he again ate some of the figs; but this time, in order to avoid being accused as he had been earlier, he took the precaution of hiding the letter under a big rock, and then felt assured that if the letter did not see him eat the figs, it could not tattle on him. Yet upon reaching his destination, the slave was berated more severely than ever; the poor fool ended by confessing his deed, and from that point on he bowed down in awe and admiration before the magical power of writing.[6]

This is a very pretty tale: each element corresponds to a recognized function of writing as described in the Lévi-Straussian version: hierarchization, exploitation, violence, economic power, inclusion of its holders in a quasi-religious secret. And yet this story also corresponds to the Derridian critique of writing. We see clearly here that the elements of exploitation on the one hand, and of corruption and deviousness on the other hand, *precede* writing; and that in the end writing functions as *pharmakos*—a violent corrective to the violence of corruption. This story illustrates the contemporary controversy of writing more effectively than any explanation offered by the most talented professor, even if he undertook to explain all of *Tristes Tropiques* and *Of Grammatology*. This is not to be construed as a reproach to Lévi-Strauss or Derrida, as I believe both authors would agree that if each of them had tried to dream up a fiction to illustrate his respective theory of writing, he could find no more fitting a scenario. *Bricolage*, or *différance* and *supplément*, comprise theory as it is currently understood; but what can we say about the tale of the Indian, and his reaction to the advent of writing? Strictly speaking, the Indian has no theory of writing; consequently he can formulate only an inadequate interpretation for what writing is or

[6] *Abrégé de toutes les sciences à l'usage des enfants*, new ed., rev., corrected, and enlarged by M. Varney (Paris: Volland, 1790), 35–36.

accomplishes.[7] Had this Indian been promoted to the rank of modern theorist, however, he probably would have produced out of this scenario both Lévi-Strauss's theory of writing and its Derridian critique.

The main point of my argument is that the Indian—as layman or as theorist—*does not draw his scenario out of a theory, but instead does just the opposite:* the scenario comes first and the theory, when there is one, follows, just as Lévi-Strauss's theory of writing is grounded in the Nambikwara writing scenario, and Derrida's critique is grounded in Lévi-Strauss's fictionalization of this scenario. In epistemological terms, the question comes down to asking ourselves how it happens that, in literature and in the human sciences, theory imposes itself as theory. A first answer is to look for a supporting scenario, for I would argue that underlying every theory there exists a corresponding scenario—real or imaginary. In general, we critics fervently want to believe that we deduce interpretation from theory; yet the overwhelming evidence shows that theory is merely the justification, *after the fact,* of a scenario—in most cases a personal scenario—which imposes itself upon an author for reasons that may or may not be related to the substance of the resulting theory.

In support of this view, all the authors examined in this book— Montesquieu, Rousseau, Sade, Freud, and Lévi-Strauss—are "theorists" who elaborated fictional scenarios, from *The Persian Letters* to *Tristes Tropiques.* The scenarios constitute an effort either to ground theoretical representations whose conceptual matrix eludes their authors, or to pursue these theoretical representations beyond their limits (with the exception of Sade, who attempts both). What is peculiar to all the aforementioned authors is the sort of *imaginary pre-text* which, even when it seems absent, continues to operate in their theoretical texts. In each of these cases, and in a precise and predictable manner, the imaginary functions as the pre-text of theory; and all the consequent theoretical texts obey—indeed, depend on—this pre-text in their economy as well as in their structure. But to recognize that imaginary scenarios infuse the very constitution of theory is tan-

---

[7] Note that, with respect to the act of interpretation, the Indian who has no theory does the same thing, but in reverse, as the critic who knows nothing but theory and who, likewise, cannot interpret any further than to repeat a theory and all of its related suppositions.

tamount to realizing that the authority of theory is rooted in personal predilection, and not in morality, or knowledge, or science, as is generally believed.

In keeping with this view of the nature of theory, I will seek to trace back each of the theories in question, in order to uncover the generative phantasms that underlie it, and thereby to "diagnose" those moments when the fictional scenario, as the product of an individual's imaginary, catches on and becomes theory. I shall not fully develop the question of *why* certain scenarios have the power to take hold and become the founding theories of widely accepted social and human disciplines. Rather, I shall concentrate on *how* the imaginary intervenes at founding moments in the constitution of certain influential "modern" theories, such as: the theory of government, originating in Montesquieu with the "metaphor" of the body; the theory of education born from Rousseau's delirium in *Emile*; the theory of psychoanalysis, which can be traced to an imaginary motivation (with regard to his dead father) that induced Freud to choose the Oedipal theory over the seduction theory of neurosis;[8] and the theory of structural anthropology, identified in a Lévi-Straussian psychodrama (in the form of a play in *Tristes Tropiques*), which can be read as the symptom of his anguish when confronted with reality. Two chapters on Sade at the center of the book analyze the operation of the theoretical imaginary as such.

The striking similarity in all of the theoretical texts examined here is that the imaginary intervenes at the same point and at the same moment—in each case, a moment of "crisis" for the author. This crisis is resolved by a scenario that marks the first step in the constitution of the theory. As I shall seek to demonstrate, the passage from personal scenario to theory depends on a fundamental repression of reality. The imaginary fulfills this function by developing scenarios that replace and preempt the real—scenarios that then produce theory by resolving or carrying

---

[8] It is no accident that Freud once remarked: "It almost looks as if analysis were the third of those 'impossible' professions in which one can be sure beforehand of achieving unsatisfying results. The other two, which have been known much longer, are education and government" (*Analysis Terminable and Interminable,* in *The Standard Edition of the Complete Psychological Works of Sigmund Freud,* ed. James Strachey [London: Hogarth Press, 1953–74], 23:248.

to another register the antinomies and complications of the real. Hence at the same time that theory claims to stand for the real, the discourse of theory inscribes within itself the very repression of the reality it promotes. This intertwining of the theoretical and the real should surprise no one, for broaching the question of theory leads necessarily to the question of the real—not only the recently debated question of its representation, but more important, the philosophical question of the *nature* of the real. It would be appropriate here to make some preliminary remarks concerning this last point.

From Proust to Beckett, from Blanchot to Derrida, from Freud to Lacan, and from Lévi-Strauss to Girard, our entire literary and theoretical modernity has been predicated upon a nostalgia for the real. Reality is accused either of never showing its true face (as in Derrida's concept of *différance,* in which the advent of the real is always deferred) or else—when reality does make itself manifest—of always falling short of itself (in Lacan's case, the symbolic is the only instance capable of revealing the real; and similarly, for Girard, the reality of desire is always elsewhere, mediated by the desire of a model). Thus the real in and of itself is void, an empty space that gains meaning not from its own manifestation, but always through allusion to an otherness. In Clément Rosset's succinct formulation: "[The real] is a negation of the here in favor of the elsewhere."[9] It would be illuminating to pursue a longer study of the link between theory and the lack inherent in the real—our conception of the real as lack—which defines our modernity. Although I will limit myself here to a tentative formulation of this link, I would like to suggest that the notion of totality—or of closure—which generally accompanies theory is one of the phantasms that serve to satisfy our metaphysical demand for a global and integral hold on the real. As a phantasm of totality, theory covers up this "lack in the real" which is inscribed at the center of our modernity.

---

[9] " . . . dénégation de l'ici au profit de l'ailleurs" (in *Le philosophe et les sortilèges* [Paris: Minuit, 1985], 39). Rosset is also quick to diagnose the reason underlying the keen interest evident on the part of contemporary criticism in problems specific to language: one of language's primary traits is that it evokes the real by means of a substitute that is *not* the real; in other words, language evokes the presence of the real through its absence.

With this in mind, I should like to conclude by recalling a famous Lacanian formula: *Le réel c'est l'impossible.*[10] For my purposes, I shall transform it into a more appropriate theoretical statement: the real is that which is impossible to grasp, at least in the discourse of theory as we know it today. Theory's incapacity *really* to account for the real or, rather, its inadequation to the demands of the real—therein lies the source of the malaise evident among contemporary theorists who are hypersensitive to this question by virtue of the fact that, even if they do not attain the real through their theories, the real gets to them, like it or not. The question is hardly new. Nonetheless it could be instructive to situate it in a different register (the realm of the imaginary or, as we shall discover, the closely related realm of narcissism) and to reformulate it—to move away from the assumption that theory faithfully represents the real, and to focus instead on the "lie" by which theory claims to uphold the real, only to suppress it.

The strategic juxtaposition of the readings proposed in the pages that follow is an attempt to bring to light—and to resolve—these concerns, and to suggest in the process a kind of genealogy of theory which nevertheless questions the credibility of the theorizing process. It is this epistemological question of theory's advent as theory which underlies the structure of *Scenarios of the Imaginary.* I have tried to bring together in this book my interest in the Enlightenment as the period in which the epistemological foundations of the human sciences were first laid down, and my concern with the nature of theory—and its natural corollary, contemporary literary theory.

[10] *Séminaire XI* (Paris: Seuil, 1973), 152; cf. also p. 253.

I

Transcoding

> Critics have the advantage of choosing their enemies, at-
> tacking their weak points, ignoring their strong ones, and
> making problematic through contradiction what the others
> had advanced as certain. They act like incompetent generals
> who, failing to conquer a country, pollute its waters.
>
> Montesquieu, *Mes pensées*

In response to the books that were inundating his desk, Voltaire
once remarked gloomily that the writer who seeks originality is
compelled to be eccentric and that the writer who wishes to avoid
eccentricity is bound to be unoriginal. The situation of criticism
today is not very different from that which Voltaire diagnosed in
the eighteenth century, for we continue to think of the opposition
between traditional and modern criticism in terms of to the two
poles of eccentricity and unoriginality, except that original criticism is today labeled deconstructive. Keeping past and present
practices in perspective, I will, first, briefly situate the critical
approach I have adopted in this book.

Over the past decade, deconstruction has rejuvenated the field
of criticism by providing its practitioners not only with the seal
of fashionability—an accomplishment not to be underestimated—
but also with genuinely original insights. It would not be an ex-
aggeration to say that we will never again be able to read a text
in the naive manner we once did, before deconstruction appeared
on our critical horizon. This is not to say that deconstructive

criticism as it is generally practiced today, even in the most sophisticated Franco-American academic circles, does not have its
drawbacks. Foremost among them is the fact that, methodologically speaking, deconstruction has led its students to an impasse:
the impasse of "interpretive aporia" whereby all deconstructive
readings repeat, in the particular way allowed by each text, the
same movement of an aporia. Such a critical stance is paradoxical
in that we, as critics, must reconcile the fundamental contradiction that governs all deconstructive readings: we must recognize
that, by its very nature, deconstructive indeterminacy undercuts
any authoritative explanation of what we say about a text. At the
same time, we must continue to find ways to *explain* those texts
that we deem indeterminate, unfollowable, or indecipherable.

Against this view, traditional criticism rests on the assumption
that originality need not be an attribute of the critic, since the
interpreter attains the meaning of the work by substituting himself for the author. As a result, any notion of original interpretation is suppressed in favor of the meaning that the author
intended for the work; and all interpretation that deviates from
the language of the author is considered deforming, because it
reflects another era, another language, and ideas that have no
relation whatsoever to the conditions of the work's production.
In the final analysis, only the author can account for the meaning
of the text, and the context—sociological, historical, biographi-
cal—enters into play only in order to reinforce one view of the
author rather than another.

Another and perhaps more fruitful way of highlighting the differences between traditional and modern criticism is to note that,
whereas the former focuses on the author at the expense of the
text, the latter tends to "forget" the text to the benefit of the
reader's or the critic's own fabulations. When we read a work
from a modern perspective, it is always *we* who read it, and given
that the work needs us in order to constitute itself, it is evident
that all literary works are read in a different manner depending
on the different epochs and the different people who read them.
Modern criticism rests on a postulate which holds that the work
does not have *a* meaning, but rather several meanings; that is,
the work constitutes a reserve of possible meanings, which readers
of each different generation will concretize into determinate significations. The corollary to the above postulate is that each time

a critic comments on a work, he discovers a part of himself in what his words express about the work in question. The critic speaks, and whether he believes that he interprets or simply states what the work is about, he inevitably says what he himself is about. Hence critical commentary functions here either as a misprision on the part of the critic about himself (*pace* Lacan), or, at the other extreme, as the critic's instance of self-recognition and self-understanding. Criticism then becomes less a search for values such as communication, a world view, an ideology, a truth, than a way for the critic to constitute himself as a "psychoanalytic" subject through the act of writing. The danger of this type of criticism is not that it does not work; on the contrary, as the most immediate form of therapy available to academics, it is an infallible enterprise. Hence the text exists only insofar as it is the object of the critic's imaginary endeavors, entrusted to any and all possible readings. One is reminded of Roland Barthes's opening lines in *S/Z*—"There are said to be certain Buddhists whose ascetic practices enable them to see a whole landscape in a bean'"[1]— where reading is defined as the importation of meaning into a text that has no meaning "in itself."

What is at stake in this conception of the text is the very essence of postmodern critical activity. Indeed, to posit that the text is a working space where meaning is in permanent migration is to declare that critical activity *cannot* receive its legitimacy from the text being commented upon. There is, however, a positive corollary to this viewpoint: criticism is not viewed anymore as a secondary activity in relation to the so-called primary text, but instead is understood as a productive activity, which "creates its subject-matter."[2] Hence, the critic is also a producer of text. Unfortunately, this notion has been stretched to the limit by many postmodern critics, who often "read" texts only to "misread" them, in order to indicate something about the power of critics to make the reader believe their own fictions.

What does it all add up to for the critic who wishes to avoid both the traditionalist pitfall, which consists of talking carefully around but not about the text, and the modernist delusion, which

[1] *S/Z*, trans. Richard Miller (New York: Hill and Wang, 1974), 3.
[2] Edward Saïd, "Roads Taken and Not Taken in Contemporary Criticism," in *The World, the Text, and the Critic* (Cambridge, Mass.: Harvard University Press, 1983), 154.

deems anything of concern to the critic as central to the text? What kind of critical alternative are we left with, in view of the recent transformations that have occurred within the field of criticism?

In an undogmatic and methodologically enlightening article entitled "La littérature, le texte et l'interprète," Jean Starobinski suggests that since all critics are essentially interpreters of texts, one would gain some insight into the nature of critical activity by going back to the etymology of the word *interpreter*—from the Latin *interpres*—which means an agent between two parties, a broker, a negotiator:

> If one is to believe historians of language, the word *interpres* originally signified someone who acts as a mediator in a transaction, a person whose assistance is necessary in order for an object to change hands, on the condition of payment of a fair price. Thus the *interpres* assures a *passage*. At the same time, he assures that the exact value of the exchanged object is recognized, and participates in the transmission process in order to vouch that the object is passed on to its new owner in its *integrity*.[3]

The interpreter-critic, according to this definition, assures the passage of a message from the language of the text into another, critical language; and during or through this passage, he is responsible for preserving what Starobinski calls the "integrity"— the nature, quality, tone, direction—of the message. The operation of passage, of transferral, of conversion, from the language of the text to the language chosen by the critic (a language borrowed from another domain, another field, or another medium, i.e., another code) is an operation of transcoding.[4]

Transcoding consists of converting the lexical network of the text into another lexicon, in such a way that the initial message, or messages, takes on another layer of meaning, in accordance

---

[3] "La littérature, le texte et l'interprète," in *Faire de l'histoire: Nouvelles approches,* ed. Jacques Le Goff and Pierre Nora (Paris: Gallimard, 1974), II, 180.

[4] "Transcoding" is a neologism constituted by the verb "to code" and the prefix "trans." According to *Webster's,* "to code" means "to transform a message according to a code"; and the prefix "trans" means "(a) on the other side, to the other side, over, across" [denoting transition or passage]; "(b) so as to change thoroughly; (c) above and beyond" [both (b) and (c) denote transformation].

with a language and value system that conforms to the intellectual needs of the critic and to the imperatives of the times. This conversion, however, is not based on a simple operation of equivalence, but rather on two simultaneous movements, of passage and of transformation, which one could subsume under the concept of translation—translation of one level of meaning dictated by the code of the text, into another level of meaning inscribed in the chosen critical code. And I use translation here in all of its etymological polysemy as defined by *Webster's Third World International:*

1. to change from one condition to another [transformation];
2. to change from one language into another [passage];
3. to change into another medium or form [conversion];
4. to put into different words; to interpret [interpretation];
5. in mechanics, the motion in which every point of the moving object has simultaneously the same velocity and direction of motion [homology].

Translated into the language of the text, "translation" means that the message would conserve its movement, its organization, its character—that is, its integrity. The notion, or the sense, of the integrity, of a text's significance does not exclude a certain transformation intrinsic to the passage from one code to the other, because the critic both transforms and produces significance, by his choice of the code into which he converts the text's message(s), and by his manner of inscribing it in the new code. In that sense, transcoding does not consist of a simple assimilation or equivalence, but rather of an activity that both broadens the domains of knowledge of the text and protects its integral nature.

But rather than pursue mere abstractions, let me give a concrete illustration of a transcoding activity by analyzing an episode from Marivaux's *La vie de Marianne* dealing with what one could rightly call the scenario of the first seduction.[5] The scene takes place between Valville and the young Marianne. Valville openly declares that he is in love with Marianne. She, however, does not take his declaration at face value. Although she suspects his motives, she refuses to see the real implications of his speech. She

---

[5] I am indebted to Eugenio Donato for bringing this passage to my attention and discussing its implications.

eliminates all sexual connotations and chooses to understand his advances as that of an obliging gentleman.

> As for Valville, I had nothing indeed to reproach him with; I had inspired him with sentiments to my advantage, but his love was not so violent as tender. When a man admires a woman in this manner in the beginning of his passion, it makes his heart honest, inspires him with virtue, makes him delight in the refined pleasure of loving and respectfully treating the object of his affections.
>
> This is the first employ of a tender, generous mind; it dresses the object of its love in all imaginable dignity and worth *[et il n'est pas dupe]*. Nor is it without its own reward, for it is attended with great delight; and where a man is incapable of this happiness, he himself is the greatest loser.[6]

When he becomes insistent, she counters with subtle rationalizations and delaying tactics. She is not, however, indifferent to the fact that Valville's desire is directed toward her body, and the ambiguity of her behavior appears clearly when he goes ahead and kisses her hand.

> In the midst of this tender pleading, he again took my hand in his *[que je lui laissais prendre]*, and with all the warmth of the most passionate lover, kissed it every moment, always begging pardon for his presumption. But the best of the joke was that I thought that was a sufficient *[fort bonne]* reparation for the fault and innocently enough *[de la meilleure foi du monde]* received it as such, when, in fact, it was only repeating the fault, though I don't think either of us perceived it: *[entre deux personnes qui s'aiment, ce sont là des simplicités de sentiment que peut-être l'esprit remarquerait bien un peu s'il voulait, mais qu'il laisse bonnement passer au profit du coeur]*.[7]

Finally, though she knows that Valville's advances demand a decision on her part, Marianne manages to avoid making any com-

---

[6] Pierre Carlet de Chamblain de Marivaux, *The Virtuous Orphan*, trans. W. H. McBurney and M. F. Shugrue (Carbondale: Southern Illinois University Press, 1965), 58–59; *La vie de Marianne* in *Romans* (Paris: Pléiade, 1949), 134. The English translation of *La vie de Marianne* is often inaccurate and incomplete. I have incorporated missing portions of the text in brackets. References will be given in the text both to the English translation and to the French original.

[7] *Orphan*, 59; *Marianne*, 135.

mitment and leaves the whole question up in the air "with the best good faith in the world" *(de la meilleure foi du monde)* as she puts it.

Most critics of Marivaux, including the best ones, have had serious problems describing Marianne's behavior, especially her flirtatious attitude toward her numerous suitors. In general, discussion has centered upon the nature of the division of the Marivaudian psyche, how it constantly oscillates between conscious and unconscious motivations, and thus results in the psychological instability of Marivaux's characters. Georges Poulet, for instance, attributes Marianne's loss of identity to her divided psyche, a situation that explains, in his view, the contradictory nature of her actions and the fact that she remains as incomprehensible to herself as she is to the reader.[8] This also accounts for her permanent state of (moral) confusion, the mixture of innocence and guilt, of knowledge and ignorance, which characterizes her. In a twenty-five-page letter-response to Poulet's article, Leo Spitzer argues that, on the contrary, Marianne follows a unified path; yet he also admits that it takes Marianne an inordinate amount of psychological virtuosity to protect her virtue from breaking down at every turn (of the page): "She follows a temporal line from which she will never deviate despite the calculations, listlessness and coquetry that she exhibits at certain moments; moreover, this line is traced by her social and moral advancement."[9] Spitzer concludes that Marianne is fundamentally sincere if at times deceptive, deeply honest even though dishonest, yet she remains somewhat honest in her dishonesty!

Their flourishes notwithstanding, Poulet and Spitzer are really not that far apart in their views, for Marianne exists on an existentially contradictory mode: Marianne really *is* what she is not, and she *is not* really what she is. So goes their reasoning. What kind of conclusion are *we* to draw from their critical acrobatics? The question is made even more acute when one realizes that the best Marivaudian critics of the last thirty years have been debating, each in his or her own way, the question of Marianne's behavior.[10]

[8] Georges Poulet, "Marivaux," in *La distance intérieure* (Paris: Plon, 1952), 8.
[9] Leo Spitzer, "A propos de *La vie de Marianne* (Lettre à M. Georges Poulet)," *Romanic Review* 44:2 (1953), 105–6.
[10] See Peter Brooks, *The Novel of Worldliness* (Princeton: Princeton University

Far away from Marivaux, some two hundred years later, let us transpose Marianne into a somewhat homologous situation, which raises an analogous problem. This similar and yet more familiar (because of its contemporaneity) situation is now articulated according to a different code, behavioral rather than sociomoral, and into a different lexicon, that of philosophy rather than that of literature:

> Take the example of a woman who has consented to go out with a particular man for the first time. She knows very well the intentions which the man who is speaking to her cherishes regarding her. She knows also that it will be necessary sooner or later for her to make a decision. But she does not want to acknowledge the urgency; she concerns herself only with what is respectful and discreet in the attitude of her companion. She does not apprehend this conduct as an attempt to achieve what we call "the first approach" . . . she does not wish to read in the phrases which he addresses to her anything other than their explicit meaning. If he says to her, "I find you so attractive!" she disarms this phrase of its sexual background; she attaches to the conversation and to the behavior of the speaker, the immediate meanings, which she imagines as objective qualities. The man who is speaking to her appears to her as sincere and respectful as the table is round or square, as the wall covering is blue or gray. The qualities thus attached to the person to whom she is listening are in this way fixed in a permanence like that of things *[permanence chosiste]*, which is none other than the projection of the strict present of the qualities into the temporal flux. This is because she does not quite know what she wants. She is profoundly aware of the desire which she inspires, but the desire crude and naked would humiliate and horrify her. Yet she would find no charm in a respect which would be only respect. In order to satisfy her, there must be a feeling which is addressed to her whole being *[personne]*.[11]

Press, 1969); Lionel Gossman, "Literature and Society in the Early Enlightenment: The Case of Marivaux," *MLN* 82:4 (1967); Nancy K. Miller, *The Heroine's Text* (New York: Columbia University Press, 1980); Ronald Rosbottom, *Marivaux's Novels* (Rutherford, N.J.: Fairleigh Dickinson University Press, 1974); and especially René Girard's "Marivaudage and Hypocrisy," *The American Society Legion of Honor Magazine* 34:3 (1963).

[11] Jean-Paul Sartre, *Being and Nothingness: An Essay in Phenomenological Ontology*, trans. Hazel E. Barnes (New York: Philosophical Library, 1956), 55.

This passage is from the chapter on bad faith in *Being and Nothingness*. In it, Sartre presents one of the three patterns of bad faith which he has identified. According to Sartre, the woman in bad faith acts on her first date in such a way as to strip her partner's behavior of its meaning by reducing him to the status of an object. Consequently, everything he says or does is perceived and received according to a "frozen" temporality, that is, fixed in a permanence like that of things. This non-possibility of temporal flux excludes de facto the possibility of any sexual development or repercussion. Yet for this woman, a desire that translates itself into feelings of pure respect is not satisfactory either, for she longs for a desire that addresses itself "to her whole being," that is, a desire that aims at her body as well. But she can only tolerate this desire to the extent that it is absorbed into more refined forms of "esteem, respect, and admiration" and thus loses its specificity. While our modern Marianne attempts to disentangle the psychological dilemma she is experiencing, the partner suddenly makes his move.

But then suppose that he takes her hand. This act of her companion risks changing the situation by calling for an immediate decision. To leave the hand there is to consent in herself to flirt, to engage herself. To withdraw is to break the troubled and unstable harmony which gives the hour its charm. The aim is to postpone the moment of decision as long as possible. We know what happens next; the young woman leaves her hand there, but she *does not notice* that she is leaving it. She does not notice because it happens by chance that she is at this moment all intellect [esprit]. She draws her companion up to the most lofty regions of sentimental speculation; she speaks of Life, of her life, she shows herself in her essential aspect— a human being [personne], a consciousness. And during this time the divorce of the body from the soul is accomplished; the hand rests inert between the warm hands of her companion—neither consenting nor resisting—a thing.

We shall say that this woman is in bad faith. But we see immediately that she uses various procedures in order to maintain herself in this bad faith.... But she permits herself to enjoy her desire, to the extent that she will apprehend it as not being what it is, and will recognize only its transcendence. Finally while sensing profoundly the presence of her own body—to the degree of being disturbed perhaps—she realizes herself as *not being* her own body, and she contemplates it as though from above as a passive object to which events can *happen* but which can neither provoke them nor avoid them because all its possibilities are outside of it.[12]

Sartre's conclusion: bad faith is the art of forming contradictory concepts that unite in themselves an idea and the negation of that idea. Bad faith takes up the two fundamental aspects of human reality—facticity and transcendence—not in order to coordinate them, but rather to affirm facticity in the mode of transcendence and transcendence in the mode of facticity, in such a way, says Sartre, that at the very moment in which an individual apprehends the one, he or she is suddenly faced with the other.

Let me now return to Marianne and try to reappraise, in the light of Sartrian bad faith, the meaning of the dualism of the Marivaudian character.

On the one hand, Marianne is an object in the world, a body, a facticity in the Sartrian code; on the other hand, she is a subjectivity detached from its physical expression—a transcendence. The dualism is obvious in the encounter with Valville. As an object in the world, her body experiences sensations that Marianne enjoys very much ("I thought that was a very good reparation [being kissed again]"), yet she refuses to take any responsibility for her action ("I received it [the reparation] as such when in fact *[sans m'apercevoir]*, it was only repeating the fault") and claims total integrity insofar as she is a subjectivity that is not corrupted by her body's behavior. Thus to Valville's question "Tell me frankly whether my [love] declaration is agreeable to you or not?" Marianne asserts that she cannot even understand the question, because she "scarcely knows what love is."[13]

Sartrian bad faith helps the reader to sort out the two distinct frames of signification (moral and social), while also showing how these two levels remain intertwined in Marianne's consciousness, in such a way that she can play on the discrepancy produced between the pure image (on the moral register) of the self for the self, and the flirtatious image (on the social register) of the self for others. Marianne thus conceives of her physical/social behavior as detached from the intentionality of her consciousness. As she sees it, her integrity—Sartre would say her *liberté pleinière*—

---

[12] Ibid., 55–56.
[13] *Orphan*, 60; *Marianne*, 135.

lies not in her social being, which belongs to the public domain, but in her inner self, which, by virtue of the dualism she maintains, can never be touched by her suitors. This operation explains why she can go on believing that she has upheld her virtue—or the image she has of it—throughout the social apprenticeship that constitutes *La vie de Marianne.* In more than one way we can see that both Poulet and Spitzer had addressed the real issue, yet neither succeeded in explaining it because each had grasped only partially the two-faced psychological mechanism that regulates Marianne's behavior.

But there is more to Marianne's bad faith. In order for her to keep steady the "distanced" quality she intends to give to her physical actions and reactions, Marianne must, as we have seen, be able to hide the game completely from herself; that is, she must *be in total bad faith.* Yet this total bad faith toward her inner self creates a situation of half delusion that leads her to play her flirtatious social role with the utmost conviction and sincerity. Consequently, her outer self behaves in the mode of good faith—*de la meilleure foi du monde,* as Marianne says. Marivaux implies, therefore, that in every situation of bad faith there is necessarily a counterpart of good faith. Valville illustrates the limiting point of this intertwining: he ends up being sincere by dint of being in bad faith. Valville, who epitomizes the seducer's bad faith throughout the scene, is no longer aware of his own actions by the end of the episode; he has sincerely fallen in love with Marianne: "I don't think either of us perceived it [the kissing mistake]: among two persons in love. . . . " Marianne's behavior illustrates the reverse, yet complementary, operation. Her frame of mind reveals that the process she is undergoing occurs at a level of consciousness that is only *half* deluded. In other words, Marianne is quite aware—that is, as much aware as she is unaware—of her situation. She takes Valville's opening move precisely for what it is, she recognizes in all sincerity that she enjoys receiving his so-called "declarations of love," and she remains well aware of the flirtatious nature of her response to him: "So sensible was the joy the dear declaration gave me. . . . This I would willingly have hid from Valville. . . . What he had just said required an answer; but joy naturally renders us silent *[ce n'était pas à ma joie à la faire],* and this sensation possessed my whole soul. I thought my present situation of mind not proper to be discovered, and I continued speechless with eyes cast down....I answered with a sigh [*Un petit soupir naïf précéda ma réponse, ou plutôt la commença].*"[4]

To the extent that Marianne recognizes and consciously assumes her flirtatious behavior, she is indeed in good faith. Yet as a consciousness that acknowledges its worldliness, she is distinct from the worldly Marianne who had faced Valville earlier. The Marianne who is sincere has "exchanged" her being in the world; she escapes her worldliness to the extent that she can contemplate it from a distance and reflect on every one of her worldly acts. At the same time, she takes pride in her sincerity, a sincerity that puts her *beyond* her worldliness, and transforms it into an exterior, "incidental" attribute; in her perspective social flirt signifies only "natural feelings that perhaps the mind would notice if it exercised itself to it, but that it prefers to forego for the benefit of the heart."[5] Thus Marianne's sincerity consists in acknowledging what she is, in order precisely not to be what she is. And she uses this kind of reasoning ("A sin confessed is half pardoned") to justify her behavior each time she commits a moral infraction in the novel.

But what, then, is objective sincerity if not a phenomenon of bad faith? Down to every detail, Marivaux intuitively demonstrates the structural similarities between good and bad faith, and the impossibility of experiencing the one without falling into the other. If, for instance, a critic wished to discuss from a philosophical point of view the concept of sincerity, he would have to go and read certain pages of Sartre's *Being and Nothingness.* But if this critic wished to see a demonstration of the workings of "sincerity in the making," Marianne's complex psychological games would provide far more interesting fieldwork for him to understand the complex complementary/adversary relationship between sincerity and bad faith. In other words, Marivaux's analyses allow us in turn to give a reverse decoding of the route traveled by Sartre in moving from his conception of bad faith to that of sincerity. I shall not attempt here to transcode Marivaux's insights back onto Sartre's conceptual argumentation; it suffices to recall Sartre's

---

[14] *Orphan,* 59; *Marianne,* 134–35.
[15] Elided in English version; *Marianne,* 135 (my translation).

concluding remarks on sincerity to convince the reader that what Marivaux had intuitively sensed, Sartre makes explicit:

> Who cannot see that the sincere man constitutes himself as a thing in order to escape the condition of a thing by the very same act of sincerity? . . . Thus the essential structure of sincerity does not differ from that of bad faith since the sincere man constitutes himself as what he is *in order not to be it [l'homme sincère se constitue comme ce qu'il est* pour ne l'être pas]. This explains the truth recognized by all, that one can fall into bad faith through being sincere.[16]

Except for the fact that Marivaux limits himself to psychological observations, whereas Sartre claims an ontological significance for bad faith, both reach the same conclusions in their respective analyses. I might also add here that each displays an equal amount of bad faith in his own endeavor: each author wants his character to retain a sense of moral responsibility for her actions (this wish is more explicit in Marivaux than in Sartre), yet each admits that his character is clearly not aware of her deepest motivations. Obviously, this is a contradiction that cannot be resolved—except on the mode of mitigated good faith, as Marivaux would say!

I have gone to such length in detailing this example of transcoding activity to illustrate the full implications of such an approach. In my view, transcoding is both a restorative and an innovative activity, because it affirms the strong identity of the "original" text and also allows it to be taken up by a new discourse that draws the text to the level of the critical discourse. Yet, to be complete, transcoding cannot be limited to a one-way passage or transformation. The transcoding activity by which one interrogates a text always includes an implicit reflection on itself. All laws that are valid for the text being transcoded are equally valid for its transcoding counterpart. Every act of transcoding is a questioning of both the transcoding and transcoded texts, for it is an activity that postulates that a text is always the transformation not only of another text, but also of another transformation. Transcoding is effective because it accounts for the most fun-

---

[16] *Being and Nothingness,* 65.

damental aspects of a text—the frames of significance that are codified into the textual network; it is incorporative because it converts what seems to be unimportant or marginal material into pertinent dimensions of the text; finally, the transcoding activity is fundamentally interdisciplinary in nature. To interpret a language through another language—be it the language of another form, medium, discipline, or symbolic system—is a necessity that will undoubtedly confront literary critics more often in the future. For if, as we have learned, the function of literature is to subvert its own language, then a critical discourse that is *solely* literary is bound to become highly problematic. Not only will this discourse lack the necessary autonomy and distantiation, but it will also soon run into a serious dilemma, because the critical language it employs to interpret literature is that very language literature itself undermines.[17] Moreover, the specificity of a purely literary approach, which can only be achieved by means of a rejection of all other fields judged to be "outside" the field of literature, is perhaps an easy but unsatisfactory way of dealing (by dismissing them) with the theories and problems of other fields. Against this view, I would argue that transcoding is one way to break out of the literary impasse that faces literary criticism. Transcoding involves borrowing model texts from other disciplines; in so doing, it establishes the passage between disciplines as a dialogue of equals and demonstrates the reciprocal power that each discipline possesses to provoke and modify the discourse of the other. Thus transcoding questions the "unwritten law" of disciplinary differences, a law that divides "all texts into two categories, the ones that do the interpreting and the ones that are there mostly to be interpreted."[18] Ultimately, one can hope that it will succeed in overturning disciplinary barriers.

Methodological purists will undoubtedly denounce the theoretical "eclecticism" called for by transcoding. To this objection, I would like to answer: first, this eclecticism is not *"pot au feu*

[17] This explains the interpretive aporias that characterize contemporary critical discourse: they reflect the critics' late realization of the subversive and ambivalent nature of literary language.

[18] René Girard, "Narcissism: The Freudian Myth Demystified by Proust," in Alan Roland, ed., *Psychoanalysis, Creativity, and Literature: A French-American Inquiry* (New York: Columbia University Press, 1978), 308.

theorizing,'"[19] for, on the contrary, it requires both conceptual clarity and methodological rigor; and second, such eclecticism is more interesting and challenging than methodological purism precisely because there is not only one direction to follow, but rather several. Consequently, the critic must choose, and to choose necessarily involves risks that critics do not like to take. To adopt an already defined approach "lock, stock, and barrel" is a much safer (if more passive) alternative. But that is more a question of critical temperament, which I shall not debate here.

Yet I should mention some of my reasons for favoring a transcoding activity. First, it obviously allows the critic to work with concepts in a less narrow fashion, and in certain cases, to retrace the path (or paths) that led to the development of these concepts. Second, the absolute noncommunication between fields, and even between schools of criticism (defended in the name of the specificity of a critical language), leads inevitably to the ossification of concepts and theories that never leave the confines of an isolated discipline. What results is a degradation of concepts into labels, and those who adhere to these labels are under the *illusion* of holding total mastery over their conceptual vocabulary. Hence concepts are no longer subject to interrogation and become, instead, membership cards. In contrast, transcoding cannot be categorized within any given ideology, field, or school: it is an activity that keeps concepts in a kind of permanent anamorphosis—an anamorphosis that allows one to revive and reinscribe an "old" concept within a different field or system. The third, and perhaps most important, reason I favor transcoding is that it is neither a technique nor a method nor a theory, but rather an approach, by which I mean a procedure of the mind. In other words, I have no "secrets" to unveil that would show which texts lend themselves to a particular kind of transcoding. If the function of a technique is to be applied, the function of a method to be transposable and repeatable, and the aim of a theory to be "true" (in the sense that theory is always dogmatic, and the function of dogma is to be true), then the function of an approach is to speculate, that is, to run the risk of being wrong. And whereas meth-

---

[19] The term is coined by Clifford Geertz in *The Interpretation of Cultures* (New York: Basic Books, 1973), 4.

odology and theory have tended, in recent years, to close our critical horizon more than they have stimulated it,[20] transcoding as an approach avoids this closure by its very eclecticism.

There are no ground rules for this two-way activity. It generally occurs according to one's range of reading. For example, I owe the Marivaux/Sartre reading to a discussion with Eugenio Donato. In the case of Rousseau, I was struck by the vocabulary that appears systematically in *Emile*—*besoin, demande, désir*—and that anticipates the very meanings Lacan gave to these terms. What would result, I wondered, if *Emile* were to be "transcoded" into an analytic situation *avant la lettre*, only with the pedagogue in the place of the analyst? That is, if *Emile* were read both as a "cure" and as a treatise on the formation of delirium and its transformation into (pedagogical? psychoanalytical?) theory? In reverse fashion, since transcoding works both ways, what does Rousseau teach us about the modalities of the pedagogical "perversion" that Lacan practiced with his students—his own "imaginary" disciples? After all, the two conceptual apparatuses are identical: Lacanian analytic practice does indeed owe much to Rousseau.

In the same vein, Lévi-Strauss should be read not as the descendant of Rousseau, as he claims, but as the descendant of Sade. When we read Sade in counterpoint to Lévi-Strauss, we understand that Sade's obsession with incest is not gratuitous. It is not the result of a personal obsession with his mother, mother-in-law, sister, or aunt; nor is it the result of the eighteenth-century literary vogue of fictionalizing incest. Rather incest, as the exemplary attribute of the father, is the key to Sade's conception of both culture and desire. Sadian incest is not only the cultural operator that illuminates Sade's philosophy, but also an operator that undoes and demystifies the exogamic construct by which Lévi-Strauss has revolutionized modern anthropology. The in-

[20] We should recall Roland Barthes's warning: "Some speak greedily and urgently about method. It never seems rigorous or formal enough to them. Method becomes Law, but as this Law is deprived of any effect that would be outside of itself (no one can say, in the 'human sciences,' what a 'result' is) it always falls short.... As a result, a work that unceasingly declares its will-to-methodology always becomes sterile in the end. Everything takes place inside the method, nothing is left to the writing" ("Écrivains, intellectuels, professeurs," *Tel Quel* 47 [1971], 9–10). It is for this reason that the master thinkers of contemporary theory—Derrida, de Man, Lacan, Foucault—appear only in the margins of my work.

sights we have gathered by transcoding Sade's incestuous construct onto Lévi-Strauss's exogamic construct are confirmed by our Freudian reading of the theory of structuralist anthropology as it is presented in *Tristes Tropiques*. In this case, however, my approach differs, in that I seek to decode both psychoanalytic and structuralist knowledge by following the very premises and procedures that are standard to psychoanalysis and structuralist anthropology.

There are other issues I could bring up as I describe my approach; but as I write, the one question that hovers in my mind is whether or not, in the final analysis, the results of any critical activity are not preconditioned from its very first step. To paraphrase Leo Spitzer, can the critic avoid concluding that to interpret always amounts to having already interpreted?[21] In making this point, Spitzer was fond of quoting the well-known remark of Pascal's God: "Tu ne me chercherais pas si tu ne m'avais pas trouvé." To which I will respond, by way of a concluding statement, with a no less well-known comment by Augustine, one that I believe better qualifies critical activity: "A considerable part of discovery is to know what you are looking for."

[21] Spitzer's formula is "to read is to have read, to understand is equivalent to having understood" (*Linguistics and Literary History* [Princeton: Princeton University Press, 1967], 87).

2

Eclectic Affinities:
Imaginary/Theory/Reality

> I hold it true that pure thought can grasp reality, as the ancients dreamed.
>
> Albert Einstein

Physical Reality and Theory

In 1966 Richard Feynman, the distinguished professor of physics at the California Institute of Technology who had been awarded the Nobel Prize the year before, gave a lecture to the American Association of Teachers of Physics. The subject of his lecture was "What Is Science?" Undoubtedly, when a paper boasts such a title and is delivered by a Nobel Prize winner there is an underlying expectation that the world will finally hear the answers to some, if not all, of the unresolved questions concerning the nature of science and scientific inquiry. One would naturally have expected Feynman to offer the most serious remarks, arguments, and demonstrations regarding his conception of science. But instead, Feynman spoke of his childhood and explained, among other things, how his father had taught him the rules of logic and of set theory by playing with old bathroom tiles of various colors, and how, as a student, he had discovered an application of one of the most difficult principles of analytic geometry—the problem of intersection—while in the Cornell

University cafeteria listening to two girls discussing how to knit argyle socks.[1] Feynman's bathroom tiles and knitting stories illustrate the kind of creative moments not uncommon to the scientific unconscious. Einstein once remarked that he was brought to the formulation of relativity theory in large part because he kept asking himself questions concerning space and time that only children would pose. And he often referred to the "wonder" he experienced when, as a child of four or five, his father showed him a simple magnetic pocket compass. In his autobiography, written at the age of sixty-seven, Einstein recalls how he was marked his whole life by this childhood experience—the mysterious constancy of the compass needle, seemingly free from any action-by-contact, yet always returning to the same direction.

There would be much to say concerning the profundity of these privileged moments for anyone interested in the genesis of scientific ideas. Gerald Holton has taken up this question in his two books on the nature of the scientific imagination.[2] Through a number of case studies he demonstrates convincingly that the process of building a scientific theory often follows criteria that lie completely beyond the sphere of science proper—chance events, personal motivations, esthetic considerations, or philosophical presuppositions—and which play a crucial role in the decisions leading to scientific discovery:

> Cases abound that give evidence of the role of "unscientific" preconceptions, passionate motivations, varieties of temperament, intuitive leaps, serendipity or sheer bad luck, not to speak of the incredible tenacity with which certain ideas have been held despite the fact that they conflicted with the plain experimental evidence, or the neglect of theories that would have quickly solved an experimental puzzle. None of these elements fits in with the conventional

---

[1] Richard P. Feynman, "What Is Science?" *The Physics Teacher* 7:6 (1969). In his recent book *Surely You're Joking, Mr. Feynman* (New York: Norton, 1985), Feynman writes that the Feynman diagrams for which he won the Nobel Prize can be traced to his observations of a young man throwing a wobbling plate in the air in the Cornell cafeteria. One can only conclude that, for anyone who seeks scientific illumination, the place to be is...the Cornell cafeteria.

[2] *Thematic Origins of Scientific Thought. Kepler to Einstein* (Cambridge, Mass.: Harvard University Press, 1973) and *The Scientific Imagination: Case Studies* (London and New York: Cambridge University Press, 1978).

model of the scientist; they seem unlikely to yield to rational study; and yet they play a part in scientific work.[3]

What is remarkable in the above passage is not the "unscientific" characteristics themselves, but the fact that circumstances that are completely independent from the empirical and analytical content of scientific work could affect, and even *preempt*, scientific decisions. Holton shows, for instance, that the willful neglect of Einstein's relativity theory of 1905 exhibited by both Henri Poincaré, who was technically the best-prepared scientist in the world to understand Einstein's theory, and Max Abraham cannot be attributed, in the case of either researcher, to scientific ignorance. Quite to the contrary, both men understood only too well Einstein's relativity theory; the problem was that, in their view, it offered a vision of reality that conflicted with their *esthetic* judgment.

> [Abraham] found the abstractions of Einstein disgusting in his very heart. He loved his absolute ether...as a youth loves his first passion whose memory cannot be erased by any later experience.... His opposition was grounded in physical, fundamental persuasions to which he, purely in accord with his feelings, held as long as possible. ...[As Abraham himself once said], against the logical coherences he had no counterarguments; he recognized and admired them as the only possible conclusion of the plan of general relativity. But this plan was to him thoroughly unsympathetic, and he hoped that the astronomical observation would disconfirm it and bring the old, absolute ether again into honor.[4]

What we learn from the Poincaré-Abraham-Einstein controversy is that scientific disagreement, or in this case antagonism, is primarily the result of diverging esthetic convictions. Abraham's accommodation of feelings and data had led him to conceive of an esthetically pleasing (to him) reality, revealed through his ether theory; Einstein's theory proposed instead a "disgusting ...unsympathetic" view of reality. And although the latter's theory was mathematically irrefutable, Abraham still hoped that observational evidence would invalidate the relativity theory and

[3] *Thematic Origins*, 18.
[4] M. von Laue and M. Born, *Physikalische Zeitschrift* 24 (1923), 52; quoted in Holton, *The Scientific Imagination*, 10.

reinstate in its place his first "love." This kind of sentimental attachment, which is anything but scientific, is not unusual among scientists. And it explains far better than many analytic arguments the obstinate character of certain scientific views. A more contemporary example is the comment of the physicist Paul Dirac, who in the face of experimental evidence remained confident in his belief that "a theory that has some mathematical beauty is more likely to be correct than an ugly one that gives a detailed fit to some experiments."[5] Before following in the footsteps of Dirac, Robert Oppenheimer had youthful ambitions to become a writer and a literary critic; he once attempted to strangle his friend, the drama critic and art historian Francis Fergusson, for mocking his prose! After this literary debacle, Oppenheimer opted for physics, not because of the advances of that science, but because it offered at the time an elegance in the formulation of problems and "a beauty that no other science could match."[6]

Poincaré, Abraham, Dirac, Oppenheimer—the list speaks for itself—thus articulated in scientific terms their own esthetic ideals and values. Einstein's attempt to restructure science went further: although his theory subscribes to an esthetic ideal of simplicity,[7] it could also be read as an attempt on Einstein's part to rememorate the state of youthful innocence during which he had believed in the reality of biblical events and dreamed of a social environment that broke with the harsh reality surrounding him.[8]

I should explain, at this point, that if I have gone to such length to describe the relationship between the personal and the scientific views of Einstein, Abraham, or Dirac, it is not because I wish to emphasize or pursue the psychobiographical track. Rather, what interests me in this interrelationship is the fact that, in all the above cases, personal vision—be it esthetic, sentimental, or dreamlike—has infused the theoretical view so as to make it

[5] Dirac is quoted in Holton, *Thematic Origins,* 26.

[6] In *Robert Oppenheimer. Letters and Recollections,* ed. Alice Kimball Smith and Charles Weiner (Cambridge, Mass.: Harvard University Press, 1980), 155.

[7] "What I'm really interested in is whether God could have made the world in a different way; that is, whether the necessity of logical simplicity leaves any freedom at all" (quoted in Holton, *The Scientific Imagination,* xii).

[8] See Holton's insightful commentary on Einstein's autobiographical account of his shattered youthful dream, in *Thematic Origins,* 109–10.

conform with each scientist's personal (and personalized) perception of reality. The individual theories accommodate feelings and sympathetic correspondences (Abraham), ideals of plenitude (Poincaré), of simplicity and purity (Einstein), or of beauty (Dirac); but none of the theories seems concerned with, or accountable to, real phenomena. Each theoretician provides a personal and thus divergent "version" of reality, but they all seem to agree on one point: there is little room in any of their theories for factual reality. Einstein is even more "extreme": he denounces Mach's theory of knowledge precisely because it supposes an overly close connection between observed facts and concepts.[9] Einstein recommends instead that one disregard "phenomenological physics" in order to achieve a theory that could attain more unity in its foundations: "Physics is an attempt conceptually to grasp reality as it is thought independently of its being observed. In this sense one speaks of 'physical reality.' "[10] If we follow Einstein to the letter, we would have to conclude that "physical reality" is *the lie by which theory assumes, and substitutes itself for, the real.* This would come as no surprise to Einstein, who analyzes this very "dilemma" in his essay "Motiv des Forschens" of 1918.[11] Some key passages from it, in which Einstein discusses his view of the motivations that lead people to do research in science, follow:

> What led them into the Temple [of science]? The answer is not easy to give, and can certainly not apply uniformly. To begin with, I believe with Schopenhauer that one of the strongest motives that leads men to art and science is flight from the everyday life with its painful harshness and wretched dreariness, and from the fetters of one's own shifting desires...

> With this negative motive there goes a positive one. Man seeks to form for himself, in whatever manner is suitable for him, a simplified and lucid image of the world, and so to overcome the world of experience by striving to replace it to some extent by this image. This

[9] "Physics and Reality," in *Ideas and Opinions of Albert Einstein,* trans. S. Bargmann (New York: Crown, 1954).

[10] "Autobiographical Notes," in P. A. Schilpp, ed., *Albert Einstein: Philosopher-Scientist* (New York: Harper, 1959), 81.

[11] This address given in honor of Max Planck appears summarized in translation in Holton's *Thematic Origins,* 376–78.

is what the painter does, and the poet, the speculative philosopher, the natural scientist, each in his own way.

The theoretical physicist's picture of the world is one among all the possible pictures.... The physicist must content himself from the point of view of subject matter with "portraying the simplest occurrences which can be made accessible to our experience"; all the more complex occurrences cannot be reconstructed with the necessary degree of subtle accuracy and logical perfection. "Supreme purity, clarity, and certainty, at the cost of completeness." Once such a valid world image has been achieved, it turns out to apply after all to every natural phenomenon, including all its complexity, and in its completeness.

The road to the "Temple" is clearly mapped out. First, the personal "flight from everyday life" produces a blockage of reality. Second, the scientist constructs a mental image of the real, which replaces the "world of experience." Note that this mental construct—this theory—must not attempt to project reality in its completeness; instead, perfection is to be achieved within the model: purity and clarity "at the cost of completeness," as Einstein says. Third, there is a leap across the gap between the theory and the phenomenal world by which the theory, miraculously, "turns out to apply *after all* to every natural phenomenon" (my italics). Einstein chooses not to elaborate on this sudden transformation—to say "after all" is not an explanation—which gives the theory the power not only to account for the real, but to account for it "in its completeness."

We can draw two conclusions from Einstein's exposé. First, he clearly believes that the real is too complex to be grasped in its own terms. Like Newton, who once remarked that he had to rely on theory because he could not understand reality from the phenomena, Einstein builds a theory that bypasses the complexity of the phenomenal world, in the intent to explain this very complexity through the theory. There is in Einstein's argument a kind of perverse logic in that the theory is built as a bridge over the scientist's *gap of ignorance* of the real, yet this same gap of ignorance comes to constitute, when reformulated into theory, the truth of reality. The conjuring trick involves one nimble operation by which reality is occulted only to be quickly restituted to our view, *but through the theory.* Two questions arise at this point, one concerning the nature of the theoretical legerdemain, the other the nature of the resulting reality: namely, in what manner does a certain ignorance constitute itself *qua* theory? And what kind of reality is reinstituted *after* the theoretical inoculation?

My second conclusion does not so much "conclude" as register Einstein's claim that the back-and-forth movement between theory and reality which he diagnoses in the case of physics applies to all disciplines: in the arts, in the humanities, and in the natural sciences. In other words, for Einstein, the difference between the humanistic and scientific imagination is negligible when one is formulating a theory—from the point of view of both mental processes and aims.[12] While generally correct, Einstein nonetheless oversimplifies the differences. Einstein is correct when he says that imagination is necessary to all scientific procedures. In order to apprehend reality, the scientist must first imagine an ideal reality. It is certainly true, for instance, that no scientific perception of space is possible without an imaginary representation of it. Yet it is equally true that we cannot simply imagine anything we please in science. By the rigor of its demonstrations, scientific activity is also an activity that regulates the imagination. Hence the figures and calculations one finds in all scientific theories tend to "image out" the real according to abstract constructs that drain out the excesses of the imagination.[13] In the limiting case, scientific constructs are paradoxically the product of an imaginary without images. Consequently, the function of rigor in science is to repress all traces of the work of the unconscious in scientific discovery. It is for this reason that, although scientific research resembles humanistic work in that feelings, esthetic considerations, and emotions play an important role in the formulation of scientific theories, such personal circumstances are nevertheless *not* an integral part of the theories them-

---

[12] For a general discussion of this problem and related questions, see the pioneering work of Wilda C. Anderson, *Between the Library and the Laboratory: The Language of Chemistry in Eighteenth-Century France* (Baltimore: Johns Hopkins University Press, 1984).

[13] In Judith Schlanger's formulation, "the image sustains the construction [of theory] like a scaffolding that will be removed later" (in *L'invention intellectuelle* [Paris: Fayard, 1983], 37).

44

selves, nor do they, in the end, determine if a theory is scientifically valid or not.[14]

This kind of resolution is not possible in domains outside science. A theoretical discourse by Montesquieu, or by Rousseau, is endowed by the very nature of its language with multiple significations. And those significations do vary according to personal "givens." But curiously enough, as we shall see, the fact that literary discourse offers us a plurality of significations which are both simultaneous and *not* incompatible with each other, allows us to raise the kinds of questions about theory and its relationship with reality that science cannot ask. By way of an introduction to the subject of this book, let me attempt to address some of these questions by focusing first on Rousseau and Montesquieu.

Theory and Social Reality

Three books dominate the "political" literature of the Enlightenment: Montesquieu's *The Spirit of Laws*, Abbé Raynal's *Political and Philosophical History of the Two Indias* (to which Diderot lent a helping hand as coauthor), and Rousseau's *Social Contract*. In the domain of political philosophy, posterity has spoken in favor of Montesquieu. Auguste Comte claims in the forty-seventh lesson of his *Cours de philosophie positive* that Montesquieu belongs to the intellectual lineage of Descartes, Galileo, Kepler, and Newton, because he is the first thinker ever to define properly the general idea of law. In turn, Durkheim canonizes *The Spirit of Laws* by writing his Latin thesis on "La contribution de Montesquieu à la constitution de la science sociale."[15] We read in the first paragraph of Durkheim's thesis that

[14] The issue is not as clear-cut as I present it here. In fact, if I have chosen to conclude this book on Freud's and Lévi-Strauss's experiences of reality, it is because their discourses, which maintain a high degree of conceptual coherence and even a certain degree of scientificity, debunk the confident assumption that all scientific conceptual constructs are born of pure scientific reasoning. In many ways, psychoanalytic theory uncovers all that is repressed in scientific theory, by showing that in science as in all other disciplines the unconscious modifies (at the level of the most basic fantasies) the path that goes from the experience of reality to its theoretical expression.

[15] In Emile Durkheim, *Montesquieu et Rousseau. Précurseurs de la sociologie*

The Spirit of Laws founded all of the principles of social science. Yet Montesquieu's wide acclaim does not imply that Rousseau has been slighted; he too has fared well in posterity's eyes, but for different reasons. Indeed, it has long been recognized that, in *Emile*, Rousseau inaugurated a new type of discourse, which produced a massive modification of the pedagogical field. According to all educators, Rousseau is at the origin of our modern scholastic institutions; whence the much-used label "father of modern education."

Montesquieu and Rousseau thus share the rare honor of being the originators of their respective fields of study: Montesquieu is the initiator of the first "scientific" study of governments, and Rousseau of "scientific" pedagogy. If I appear to insist on the scientific aspect of their work, it is because (1) their work is historically perceived and received as "scientific," and (2) both of them define the parameters of their fields, the nature of their object of study, and their respective methods, in terms that *seem* to meet the conditions necessary for the establishment of scientific disciplines. But before pursuing this question any further, let us first recall that there is a very close kinship between education and government, in that both address the same issues: family, religion, morality, the place of man in society, and so on. In other words, both disciplines are grounded in the global network of social life. Thus pedagogy and political theory, each in its particular way, are concerned with manifestations of social reality, that is, with the exploration and interpretation of social reality. In the words of Durkheim: "Social science [he refers here to Montesquieu] is concerned with things, with realities; without an experiential given to describe and to interpret, social science is empty at its core. In effect, the only suitable subject [for the social scientist] is the description and interpretation of the real, and nothing else."[16] But we remember that Einstein's physics turned out to be concerned with a very particular "physical reality." The questions to ask of Rousseau and Montesquieu are no different: what kinds of social and political realities do their works

(Paris: Marcel Rivière, 1966). Durkheim's thesis was originally published in 1982 under the title *Quid Secundatus politicae scientiae instituendae contulerit.*

[16] "La contribution," in Durkheim, *Montesquieu et Rousseau,* 29.

yield? And how do their respective theories affect their descriptions and their interpretations of the "real"?

"Childhood is unknown *[on ne connaît point l'enfance]*. Starting from the false idea one has of it, the farther one goes, the more one loses one's way. . . . Begin, then, by studying your pupils better. For most assuredly you do not know them at all.'"[17] Rousseau goes to the heart of the problem from the very first page of the preface to *Emile*. His book is about childhood and, by extension, about the art of educating men: pedagogy. But a few lines later he adds: "As to what will be called the systematic part, which is here nothing but the march of nature, it is the point that will most put the reader off. . . . He will think that what he is reading is less an educational treatise than a visionary's dreams about education" (*E*, 34). At the precise juncture at which one would expect education to demonstrate its kinship with the real— "the march of nature"—Rousseau inexplicably shifts gears, shying away from the real to the benefit of reverie. There is, thus, a sudden discrepancy between education perceived as an *objective* phenomenon and the *subjective* importance Rousseau seems to be attributing to his reverie. The reader may even be entitled to wonder where the significance of *Emile* really lies. Luckily, Rousseau is quick to provide the answer: "What is to be done about it [his reverie]? It is on the basis not of others' ideas that I write but on that of my own. I do not see as do other men. I have long been reproached for that" (p. 34). If we follow Rousseau's logic, it would appear that his reverie takes precedence over education proper. Or to be more precise, one might say that Rousseau's reveries on the subject of education are more important than education itself. It is the projections of the imaginary—which happen to focus on education—that should be noted: "This is the study to which I have most applied myself, so that even if my entire method were chimerical and false, my observations could still be of profit" (p. 34). The reader will have undoubtedly discerned from these remarks the typical Rousseauian narcissistic

[17] Jean-Jacques Rousseau, *Emile, or On Education*, trans. Allan Bloom (New York: Basic Books, 1979), 34. All further references to *Emile* will appear in the text with the abbreviation *E* (unless the source is obvious), followed by the relevant page number.

47

pattern, which ordains that all of his projects be transformed into unique and exceptional events.[18]

If I have chosen to broach the question of narcissism, it is not out of interest in the narcissistic operation per se, but rather because narcissism entertains a very close cause-and-effect relationship with the real. The question is whether narcissism *determines* an individual's indifference to reality, or whether narcissism is the *consequence* of his indifference to reality. In a perceptive study of literary narcissism, Clément Rosset argues that narcissism's dominant trait is the individual's capacity to ignore the real, and that complacency about the self is simply the consequence of this lack of interest in the outside world:

> Narcissism is worrisome in its capacity to ignore the real, and not so much in its complacency to concentrate on nothing but itself. While it is true that either of these aspects is hard to conceive of without the other, it seems necessary to grant psychological priority to the first. It also seems clear that the depreciation of the real which is characteristic of narcissism is more a cause than a consequence of the excessive valorization of the self... the excess of indifference to the real is primary, and the excess of self-love occurs only as an aftereffect.[19]

In order to explain why narcissism is primarily a phenomenon of blockage of reality, Rosset goes on to argue that narcissism results from a discrepancy between the real and the narcissist's representation of it, especially when this discrepancy leads to an extreme valorization of the representation at the expense of reality: "The discrepancy between the real and its representation culminates in a grandiose valorization of the image to the detriment of reality.... The image is rich in connotations and significations that it adds to the real, so as to make the real, according to the case at hand, flattering (as in the case of narcissism) or unbearable (as in the case of violence, that is, wounded narcissism)."[20] In effect, by collapsing the image (offered to the other, and to the self by way of the other) onto the real in the narcissistic operation,

[18] Cf. the classic example of *Les confessions:* "I am commencing an undertaking, hitherto without precedent, and which will never find an imitator" (trans. Ernest Rhys [London: J. M. Dent, 1931], 1).

[19] Clément Rosset, *Le réel. Traité de l'idiotie* (Paris: Minuit, 1977), 111–12.

[20] Ibid., 112–13.

representation claims for itself the role of exclusive guarantor of reality and of truth. This explains the phenomenon by which anything and everything that crosses the narcissist's imaginary becomes, in his mind, an event worthy of everyone's attention.

We have a clear example of the above situation when Rousseau assures his readers that his "visionary's dreams" are the definitive statement on the subject of education. At first, Rousseau judges his reveries only in function of their existence as dreamlike productions. Yet, because the narcissistic representation carries with it the seal of reality, the reveries soon become "reality," thus allowing Rousseau to dispense with objective reality. Coincidental with his disengagement from reality, Rousseau shifts his focus to the "quality" of the representation of his pedagogical project. It is important to note in this respect that Rousseau's denunciation of past pedagogical practices is not a function of their being wrong or harmful to citizens. Rather, pedagogy becomes the object of a narcissistic operation that displays Rousseau's personal vision of education: "My vision of what must be done may have been very poor, but I believe that I have seen clearly the subject on which one must work.... Now if you read this book with this in view, I believe that it will not be without utility for you" (*E*, 34). The visual terminology is relevant here, for what becomes crucial for Rousseau is not the *real*, but the *imaginary* status of the pedagogical enterprise, that is, the status of Rousseau's *narcissistic image* of it—what has come to be viewed, paradoxically, as Rousseau's contribution to scientific pedagogy!

Now, whether or not *we* have any doubts about the status of the theory, Rousseau himself apparently has none. He specifically emphasizes in *Emile*'s preface the peculiarity of his method:

In every sort of project, there are two things to consider: first, the absolute goodness of the project; in the second place, the facility of execution.... The second consideration depends on countless circumstances that are impossible to determine otherwise than in a particular application of the method to this or that country, to this or that station. *Now all these particular applications, not being essential to my subject, do not enter into my plan.* (pp. 34–35, my italics)

Thus from the very first lines of *Emile,* Rousseau refuses to relate his system to those "particular applications" it should logically entail. The theory sustains itself *outside* of the examples: "In any case, my method [my system] is independent of my examples" (p. 192). Hence the function of theory, as Rousseau conceives of it, is to reinforce the divestiture of reality from his pedagogic enterprise. We rediscover here a procedure analogous to that described by Einstein in the production of the "physical reality." There is, nevertheless, the obvious difference to which I have already referred: a scientific theory, even though it must bypass reality to constitute itself as theory, cannot altogether clash with the facts. The epistemological demands of science require that the theory be subject to verification (or nonverification). These notions as we understand them in the sciences do not apply to a theoretical discourse such as Rousseau's, which is open to interpretation and which, furthermore, does *not* claim to account for the reality of the social situations it depicts. And yet we have come to accept over the years, in the face of the evidence, that Rousseau is the father of "scientific" pedagogy. How did such an identification develop? How did Rousseau develop a pedagogical theory that is perceived as scientific—that is, accountable both for its internal rigor and for a minimal degree of accuracy in presenting and analyzing social reality—from principles that take literally no account of relevant examples and real situations? What is the meaning of a pedagogical theory, or any theory, developed under such conditions? What would be the status of this theory? Finally, what happens to Rousseau's world of experience, to his everyday reality, as it comes into contact with such a theory? Montesquieu will bring us one step closer to answering these questions.

The same Rousseau who so eagerly promotes his theory-reverie on education in *Emile* accuses Montesquieu of having failed in his attempt to establish a political science, because he had favored empirical facts over theoretical principles: "The science of political right is yet to be born.... The only modern [author] in a position to create this great and useless science was the illustrious Montesquieu" (*E,* 458). Rousseau adds, however, that Montesquieu was too much of a positivist to become a good political theorist: "But he was careful not to discuss the principles of political right. He was content to discuss the positive right of established governments, and nothing in the world is more different than these two studies" (ibid.). Indeed, Rousseau should know the difference between empirical evidence ("positive right of established government") and theoretical speculation ("principles of political right"). Yet what is most peculiar in Montesquieu's case is that Enlightenment critics tended to dismiss *The Spirit of Laws* for precisely the opposite reason: its lack of empirical objectivity! Voltaire, for instance, accused Montesquieu of using approximations and vague generalizations in his choice of examples, of falsifying facts to fit his abstract theses, and of drawing his conclusions based on faulty reasoning.[21] And at about the same time, Anquetil-Duperron criticized the factually misleading nature of Montesquieu's tableau of social life in the Orient.[22] Indeed, according to Montesquieu's conceptual "model" of despotic government—as formulated in *The Persian Letters* and *The Spirit of Laws*—Orientals could not have a good life. Consequently, even if the more reliable eyewitness accounts of the time give a picture of a relatively peaceful China under a somewhat stable, paternalistic brand of despotic government, Montesquieu ignores these accounts—which he attributes to the willful gullibility of Jesuit missionaries—and goes on to conclude, against the evidence, that China, like all despotic governments, "is therefore a despotic state, whose principle is fear."[23]

Montesquieu would be the first to agree with Voltaire's and Anquetil-Duperron's *factual* objections. In fact, he makes it quite clear in the preface to *The Spirit* that the book's objective is not to study the empirical factualness of historical and political phenomena. Montesquieu even suggests that the idea of factualness

[21] "His [Montesquieu's] examples are misleading, the inductions that are drawn from them are often poorly applied, and the citations he uses to make his work striking are often faulty.... When he quotes something, he always mistakes his imagination for his memory" ("Idées républicaines par un membre d'un corps," in *Mélanges* [Paris: Pléiade, 1961], 519).

[22] See Jean Ehrard's foreword to *The Spirit of Laws* (Paris: Editions sociales, 1977).

[23] *De l'esprit des lois,* in *Oeuvres complètes* (Paris: Pléiade, 1951) vol. II, bk. VII, chap. 21, 368. Except for certain untranslated sections of *De l'esprit* for which I use the Pléiade edition, all references will be to *The Spirit of Laws,* ed. and trans. David Wallace Carrithers (Berkeley: University of California Press, 1977). All further references will appear in the text under the abbreviation *SL* (unless the source is obvious), followed by the book number (in Roman numerals), and chapter and page number.

itself is problematic, as laws and mores do not correspond in their everyday reality to the appearance of things—the images *(fantaisies)* men have of them (pref., 91). In other words, as Montesquieu explains in Book 1, 3, the positive laws that make up sociopolitical reality are too complex and diverse to be fully grasped by the human mind. To understand laws properly, one must consider them in relation to innumerable factors: political, historical, physical (climatic and geographic), economic, moral and religious, among others. This in itself is an impossible project; and, even if one were to assume for a moment that it were feasible, one would soon reach an impasse. For after tallying all of these "givens," the researcher would discover that laws also maintain relationships among themselves, and that these relationships are in turn determined by still other laws.

Montesquieu's solution to this dilemma is to leave aside positive laws and to focus instead upon the *relationships* that they maintain both with things and among themselves: "This is what I have undertaken to perform in the following work. These relations I shall examine, which form all together what we call the *Spirit of Laws*" (SL, 1-3, 105). Montesquieu discovers at this point that these relationships, which constitute the spirit underlying the laws, are as stable as those that regulate physical laws: "These rules are a fixed and invariable relation.... Each diversity is *uniformity*, each change is *constancy*" (1-1, 99).[24] Montesquieu can thus dismiss the objections of his contemporaries by asserting that he goes beyond the details of positive laws. The novelty of his "misunderstood" project lies in the new object of study he has just defined: the order of relationships which subtends empirical laws.

How does one go about studying an order of relationships? Montesquieu's method is to favor principles over facts: facts will be sacrificed whenever they do not accord with principles, regardless of empirical evidence. For within Montesquieu's political vision, facts are only "particular cases," which must obey the higher and more rigorous logic of principles: "I have laid down the first principles, and have found that the particular cases follow naturally from them; that the histories of all nations are only consequences

---

[24] I shall discuss, in the Montesquieu chapter, how he understands political laws according to the physical laws that regulate the human body.

of them" (*SL*, pref., 91). In other words, in the face of the complexity of historical and political reality, which he recognizes as impossible to systematize (the table of contents of *The Spirit* is a good index of the multiplicity and diversity of the empirical real), Montesquieu proposes to establish theory as primary in the order of sociopolitical knowledge. One might object that Montesquieu denies being overly "theoretical" by asserting in this same preface, "I have not drawn my principles from my prejudices, but from the nature of things" (pref., 92). Yet what is entailed in this "nature of things" which Montesquieu seems to posit at the origin of the explanatory principles of *The Spirit of Laws* remains to be seen.

Let us consider the example that Montesquieu provides in Book II-I ("Of the Nature of the Three Diverse Governments") in order to illustrate his line of reasoning. How, then, do we grasp "the nature of government" (which, in this political example, stands for "the nature of things") from which, according to Montesquieu, all fundamental laws emanate? Through the description of a given government? Through concrete observations? Through empirical facts? Predictably, the answer is negative in all three cases. Here is Montesquieu's unpredictable explanation: "There are three species of government: *republican, monarchical,* and *despotic.* In order to discover their nature, it is sufficient to recollect the common notion of these species held by the least educated of men. I suppose these three definitions . . . [he then proceeds to define each type]. This is what I call the nature of each government" (II-I, 107).[25] Montesquieu moves from an alleged statement of fact (there are three governments) to a hypothetical ("I suppose") general definition of the three types of government; and he concludes by asserting that the "nature of each government" is the aforementioned definition. Hence "the nature of things" is not at all what we would normally translate as "the reality of

---

[25] Louis Althusser challenges the testimony of this typical witness who is called on to validate an institution: "It is to this evidence that Montesquieu appeals . . . one need only open one's eyes upon the world to perceive these facts—and, likewise, to perceive immediately forms, objects, groups, and movements. This evidence, which forsakes knowledge, can nonetheless make a claim to knowledge and assume that it *understands* what it only *perceives*" (*Montesquieu: La politique et l'histoire* [Paris: Presses Universitaires de France, 1969], 106). Obviously Althusser takes the eyes of the mind, in this case, for *factual* evidence—which is not at all Montesquieu's objective.

things." Rather, it is the result of a semantic operation by which a general definition becomes the constitutive principle that regulates and explains the fundamental laws "that follow directly from the nature of each government" (ibid.). Montesquieu first defines the three hypothetical models of government, and then offers examples and facts that, as he acknowledges, may or may not correspond to the theoretical model.[26]

Thus when Montesquieu claims that he has drawn his principles from "the nature of things," what he is in fact proposing is a type of political knowledge whose veracity is grounded in his reasoning process *independently* of the empirical details. This reasoning process functions according to a semantic field that is constructed upon a network of personal concepts—"principles," "nature of things," "general causes," "particular cases," "spirit of laws," etc.—which exist only by virtue of having existed in Montesquieu's imaginary. Consequently, the definitions and significations of these concepts need not be verified by empirical circumstances. This amounts to saying that, for Montesquieu, any meaningful apprehension of sociopolitical reality must be preceded by an imaginary representation—a construct that is the product of self-enclosed reasoning—of this reality. Historical reality, or rather its simulacrum (since that is all we can hope to attain), is hence the embodiment of imaginary models that must, by definition, always precede reality. It should be emphasized that the imaginary model—the representation—need be neither a reflection nor an image of reality. Yet the imaginary model remains, under any circumstances, the *necessary condition* for attaining access to the real. It is for this reason that Montesquieu insists throughout that "in the beginning" there were "principles":

---

[26] As Montesquieu says in Book IV-11 ("A Reflection on the Above Thoughts"): "These are the principles of the three governments, all of which does not imply that, in a particular republic, everyone is virtuous—but that everyone should be. Nor do these principles prove that, in a given monarchy, the subjects are honorable, or that in a given despotic state, they are fearful—but that they should be, failing which the government would be imperfect" (*Oeuvres complètes*, vol. II, 261). Then again, Usbek had already pointed out the impossible adequation between a theoretical model and historical reality: "The majority of the governments in Europe are monarchies, or rather, called so, for I am not sure that there have ever been *any real ones*. At least, it is difficult for them to have existed very long in a pure state" (*The Persian Letters*, trans. J. Robert Loy [New York: Meridian Books, 1961], Letter CII, 190).

"Often have I begun, and as often have I laid aside this under-taking.... I have followed my object without any fixed plan.... I have found the truth, only to lose it again. But when I had once discovered my first principles, everything I sought for appeared" (*SL*, pref., 93).

Indeed, Montesquieu's imaginary models can be formulated only through "his" principles; and, paradoxically, Montesquieu believes that these ideal representations will then provide him a total understanding of historical reality.[27] The conclusion of the preface to *The Spirit* reinforces this last view. "If this work meets with success," remarks Montesquieu, "I shall owe it chiefly to the grandeur and majesty of the subject. However I do not think that I have been totally deficient in point of genius.... 'And I also am a painter!' I have said with Correggio" (p. 94). Obviously, the majesty of the subject of *The Spirit* is less the historical real per se than the historical tableaux Montesquieu paints for the reader. For these representations, produced by a conceptual machine that does not lack "genius," as he puts it, are rich in significations that make the historical real interesting and majestic, while the real itself remains, at best, boring.[28] Einstein had said the same thing, in his own terms. The scientist, like the painter, must move beyond the confines of reality to pass to the other side of the looking glass. It is this "leap" into the imaginary that is illustrated by our reading of the preface of *The Spirit of Laws*. Thus, Montesquieu is the founder of political theory only because he is the first thinker to produce a theoretical discourse on political reality which, paradoxically, is completely indifferent to the real workings of government. It is instead acutely attentive to the productions of Montesquieu's (political) imaginary.[29]

One is reminded here of a famous remark by Pascal in the *Pensées*: "Painting is such vanity; it wins our admiration for its

---

[27] Cf. the passage cited earlier: "I have laid down the first principles, and have found ... that the histories of all nations are only consequences of them" (*SL*, pref., 91).

[28] "The more we enter into particulars, the more we shall perceive the certainty of the principles on which they are founded. I have not given all these particulars, for who could mention them all without a most insupportable fatigue?" (*SL*, pref., 92).

[29] Voltaire was indeed right, but for the wrong reasons, to accuse Montesquieu of always mistaking his "imagination for his memory" (*Mélanges*, 519).

likenesses of things whose originals we do not admire at all."[30]
This thought is an eloquent commentary on the power of representation to create a gap in the real through which the real can appear. Thus if we grant that the real signifies only when it takes on the value assigned to it by representation—that is, it signifies only by virtue of a detour through the imaginary—the following question naturally comes to mind: what is it that makes the imaginary signify? Or rather, *how* does the imaginary signify?

The Theoretical Imaginary

It would be fitting at this point to specify the special status I wish to give to the imaginary. The question is too broad to be treated comprehensively, and it would be absurd for me to undertake the kind of compilation that attempts to account for all of the theories—from Descartes to Bachelard, and from Sartre to Rosset—and all of the research (particularly in psychoanalysis) which pertains to this subject.[31] For the same reasons, I shall not attempt to sketch a theory of the imaginary; given the nature of the imaginary, such a theory would inevitably miss the mark. Rather, I shall simply define the concept of the imaginary that I espouse: it is essentially a semiotic concept and fulfills an operative function. By cutting the imaginary down to size in this way, I hope to establish clearer working parameters, and thereby ensure a kind of focus that is generally lacking when one speaks of the imaginary. In this book, I consider the imaginary in the light of texts that contribute (sometimes explicitly, but more often through our interpretation of them) to such an operative definition.

What, then, is the imaginary? In itself, it is nothing, and every-

---

[30] "Quelle vanité que la peinture, qui attire l'admiration par la ressemblance des choses dont on n'admire point les originaux" (quoted in Rosset, *Le réel*, 113).

[31] I have tried to steer clear of psychoanalytic theory—whatever the school, the label, or the practice, there being so many of them today—because I am not concerned with the psychoanalytic operation proper (i.e., its concepts, its techniques, its successes or failures). If I do, on occasion, use certain psychoanalytic notions in my critical readings, I do so because I find them useful in articulating the kind of *textual* imaginary that I seek to delineate. As I hope to demonstrate, this imaginary differs from, and exceeds, the authorial imaginary—the individual's drives, identifications, obsessions, etc.—as it is discussed by psychoanalysis.

thing. The imaginary world is always with us, as a parallel to our world; there is not a single moment of our existence which is not imbued with the imaginary. Yet, even if all of its "markers" refer back to reality, the imaginary does not belong to reality proper. The imaginary is neither a lie nor an illusion that distracts us from the real (as dreams do); it is neither reality's "negative" nor the "unreal" of reality.[32] The closest one can get to describing how the imaginary stands in relation to the real is to refer to the familiar Saussurian image of the sheet of paper whose front cannot be cut without its back being cut at the same time. In like manner, the real cannot be separated from the imaginary or the imaginary from the real: any such division could be accomplished only abstractly, and the result would be either pure representation or reality in its raw state—imageless, and therefore meaningless. Thus if we were to define the imaginary according to clear-cut categories, we would reach a dead end, for the imaginary is always ambiguous; it functions as an ever-present "otherness," persistently soliciting the real. Similarly, it is impossible to formulate an appropriate behavior for dealing with the imaginary given that, when faced with "images," we cannot do much: an image cannot be possessed in the manner of an object; most often, it possesses us. Hence we cannot claim to enter willingly into the realm of the imaginary (Sade provides an exception to this rule); on the contrary, we are subjected to its images, which take us over to this "other scene" of the real, in the words of Octave Mannoni.[33] Yet if the imaginary strives to work not in opposition to the real, but rather in accordance with it, how can we differentiate between those two mirror images in order to delimit the proper realm of the imaginary?

Instead of defining the imaginary as another reality, a nonreality, or the "other scene" of reality, it might be more fruitful to focus on the essential trait of the imaginary; that is, the fact that it "speaks" through images. Unfortunately, it would seem that we can only speak of the image in the same terms we use to discuss the imaginary. The image does not exist in the same

[32] This runs counter to the many dictionary definitions that oppose the imaginary and the real: "in its various accepted meanings, the imaginary is opposed to the real." P. Foulquié and R. Saint-Jean, *Dictionnaire de la langue philosophique* (Paris: Presses Universitaires de France, 1962), 344.

[33] *Clefs pour l'imaginaire ou l'autre scène* (Paris: Seuil, 1970).

capacity as does an object in the world, for it cannot be reduced to an "objective" reality. The image exists only insofar as it signifies (by virtue of its resemblance) something other than itself, something absent. This is the traditional notion of the image: an image depicts not the real *in itself*, but rather the real *in its absence*, that is, stripped of reality. According to this view, the image reproduces the real, and the imaginary is therefore a real that is spatially and temporally out of sync with the real proper. This is the accepted definition of representation. Representation is always posterior to the real it conveys. Because representation is a copy of the real, it follows that one's consciousness of the real, attained through representation, is always *second* to the real proper.

If, however, I have correctly read the passages quoted earlier from Rousseau, Montesquieu, and even Einstein, they suggest precisely the contrary. According to them, the image (representation) does not refer back to the real that it allegedly reproduces, but rather points to the real by means of the network of signification it lends to the real. These authors seem to hold that we must reverse the relationship of anteriority and resemblance between thing and image, implying by this reversal that *there is no experience of the real without an image*. In order for the real to signify, it must borrow its meaning from the image-inary.[34] In other words, we must think of the real's "coming to conscious-

[34] For instance, Condillac announces just such a theory of the imaginary in the *Essai sur l'origine des connaissances humaines* (Paris: Galilée, 1973). In the chapter on "the vices and advantages of the imagination," Condillac defines two types of imagination, one reproductive and one productive. The productive imagination is axiomatically determined as a movement toward mastery of the real: "There is nothing in the imagination that cannot take on a new form. By transferring the qualities of one subject to another with such a free hand, the imagination gathers in a single subject the qualities which nature employs to embellish several" (pp. 142–43). A few pages later, while discussing the notions of pleasure and suffering, Condillac confirms that the productive imagination is the strategic operation for capturing the real: "The perception of suffering awakens in my imagination all of the ideas with which it is closely linked.... I see danger and I am seized with fear, I am overwhelmed, my body can barely resist, my suffering becomes sharper, my affliction mounts, and it is possible that, by the mere fact of having had my imagination struck, a simple incipient illness can end by leading me to the grave... through this explanation, we can see that the pleasures [and sufferings] of the imagination are *just as real and as physical* as any others even if people generally assert the contrary" (p. 147).

ness" not in terms of a memory or return, but rather as an *advent*—an "arrivée du réel"[35] through the image which brings into being the real's "will" to consciousness. Thus we operate a fundamental conversion in terms of reality, which consists not of paring the image down to fit the dimensions of reality, but rather of fitting the real to the dimensions of the imaginary. In contrast to Sartre, who views the imaginary as the correlative consciousness of the real, I would argue that the real is the correlative consciousness of the imaginary.[36]

This is one of the central issues addressed by this book, and it is crucial for the following reasons. We have a tendency to think that an individual "takes refuge" in the imaginary in order to avoid confronting the real. This kind of reasoning stems from a confusion of dream and imaginary.[37] In fact, because it drives back our consciousness of the real, a dream is a place of evasion. We cannot say the same of the imaginary, for it always brings us back to some "form" of reality. Hence although the imaginary does

---

[35] Rosset, *Le réel*, 130.

[36] Sartre's itinerary is paradoxical in that, after criticizing in *L'imagination* (Paris: Felix Alcan, 1936) both classical and Bergsonian theories of the image as theories of an imagination *lacking* images, he in turn devaluates the image in *L'imaginaire* (Paris: Gallimard, 1940). Sartre's vocabulary betrays the negativity that characterizes the image: "nothingness," "shadow of an object," "phantom object," "there is a kind of essential impoverishment in the image" (p. 24); and again, "negation *[le ne pas]* would be the category of the image" (p. 32).
I am also aware that my conception of the real as the correlative consciousness of the imaginary calls for a reorganization of the well-known Lacanian theoretical configuration, which consists of the classical notions of real and imaginary (as illusion), to which Lacan adds the third dimension of the symbolic. This last dimension is valorized in its relation to the real and the imaginary: first, the relation between the symbolic and the phantasmatic real is a relation of structure to lack, the real remaining foreclosed from the analytic experience, which is an experience of speech; second, whereas the imaginary is the realm of alienating identification, the symbolic register is that of normal subjectivity. Henceforth it is the symbolic, not the imaginary, that is seen to be the determining order of the subject; to be more precise, the subject, in Lacan's sense, is himself an effect of the symbolic. In my view, however, the imaginary is not the seat of (Lacanian) specular illusion; on the contrary, the theoretical imaginary (which I will define shortly) founds the principles that organize the order of the real. It is thus the imaginary, and not the symbolic, which compensates for the lack of the real.

[37] The distinction is made even more difficult by the fact that the imaginary employs all of the working procedures of a dream: representation of a conflict within an "other scene," dramatization of a repressed desire, figuration, displacement, symbolic substitution, etc.

offer a "refuge," this refuge is not completely cut off from the real, as in a dream. (For instance, Rousseau remains acutely sensitive to his surroundings in *Emile*.) To state that *Emile* is a reverie emanating from Rousseau's imaginary does not amount to saying that it is the enactment of a dream. If *Emile* were no more than a dream, it would be merely Rousseau's means of personal satisfaction, built upon a momentary dream state of unreality. The lasting effect of *Emile* attests to the fact that it has not been read simply as a dream. I shall return to this point, but wish first to establish a distinction between the imaginary and yet another concept with which it is often confused: imagination.

The main difference between the imaginary and imagination lies in the kind of knowledge of reality that each concept carries. The imagination is as vague as the imaginary is precise in relation to reality. In other words, just as the imagination is a purely intuitive and primitive mode of knowledge, so too the imaginary is subject to laws that are as strict as those of reality (since it deals with the same real, simply displaced onto the "other scene"). The imaginary proceeds methodically: it sets down rules that permit it to signify the real, precisely in order to avoid straying into the illusions created by the imagination. Yet, as with the real, logic always rules but does not always govern the imaginary, ceding some of its powers to the imagination. That is, the imaginary offers, among its many paths and images, some that also lead to illusion (Rousseau is a case in point). Hence we are inevitably forced to choose which clues will put us on the right track.

I shall define two types of imaginary: the theoretical imaginary, in which theory constitutes the key element in structuring this imaginary; and, in opposition, the dreamlike imaginary, prototype of the ordinary individual. (It will come as no surprise that I discuss mainly the *theoretical* imaginary in this book.) "In opposition" does not mean "to the exclusion of," for theoretical and dreamlike imaginaries can and do coexist (witness again the case of Rousseau). But in general, one clearly dominates the other. To give an example of a dreamlike imaginary: when Pascal condemns imagination by calling it "maîtresse d'erreur et de fausseté," he is denouncing not the theoretical imaginary, but rather an imaginary that grants the imagination free reign in producing the illusions and mirages of dreams, to the exclusion of the real. In contrast, the theoretical imaginary does not negate the real, but instead rigorously subsumes it *on its own terms;* that is, under the condition that the real will appear wearing the signifying cloak of the theory produced by this imaginary. This entails no rejection or evasion of the real; on the contrary, by subsuming the real, the theoretical imaginary displaces it ever so slightly, so as to institute, behind the sheltering veil of theory, a buffer zone between one's experience of the real and the real in its brute state. As a result, theory—be it political, social, pedagogical, anthropological, or psychoanalytical—allows the individual subject to reassume the real, but a real stripped of certain undesirable or obtrusive characteristics, according to the case at hand.

So how does the theoretical imaginary function? In order to use it as an operative concept that we can talk about, we must organize its effects—the structure that makes the imaginary manifest—into a system. Obviously, it is fiction that actualizes the imaginary, insofar as any writer or thinker must resort to fiction in order to resolve the paradoxical situations the real imposes on him. Thus as the "countercode" of reality, the imaginary provides a reserve of meaning that engenders fictional scenarios. (In this sense, the imaginary is a text—literature—yet also belongs to reality, because, as we have seen, the scenario produces what Barthes calls "effets de réel.") As long as its code is inoperative, the imaginary remains a virtuality, a passive abstraction that coexists with the real. The code becomes operative when it receives a series of images or ideas which it transforms into a scenario. The originality of the imaginary lies in the *operativity* of the code that engenders the scenario, and in the *strict adequation* of the code to the material in which it is expressed.

I should stress that I do not intend to discover either the nature of the code, or codes, of the imaginary—that work is the domain of psychoanalysts—or its secrets (one of the most widely held literary fictions consists in believing that the imaginary holds "deep" secrets). No, the imaginary has no secrets: it is a signifying surface upon which individual experiences and the ambient culture commingle in the form of scenarios. In keeping with my working definition of the imaginary as a semiotic, operative concept, I aim: (1) to reveal, through such scenarios, the *working strategies* of the imaginary, in particular the way in which theory is embedded in the imaginary; and (2) to discuss the manner in which this imaginary intervenes and hence transforms the meaning of reality. With this in mind, I shall briefly recall the "whys," "whens," and "hows" involved in the occurrence of imaginary scenarios.

The scenario is often a symptom of a crisis whose severity varies according to the circumstances. For instance, in Rousseau's as in Sade's case, it is a lifelong crisis, whereas for Freud and Lévi-Strauss the crisis lasts only as long as is necessary to bring about a satisfactory resolution, and in Montesquieu's case there is no crisis to speak of. In this respect, a scenario can either resolve the problem it raises (Freud, Lévi-Strauss, Marianne); or, at the other extreme, plunge the subject into melancholy or lead that person to the brink of death (Usbek).[38] The resolution could suddenly surface like a daydream, in which case it suffices simply to register the message in order to change objective reality (Freud, Lévi-Strauss). Or the scenario might provoke an abrupt return to reality and thus cause more or less chronic problems (Rousseau, Usbek). Or, perhaps, the scenario might aim to turn reality inside out by seeking to signify an entirely different reality (Sade). Whatever the nature of the resolution adopted, the scenario's outcome effects a considerable change in the subject's experience of the real.

Finally, let me add a word concerning the scenario's materiality. The scenario is never a homogeneous or completed text. The refinements or revisions that are added prior to publication can also be read as the handiwork of the imaginary. Freud and Rousseau explicate the circumstances that produced their respective scenarios; Lévi-Strauss looks back at his scenario in the light of his professional preoccupations; and Montesquieu highlights his with an answer to the anticipated objections of his critics. In the

---

[38] At this level, I do not differentiate between authors and their characters, because it is the text of the imaginary (and also the imaginary of the text) which interests me, and not the psychic makeup of each author. In other words, the crisis I refer to above is not a crisis to be understood as an author's personal psychological crisis, but a construct *within* the fiction. This construct of the imaginary uses fictional characters as tools to work through the crisis. Sometimes an author embodies himself in one of the characters, but that does not make the fiction a psychological working out of the author's problems. Rather, the crisis construct is used to solve various epistemological problems, among which, as in the case of Freud, the problem to be resolved may be a psychological one. What has priority in my perspective are the "characters"—the author is only one among them—for they are the ones who delineate through the fictional scenarios the topology of the imaginary while uncovering some aspects of its functioning.

extreme case of Sade, his fantasy is so highly stimulated by his multiple scenarios that, during interruptions in his narration, he grafts other imaginary scenarios onto the first, to produce meta-scenarios that activate in turn meta-meta-scenarios, and so on and so forth. As a result of the "writing strategies" of the imaginary, the scenario can attain the proportions of a novel (Rousseau, Montesquieu), or take the form of a play (Lévi-Strauss) or a series of scenes (Sade) or a short dream (Freud) or even a monologue like that of Marianne, who elaborates very effective imaginary scenarios both in front of her mirror and in her tête-à-tête with Valville, for instance. The emplotment of each subject's conflict with the real obeys the conventions of literary genres, and thus *necessitates* some form of resolution—an end, or a solution to the problem. Through the scenario, the theoretical imaginary produces resolutions that have far-reaching consequences for the real; yet, paradoxically, these resolutions can only take place on the scene of the imaginary. It remains for me to spell out these strategies, and the resolutions offered by the imaginary, in the specific examples that are treated in the following pages.

Montesquieu's perception of the political history of despotism is first expressed in his fiction of the seraglio, *The Persian Letters,* which I read as the imaginary scenario that theorizes the progressive degradation of absolute power into despotic power. *The Persian Letters* demonstrates that all political systems gain in strength and in "stability"—at least in the short term—as the people's imaginary shapes up their reality principle.[39] In the limiting case of despotism, the real must be completely taken over by the imaginary. A consideration of the process by which the *image* (of Usbek's body) comes to serve as "reality principle" in seraglio life will help us to understand the mechanics of Montesquieu's political imaginary—especially the nature of despotic power—as it is presented in *The Persian Letters* and *The Spirit of Laws.*

The Rousseauian imaginary differs in that it fulfills above all

[39] For an example of a people's imaginary at work, see Marie-Hélène Huet's incisive analysis of how the script of Louis xvi's trial captures, on a tragic theatrical mode, the French Revolution's imaginary (*Rehearsing the Revolution* [Berkeley and Los Angeles: University of California Press, 1982]).

a function of compensation.[40] However, Rousseau's imaginary also seeks to establish itself as the law in every domain that the author approaches—political theory, social theory, theory of education. I will limit myself here to studying Rousseau's pedagogical imaginary as he describes it in *Emile*, to show that the book is part of Rousseau's effort to cure himself (in the psychoanalytic sense of the term), through an operation of the imaginary, of his obsessive need for recognition. As the first to theorize an imaginary practice of pedagogy as a form of cure, Rousseau produces a "pedagogy" that has nothing whatsoever to do with pedagogical practice as it is commonly understood. If everyday pedagogical practice could speak, it would have much to say about all that Rousseau's system silences, excludes from its field, or renders unthinkable for anyone who accepts it at face value. But practice—reality—is kept silent, because truth, for Rousseau, always falls under the aegis of (imaginary) theory.

With Sade, I address the question of the constitution of the libertine imaginary. As the monk Clément explains to Justine, the libertine imaginary is the product of an optical illusion.[41] The important point here is not that the imaginary is a distorting mirror, but that it is itself distorted at its origin: "The human imagination is an intellectual faculty in which, through the work

---

[40] The reader will recall this famous remark from *Les confessions*: " . . . my restless imagination entered upon an occupation which saved me from myself. . . . This consisted in feeding it upon the situations which had interested me in the course of my reading, in recalling them, in combining them, in making them so truly my own that I became one of the persons who filled my imagination, and always saw myself in the situations most agreeable to my taste; and that, finally, the fictitious state in which I succeeded in putting myself succeeded in making me forget my actual state with which I was so dissatisfied. This love of imaginary objects, and my readiness to occupy myself with them, ended by disgusting me with everything around me, and brought about that liking for solitude which has never left me" (pp. 34–35). The technique Rousseau uses to activate his imagination is not very different from that advocated by Sade in the formation of the libertine imaginary. I discuss extensively this aspect of the question in the first of my two chapters on the Marquis de Sade.

[41] "Let me give a comparison to clarify my point. Have you not seen, Justine, mirrors of various sizes, some of which shrink objects—thereby lending them certain charms; others that expand them—thereby making these objects hideous? Now, do you not grant that, if each of these mirrors brought together the creative faculty with the objective faculty, it would reflect a very different image of the same man who gazed at himself in that mirror?" (*La nouvelle Justine, Oeuvres complètes* [Paris: Pauvert, 1968], XVI, 203).

of the senses, objects are depicted and modified, and consequently compose thoughts, based upon the first glimpse of these objects."[42] The imaginary as the seat of imagination is a reflecting surface that not only reflects, but also provides a ground upon which the subject *originally* inscribes himself. Hence the imaginary is not reality's accessory support; on the contrary, it is the fundamental structure that grants the libertine subject his specificity. In elaborating his conception of the libertine imaginary, Sade himself provides the methodological concepts—the theoretical imaginary and the fictional scenario—which I have developed for my own purposes; however, he does so in order to construct the notion of a perverse imaginary that challenges the traditional premises of the Western imaginary.

The present book concludes with a study of two dreams that are very different in their content, yet quite similar in their implications. The first is a dream that Freud had about his dead father, a dream that shows how Freud's profound ambiguity toward Jakob led him to produce an imaginary scenario—the theoretical fiction of the Oedipal complex—which has become the foundation of the psychoanalytic institution. In the case of Lévi-Strauss, we find not so much a dream as an extremely rich "delirium" whose genesis, progress, detours, and (non)conclusion are all dutifully noted by Lévi-Strauss. He gives us an unedited version of this delirium in a play entitled "The Apotheosis of Augustus," a chapter in *Tristes Tropiques*—the book itself could be read as a retrospective version of the play—which offers us an opportunity to study the organizing principles of structuralist theory in the context of Lévi-Strauss's theoretical imaginary, whose rigor is matched only by its inventive versatility.

In seeking the organizing principle of my book, I followed these authors' diverse attempts at situating themselves in the realm of the imaginary. All of the theories produced by these authors are grounded in imaginary scenarios whose very function is to preempt the real. They all obey—in varying manners and degrees[43]—the rigorous laws of the imaginary. And yet, as I have

---

[42] Ibid.

[43] For my purposes, I do not differentiate between, on the one hand, authors such as Montesquieu or Sade, whose theoretical imaginaries conform to the scenarios they propose; and, on the other hand, those like Freud and Lévi-Strauss, whose scenarios "undo" their theories, thereby revealing a deep misprision. As

said before, this does not imply that we can construct a theory of the imaginary, for the imaginary is not a theoretical field in the usual sense of the term. Rather, the imaginary is kept alive and well by the exigencies of the real, a real that it seeks to elucidate and to implicate by means of successive theoretical scenarios. At times fragmentary, at times incomplete, always strictly logical, but never rigorously *demonstrable*, the imaginary cannot be formalized or constructed—it only invents itself.

---

for Rousseau, his bad faith contaminates even his imaginary, so that he can claim affinities for both camps while truly belonging to neither.

3

The Eunuch's Tale:
Montesquieu's Imaginary of Despotism

> We never judge of matters except by a secret return we make
> upon ourselves.
>
> Montesquieu, *The Persian Letters*

Do you see what I see?

I discussed in the opening chapter the question of Marianne's
mitigated good faith as illustrative of her half-conscious self-de-
lusion about her identity. But we could also view the problem of
Marianne's identity as a question of the nature of the fictional
real. The mirror play in *La vie de Marianne*—the doubling of the
old Marianne (now writing her memoirs) observing the young
Marianne observing herself playing a role before the gallery—is
so complicated that it is impossible to distinguish the "real"
Marianne from the image that she seeks to project; and because
the entire novel takes place from the perspective of the narrator's
subjective consciousness, there is nothing that might help us to
determine what is, or is not, the index of reality. When Marivaux
wants to describe for the reader the discrepancies between Marianne's imaginary rationalization of events and the "real" status
of these same events, he presents her practicing some kind of
introspection. Marianne's introspection takes the form of interior
monologues that are often held in front of the favorite Marivaudian instrument of self-awareness: the mirror. Let us focus for a
moment on Marianne's first encounter with the mirror:

I put on my clothes in the most modest and grave manner, before a little silly looking-glass, which could scarce show me half of my person. But that half appeared smart and charming *[bien piquant]*. I then began to dress my head, that I might enjoy at once all my ornaments. I could not look upon my growing beauty, which seemed to increase in proportion as I advanced in dressing, without feeling a kind of pleasing palpitation at my heart *[Il me prenait des palpitations en songeant combien j'allais être jolie]*, whilst my hand trembled at every pin I stuck. I made as much speed as I could to finish my agreeable employment, yet without being over-hasty, for I was willing to have nothing imperfect . . . [1]

What should we make of this face to face exchange with the mirror? First of all, we see that Marianne is fascinated less by the outfit that graces her figure than by the enhanced self-image that *she imagines*. The mirror sends back not what is familiar—the real—but instead something unexpected, an "embellished" virtual image. The image that Marianne sees in the looking glass is neither objective reality nor even the image of the "real" Marianne; it is the image that she projects through her visual imaginary: "Il me prenait des palpitations *en songeant combien j'allais être jolie.*" To her surprise, and jubilation, Marianne discovers that the discrepancy in representation works in her favor, because she soon realizes that her "being in the world" does not exist outside of the imaginary representation that she projects in the mirror. She also learns that one does not enter the social circuit as a "being in itself," but rather as a "being in the world," that is, luckily for her, as the embellished image that she projects for herself and for the Other. Finally, Marianne's social education is completed the moment she discovers that she does not need a mirror to see herself, because the eye of the Other—her rivals—provides an even better means of self-awareness.

Now, let us imagine for a moment someone who is ignorant of the image he is projecting in society. Let us suppose further that this person has no mirror and consequently cannot see his image, his disguise, by himself. Let us call this person Rica, give him a Persian identity, and transplant him to Paris. One day, Rica is happily strolling through the Ispahan of Europe when he suddenly

---

[1] *The Virtuous Orphan,* 46–47; *La vie de Marianne,* 117.

discovers that the eye of the Other is not producing any image
of him at all! What happens then?

Most readers recall the famous passage of *The Persian Letters*
in which Rica writes of his distress at having lost his Persian
identity on the day he decided to trade his Persian "image" for a
French outfit. "This test," says he, "made me understand what I
was *really* worth... for I immediately fell into a frightful *nothingness [néant].*"[2] But in reality, Rica is *réellement* Persian! We
may glean from his unfortunate experience that the real "worth"
of the Persian real—of any real—is to be found in the image rather
than in the reality. This we could have predicted. Objective
knowledge of things "such as they are" is not accessible to anyone,
for there is nothing outside of representation. Even the epistemological privilege that is characteristic of the foreign observer
(so often singled out by Montesquieu's critics as a main point of
his novel) does not hold when one seeks to go to the "heart" of
things. What happens to Rica in this respect? He realizes that,
whereas he had believed that there exists a "secure" Persian real,
there is in fact nothing. What is worse, however, is the loss of
his self-image. Marianne's jubilation at the advent of her image
in the mirror is matched only by Rica's terror when he sees (or
does not see!) that he is not portrayed by any representation—
neither mirror nor the Other's eye—which might allow him to
pass over to the image; in other words, to the world and to himself.
Let us note that in this episode, first, the "advent" of the real
coincides with the loss of the image; and second, Rica experiences
the loss of his image as the loss of his life ("I fell into a frightful
nothingness"). It follows deductively that the real is intimately
linked to death: like the real, death implies the disappearance of
the image, because it is that which we cannot imagine. The ca-
tastrophe that threatens Rica is, in truth, the possible *return of
the Persian real*, which is equivalent to some form of "death."
This point will prove crucial to my argument.

If there is a central episode in *The Persian Letters*, it is indeed
that of Rica. Paul Valéry was the first to recognize this when he

---

[2] "Cet essai me fit connaître ce que je valais *réellement....* J'entrai tout à coup
dans un *néant* affreux" (*The Persian Letters*, trans. J. Robert Loy [New York:
Meridian Books, 1961], xxx, 88). All further references to *The Persian Letters* will
appear in the text using the abbreviation *PL* (unless the source is obvious), followed
by the letter number (in Roman numerals) and the page number.

reformulated the question asked of Rica ("Comment peut-on être Persan?")[3] into its contemporary philosophical equivalent: "Comment peut-on être ce que l'on est?"[4] How can anyone be himself, that is, how can one achieve self-autonomy?[5] It was this question that provoked Usbek and Rica to leave Persia—to discover the meaning of truth and freedom for the self. Of course, the logical outcome of the question is death: the point at which the self is freed of everything beyond itself. But by an unforeseen turn of events, Rica prematurely stumbles upon the truth—in its Persian version—which Usbek will only discover at the end of the novel.

Let us focus on the language that conveys Rica's experience. His ordeal is expressed in terms of what he calls "a frightful nothingness"—*un néant affreux*. The word *néant* and its derivative *anéanti* (annihilated) appear three more times in *The Persian Letters* (Letters II, CLV, and CLVII). Each time it is used, *le néant* is associated with the figure of the eunuch; each time it signifies a real or symbolic castration. It is certainly clear for the informed reader that one of the peculiarities of *The Persian Letters* is that the symbolic field in which the novel occurs is not that of biological sexuality, but rather that of castration. All the characters castrate and are castrated symbolically: Usbek does to the eunuchs what the eunuchs do to the seraglio wives, and ultimately, what the wives do to Usbek. It would be a mistake to assume that, in this operation, the eunuch can be simply categorized as castrated: on the contrary, he is the "blind spot" around which the whole system revolves. The eunuch is at the center of the novel's system of meaning just as he is at the center of the seraglio's chain of command; hence this center is symbolically and structurally empty, constituted by a lack—castration. If Rica's experience is central to the *Letters*, it is because, in the flash of an instant, Rica apprehends the symbolic truth of the eunuch, of "being separated forever" from his image, that is, from himself.[6]

Rica's Parisian episode anticipates symbolically the hermeneu-

---

[3] "How can anyone be a Persian?" (XXX, 88).

[4] Valéry, "Préface aux *Lettres persanes,*" *Variété II* (Paris: Gallimard, 1930), 65.

[5] Cf. Lionel Gossman's short but incisive note on that very question, which appears as the text of a review of J. R. Loy's translation of *The Persian Letters,* in *MLN* 77:4 (1962), 322–25.

[6] The First Eunuch refers to his castration in terms of "being separated forever from myself" (IX, 55).

tic truth of the Persian real—the real nature of despotism—which
Usbek will reach at the end of the novel. Thus Rica and Usbek
find the true meaning of self-autonomy in two different registers:
symbolic and hermeneutic. Montesquieu succeeds in combining
these two paths to truth so as to make them fuse into one ultimate
discovery. Roland Barthes discusses a similar convergence in his
analysis of Balzac's short story *Sarrasine:* "Its success hinges on
a structural artifice: identifying the symbolic and the hermeneutic, making the search for truth (hermeneutic structure) into the
search for castration (symbolic structure), making the truth be
anecdotally (and no longer symbolically) the absent phallus."[7]
Usbek discovers the symbolic truth about himself ("le phallus
perdu") at the very moment that his *tale* is silenced (hermeneutic
truth). He never answers Roxane's letter.

I shall elaborate in the following pages on the meaning(s) of
this end, and in the process, discuss Usbek's political imaginary—
the structure of the seraglio and the nature of despotic authority—
in terms of the body's representations. For it will become clear,
as we proceed with our reading, that the topography of the body
in *The Persian Letters* serves as the symbolic figuration of a political *topos,* in the etymological sense of the term.

The Politics of the Body

Despotic authority depends on the forms submission takes.
Hence I shall address this question by analyzing, first, how submission in the seraglio propagates itself; and second, how, by an
act of legerdemain on the part of the despot, the wives' submission
is transformed into a *desire* for submission. The passage from
imposed submission to a desire to submit follows precise steps
that, when considered together, produce the discourse of despotism—a discourse that holds the knowledge necessary to legitim-
ize despotism and assure that even the most distant subjects
submit to the master. This "science" of power, which enables the
despot to capture and captivate his subjects, rests on an unshak-
able belief: "faith in love."[8] The success of any doctrine espousing

---

[7] *S/Z,* 164.
[8] Discussing the nature of Chinese despotism in Book XIX-19 of *The Spirit,*

submission depends on the subject's necessary shift from imposed to voluntary subjection. And this shift is characteristic of despotism, which perfects and formalizes faith in love as a kind of sexology that rules the sociopolitical economy of the seraglio through its sexual economy.

What is faith in love, and how does it regulate the subject's imaginary so as to bring about the desire for submission? On one level, faith in love is an art of murmuring comforting but empty declarations, as Usbek's letters to his wives demonstrate. More important, however, it is a way of imaginarily representing the real object of the wives' desire—the despot's body. Because the wives' imaginaries are systematically fixed upon the body as object of desire, their faith in love becomes an obsession with the despot's body, and they end up confusing their love for his body with the social authority it represents. As a result, the body is granted the legitimacy of an absolute law—the Law. The reading that follows aims to show how the social order of the seraglio is built upon a particular representation of the despot's body, a representation that depends on a manipulation of the subjects' imaginaries, and which results in forms of political submission such as those that one finds in despotic governments. As a model of despotic institution, the seraglio fabricates an *image* of the body—the image both embodies the Law and makes it manifest—which is idealized by means of a number of complex operations. These operations allow us to see how the code of the imaginary is organized, and how this code conveys and legislates both the subjects' imaginaries and, by a certain turn of events, the despot's imaginary as well.

As a background to our analysis of the structure and functioning of the seraglio, it might be useful at this point to remind ourselves that the key to the plot of *The Persian Letters* lies in the gradual changes that Usbek undergoes, more specifically the changes that his body undergoes as he visits Paris. These changes, which will be the focus of our analysis, are reflected in the tone of his language and in the content and nature of his letters home. But before

---

Montesquieu uses the formula "love relation *[rapport d'amour]* between the prince and his subjects" (*Oeuvres*, vol. ii, 570). I prefer the concept "faith in love" because of the religious shadings it gives to the nature of love in the seraglio.

analyzing the figurative and symbolic configurations by which Montesquieu stages power relationships in the seraglio, let us take a little detour by way of *The Spirit of Laws.*

We recall from *The Spirit* the difference between the nature and principle of government: "its nature is that by which it is constituted, and its principle that by which it is made to act. One is its particular structure, and the other the human passions which set it in motion" (III, 117). In Book III-8, Montesquieu adds that the principle of government is the "mainspring of the whole machine,"[9] thus implying that, by definition, a principle must be shared by those who govern and those who are governed. The mechanics of power require reciprocal and reversible relationships if the system is to function at all. In this sense, the seraglio, understood as a structure of power, satisfies all the requirements of a political machine. All of the characters are situated and interlinked within a master-slave dialectical chain: all command and all obey. Yet the seraglio is a peculiar machine in that the motivating principle that regulates all sociopolitical rapport is the *noncirculation* of bodies, rather than their circulation. Hence the effective principle of power by which the seraglio functions is reduced to the symbolic efficiency of the despot's body.

Regarding the "nature" of the seraglio, we will propose an explanation by way of an analogy, or rather, a metaphor: Montesquieu's metaphor of the seraglio-machine.[10] We should note here one very simple, even elementary, point: the seraglio is rigidly codified. Not just anyone can gain access to it in any way that one pleases. The arbitrary and the unexpected are vulgar notions that have no place in the seraglio, for everything occurs according to a regulated mode of functioning, followed punctually by all participants. "One must admit," writes Usbek, "that the seraglio is made more for hygiene [santé] than for pleasure. It is a uniform

---

[9] I have examined elsewhere how Montesquieu uses the machine analogy to communicate his understanding of the political world. See the entry "Montesquieu" in *European Writers: The Age of Reason and the Enlightenment,* ed. George Stade (New York: Scribner's, 1984).

[10] This aspect of the seraglio is perceptively developed by Alain Grosrichard in *Structure du sérail: La fiction du despotisme asiatique dans l'Occident classique* (Paris: Seuil, 1979). I am particularly indebted to his reading in the chapter entitled "La machine," 91–106.

existence, without excitement. Everything exudes obedience and duty. Even the pleasures taken there are sober, and the joys severe" (xxxiv, 91). However, to understand Montesquieu's homology of the seraglio and the (political) machine, we must determine how and to what end it functions: first, by situating its source of energy; second, by analyzing the manner in which energy circulates; and third, by establishing what the machine produces and for what purpose.

The reader of *The Persian Letters* will undoubtedly diagnose, at least on a thematic level, all of the components that constitute the seraglio-machine. The motor ("mainspring" or "driving force" in Montesquieu's vocabulary) is the erotic body of the despot— "the flattering voice of that sex which extracts a hearing from the rocks and stirs even inanimate objects" (xxvii, 83). At the organic level, this erotic body is the mainspring of power, in that it produces, for each of its subjects, the needed conditions for vitality, harmony, and proper functioning; yet it also represents the *language* of power, because it speaks and transmits, in a "flattering voice" the ultimate knowledge that can even give life to "inanimate objects." However, this body that claims to "extract a hearing from rocks" is deceptive. The despot's body speaks not through its sexual exploits, but rather through a delirious discourse whose nature we shall soon specify.

To return to the machine homology, Usbek's body is the motor that feeds the machine with negative energy—negative because it originates from an illusory source, that is, an illusory body. At a level below that of the despot, the eunuchs are those who possess the technical expertise to operate within the machine. "In the seraglio it is as if I were in a small empire,"[1] says the chief eunuch, who continues, "I can see with pleasure that everything turns on me and that I am needed at every moment" (ix, 56). To minimize the risk of disturbances and to assure that the seraglio functions smoothly, it is important to provide replacement parts.

---

[1] In Montesquieu's anatomical imagery, and later in his political imagery, the terms *empire*, *body*, and *machine* are often used as synonyms. See, for example, this early passage from the *Discours sur l'usage des glandes rénales* written in 1718: "When we study the *human body* and become familiar with the immutable laws that govern *this little empire*, when we consider . . . this *machine* which is so simple in its action and so complex in its moving parts . . . what grand examples of wisdom and economy!" (*Oeuvres complètes*, vol. i, 15).

Thus, in order to be replaceable, all of the machine's components must be interchangeable: the eunuchs are interchangeable by virtue of their sexual nullity, and women are interchangeable because of their sexual servitude.[12] To this end, the seraglio presents two perfectly symmetrical lines of political submission: the first is based on "sacred" love (the women), and the second is based on "political" love (the eunuchs). Finally, this machine, which runs according to the personal regimen of the despot, produces nothing but the same: images of the self. Indeed, the despot cannot conceive of an otherness except as a means of satisfying his own self-image and felicity: "For what are all of you if not base tools that I can break at my fancy . . . who draw breath only so long as my happiness, my love, and even my jealousy exist . . . who can hope for no other lot but submission, no other soul than my desires, no other hope save my felicity?" (xxi, 75).

This passage accentuates an essential point: Usbek holds the only discourse possible in the seraglio. He is the voice of the Law—the Law that dispossesses any subject of the claim to have something to say outside of the Law's message. By personifying the Law in the eyes of his subjects, Usbek comes to occupy a sacred position in the seraglio: he represents the all-powerful and absent god (just as He is absent in religion) in which all the subjects must believe, in order to live and "flourish." All of Usbek's edicts are final, for Usbek is, and speaks, the Law. Despotic discourse echoes Louis xiv's famous proclamation "L'Etat, c'est moi," yet with a twist: it declares repeatedly, "La Loi, c'est moi," in order to (re)confirm at every moment the despot's legitimacy and to perpetuate the cult of his personality.

Having described the structure of the seraglio as a political machine, it remains for us to explain the dynamics of power and the principles by which its subjects are made to act and interact among themselves.

The formal closure of the seraglio—a place where "no man has ever soiled you with his lascivious regard" (xxvi, 80)—corresponds to a specific disposition of the body. Just as the step, cadence, and movement of the Oriental body are regulated in all of their expressions, so too the order of the seraglio is organized with the purpose of instituting a state of bodily rest and innocence "far from the

---

[12] Cf. on this point Letter ii from Usbek to the First Black Eunuch.

reaches of all human beings" (xxvi, 80). We witness here something quite different from an ordinary exercise of control over the body; what is taught in the seraglio is a kind of grammar of submission. The body of the woman is treated ceremonially, the better to signify submission. The eyes, hands, and face of Usbek's wives, which must never be seen by anyone but him, signify an explicit recognition of their own submission. A happy submission, I might add, because the seraglio conceives of this "policing" of the body in the modern sense of the term *police*: it is a power that protects the social well-being of its citizens. The social code of the seraglio, whereby no woman can be seen, aims in this way to ensure the wives' happiness: its prescriptive interdictions are a reglementation of happiness. "How fortunate you are, Roxane, to be in the gentle country of Persia. . . . You dwell in my seraglio in a continuing state of innocence. . . . You are in a joyful state of happy inability to transgress. O happy Roxane!" (xxvi, 80).

Yet, to be operative, the social code depends on the sexual code of the seraglio. The social law of happiness has its sexual requisite, which states that a woman can experience happiness only to the extent that her body conforms to the needs of the master's body. The regulated gestures and countless little rituals that the women must follow are a manner of formalizing the female body, so that the Law of the master will resonate all the more. We might even call this a daily training intended to make the female body "dance" to the tune of the despot's body. This process aims at preventing the woman's body from imagining independent pleasures. That is, the feminine body's imaginary cannot be its own master: it can only express itself in the code of Usbek's own "perfect" body. The results are quite telling; they illustrate the passage from submission to the desire for submission in the name of "faith in love": " 'Even were I permitted to leave this place where I am enclosed by the necessity of my calling [writes Fatmé to Usbek]; were I capable of eluding the encircling guards, were I able to choose among all the men living in this capital of nations, Usbek, I swear it, I should choose only you. In all the world, there can be only you worthy of being loved' " (vii, 52).

Considered from this perspective, the seraglio is a disciplinary machine that distributes pleasure to all its subjects by concentrating it in a central point: the transcendent Body of the despot. This conception of the body as Body is required for the orderly

76

functioning of the seraglio; moreover, all other participants in this despotic machine are distributed in terms of their relationship to this principle of transcendence. Each individual belongs to a class that is defined by a lack, a lack that is specifically brought into contrast with the master's perfect body. Eunuchs, women, children—all members of the seraglio—represent *negatively* the one feature particular to the master; thus they provide both the visible emblem of his body's infinite superiority and the tangible reminder of his presence, even when he is not there.

The Chief Eunuch, the white First Eunuch, and the Black Eunuch hold positions that give them a provisional power, that give them, in fact, all the power, save the absolute power of the body. "Vain semblance of an authority that is never entirely communicated," remarks the First Eunuch, "we represent but weakly half of your own self" (xcvi, 183). The authority of these "master-eunuchs" is paradoxical, for they are the relays and not the sources of power.[13] They share the power of Usbek in the chain of command, and in that sense they are his doubles—they use symmetrical means to implement the wives' submission, and share Usbek's knowledge of them. Nevertheless, as the eunuchs take great pains to remind us, they are dispossessed of their desires by dint of their sexual nothingness and are, consequently, Usbek's first victims as well as his doubles. Thus the eunuchs only exercise power inasmuch as they convey Usbek's desires and orders. They represent, but do not *replace,* the master: in that way, they provide simulacra of authority which draw attention, by analogy, to their false sexuality. It is precisely because they are impotent, cut off from all sexuality and "separated forever from themselves," that they seek to compensate for their central lack by blindly identifying with the master's body. This is accomplished, in the eunuchs' sexual imaginary, by an association with the master's eye. It is not simply the erotic symbolism associated with the eye that I wish to evoke here. Rather, I would argue that the eye in *The Persian Letters*—considered as an authorized *regard* (gaze), or as the maniacal eye that sees all—is the privileged organ

---

[13] Jaron, Nessir, Solim, and others become masters only because they have "at birth" renounced any claim to absolute mastery. "Remember always the void *[néant]* from which I drew you. . . . But, by an exchange of authority, you command as master like myself," writes Usbek to the First Black Eunuch (ii, 48).

of sexual fantasy, and even more significant, the agent of despotic tyranny.

There is, at a first level, a confirmation of the symbolic function of the eye, in that it literally becomes the organ of love. Usbek's sexual climax—and authority—are explicitly achieved through the eye. "We had to present ourselves to your view in the simplicity of nature," writes Zachi to Usbek as she recalls their first encounter. "Happy Usbek, what charms were displayed before your eyes! We saw you wander from one delight to the next... you extended your curious regard to the most secret spots; in a trice, you made us assume a thousand different positions—ever a new command and ever a new submission" (III, 49). And as Usbek reminds Zachi in turn, the *regard* is penetrating: "You diminish my honor by exposing yourself to glances" (xx, 73).[14]

In contrast, and for good reason, the eunuch's gaze is an indifferent blank stare: "I behold women with indifference" (IX, 56), says the First Eunuch, who adds later, "I am all the better a judge of women since they never take me by surprise" (XCVI, 182). Dead or blind to sexual curiosity, the eunuch's eye becomes a maniacal eye, obsessed with detail: it dissects but does not see. The eunuch deciphers indices of beauty in a woman's body, without having any possible sexual curiosity himself. The Great Black Eunuch reminds Usbek that he is a kind of "anatomist" of vision: "I... undressed her, and examined her with the eyes *[les regards]* of a judge. The more I examined, the more charms I found" (LXXIX, 161). This scene takes place while he is looking to purchase a new slave for Usbek's seraglio. Once his decision is made, his penetrating gaze dies instantaneously: "As soon as I had judged her worthy of you, I lowered my eyes and threw a scarlet mantle over her" (ibid.). Eunuchs and wives never exchange glances, because the *regard* is sexual and hence reserved only for the despot.[15]

Yet the eye operates on a double register: as the substitute judge for the gaze of the despot, the eunuch's eye functions *in all circumstances* as his master's eye. The eunuch cannot be the mas-

[14] In both examples, the pleasure principle gives way to the motif of obedience. In the case of the eunuch, on the other hand, vision becomes ultimately punitive. For instance, Usbek tells Zachi, "You cannot stand the chief eunuch because he always keeps an eye on your conduct" (xx, 74).
[15] Usbek writes to the First Eunuch, "You... cannot without committing a crime, raise your eyes on the fearless objects of my love" (xxi, 74).

ter's "flattering voice," but as the agent of surveillance in the seraglio, he *is* his master's eye. Narsit writes to Usbek: "Be sure that nothing will happen here [in the seraglio] that your eyes could not behold" (CLII, 273); and disaster strikes when the Great Eunuch confides to Solim that "the only grief I feel upon leaving this life is that my last glances have found my master's wives criminal" (CLI, 272). This merging of the eunuchs' eyes into the master's eye has formidable political consequences. It is the fundamental ingredient of the fear produced by knowing that *authority is always watching you*. It is only at the *level of vision* that the distinction between Usbek and his eunuchs alluded to earlier breaks down. This is for the obvious reason that by converging into a unifying vision, the multiple eyes constitute the despot's universal, omnipotent Eye: the reign of despotic fear.

At all other levels, however, the function of the eunuch is systematically to emphasize the absence of the master: the eunuch accentuates what he *lacks* by contrast to what Usbek *has*. In a letter to Usbek, Zélis mocks the White Eunuch's request to be allowed to marry Zélide, calling it a "false marriage": "What does she propose to do with that unhappy fellow...who will always remember what he was and thus make himself remember what he is no longer....Live always and only in images and in phantoms. Live only to imagine!" (LIII, 119). And yet, as the simulacrum of the master, the eunuch performs what is perhaps the most important function in the seraglio. Paul Valéry was again the first to note, with a certain perplexity, the disproportionate place assigned to eunuchs in *The Persian Letters*: "Who will explain these eunuchs to me? I have no doubt there is a secret and profound reason for the almost obligatory presence of these characters so cruelly separated from so many things, and in some way, from themselves."[16] I will address Valéry's question by discussing the eunuch's role in the sexual and imaginary economy of the seraglio.

The eunuch occupies a precise place. He is *in the place* of the master; he represents and commands in the name of the absent. At this level, he is responsible for the task of supervising the

---

[16] "Préface aux *Lettres persanes*," 71. J. Robert Loy has a most suggestive commentary on the central role of the eunuch in his *Montesquieu* (New York: Twayne, 1968), 48–52.

production of pleasure for the master: "I take aroused *[irritées]* women to my master's bed" (IX, 57). But by virtue of his own sexual separation, the eunuch is, as we have seen, all the more astute as a judge of women. Consequently, and paradoxically, the eunuch becomes the principal coordinator of sexual relations, the professional coupler who restores sexual harmony and provides for peace in the seraglio: "Disorder arose between the sexes because their rights were reciprocal. We have entered upon the plane of a new harmony. We have put between women and ourselves, hate, and between men and women, love" (XXII, 75). In this sense, the eunuch holds the keys to the happiness of the "subjects," for it is he who directs his master's choice of wife on any given night (LXIV, 226).

On a more profound level, however, the eunuch performs an even more fundamental operation—fundamental in that it touches everyone in the seraglio. It is precisely because the eunuch is unable to compensate for his lack that the women have no choice but to keep imagining the master's "beautiful" body. Thus it is the eunuch's inadequate corporality that keeps the master's body alive in the wives' memory. "I do not count as men those frightful eunuchs whose least fault is the very fact that they are not men at all," writes Fatmé, who adds that, by contrast, "My imagination furnishes me no more delightful idea than the enchanting charms of your [Usbek's] person" (VII, 52). By maintaining the illusion of Usbek's presence in his absence, the eunuch is the cornerstone of the seraglio's imaginary economy. Furthermore, if we grant that it is essential for the despot to perpetuate a positive image of a transcendent presence, we can then understand that the multiplication of the "negative" relays provided by the eunuchs is an operative strategy intended to create transitory supports for the image of the despot. Each relay (eunuch) recalls by opposition Usbek's power—now a symbolic one only, but all the stronger for being unconfirmable in reality. The eunuch is therefore the central agent in the process by which the women's imaginaries produce and substitute fictional scenarios for the reality of their life in the seraglio. Jaron, Nessir, Narsit, and others are thus the subtle spokesmen for the power of representation to pass absence off as a certified real.

Montesquieu is undoubtedly the first writer to have staged an erotico-political fiction to demonstrate that all political systems gain in strength and stability—at least in the short run—as the imaginary realm increases at the expense of the reality principle. In the limiting case of despotism, I would argue, the real must be completely annulled. For it is the complete takeover by the imagination that makes the seraglio-machine so effective. It can operate at full capacity precisely because everyone, from Usbek to the least of his subjects, fails to recognize the imaginary game in which all participate and from which none may escape once they have been taken in. Hence Montesquieu's correlative political maxim: "The reason that princes usually have such a mistaken idea of their greatness is that those who educate them are themselves dazzled by it; they are the first to be duped, and princes are only duped as an aftereffect."[17]

The same voluntary relation of "dupes" can be found at the beginning of *The Persian Letters* among Usbek's subjects, and first of all among his wives. They represent interchangeable sexual objects (Zachi, Zephis, Zelis, Zelide[18]—even their names remind us of their equivalent status in the seraglio), and in that sense it is clearly less a question for Usbek of possessing his individual wives than of possessing the other sex. Nevertheless, in the early days after his departure, the idea of Usbek's body so pervades the wives' minds that, even in his absence, they dress and prepare themselves as if in anticipation of his imminent return. But Usbek's absence lasts nine years! And in the meantime, there is no new satisfaction, no other "presence" in sight for these women, who live, says Fatmé, "deprived of him who alone can satisfy them" (VII, 53). Thus they fall back on what has gone before. Fatmé takes refuge in the imaginary realm and invests Usbek's body with all the prestigious attributes her imagination can produce: "I remember those happy times when you would come in my arms. A happy dream, seducing me, brings before me the dear object of my love. My imagination is lost in its own desires" (VII, 53). Zachi wanders "from apartment to apartment, seeking you always, finding you never," but finding instead memories of past adventures that obsessively come to haunt her mind: "everywhere falling upon the cruel memory of my past felicity" (III, 48).

---

[17] *Mes pensées, Oeuvres complètes*, vol. I, 1440.

[18] Cf. Jean Starobinski's suggestive commentary on the sinuosity and sensuality of the letter Z, "Préface," *Les lettres persanes* (Paris: Gallimard, 1973), 20.

The intensity of such image-memories erupts vividly in the correspondence. Zachi's letter in particular refers explicitly to the elaborate theatrical games staged by the seraglio wives as a competitive measure to capture Usbek's favors. However, suspending her sentence in midcourse, Zachi suddenly catches herself succumbing to the effect of her imagination: "But where have I strayed? Where does this empty recital take me?" (III, 49). It is clear that, short of indulging themselves in forbidden pleasures, the wives must resort to letter writing. And although the images transcribed on paper cannot be "translated" into real objects, they provide the women with their sole means of conjuring the missing body back to the seraglio. By the work of the imaginary upon her memory, Zachi transfigures the past by projecting it onto the present (III, 48). The phenomenon is even more striking in the case of Fatmé, who writes: "I run about throughout the whole harem as if you were still here.... Nights pass in dreams that belong neither to sleep nor to waking; I seek you at my side and you seem to be fleeing me" (VII, 52–53). Hence Usbek's body is endowed, through the force of the imagination, with an exorbitant power: "Fire is flowing in my veins.... In such moments, Usbek, I [Fatmé] should give the dominion of the whole world for a single one of your kisses" (VII, 53).

In its new imaginary life, the body becomes Body—all the more dazzling the longer it is absent. It must be emphasized here that the transcendent sexual force that the women recognize as an attribute exclusively held by Usbek is the symbolic means by which his power is rendered absolute. By becoming an object of faith—because his body has been divested of any meaning in reality, the wives must believe in it all the more—Usbek's Body also becomes the principle of obedience and order around which the seraglio's hierarchies are established. This principle illustrates Montesquieu's political belief that, in despotic governments, power must operate on the basis of two complementary notions: love and fear, or faith and obedience.[19] I will explain this last point, namely how the imaginary of authority represented by the

---

[19] For a discussion of the relationship between despotic and religious authority, see *The Spirit of Laws*, bk. III, chaps. 9 and 10, "Of the Principle of Despotic Government" and "Difference of Obedience in Moderate and Despotic Governments."

despot is consecrated, so that love of the Body becomes love of the despotic institution.[20]

The version of this operation Montesquieu describes in *The Persian Letters* depends on the rigorous manner in which the imaginary, of subjects and despot alike, is organized around the representation of the Body. For the women, the despot's body undergoes a first stage of consecration in which it is fetishized; it is then transformed, by being honored with great ceremony, into an extraordinary body that surpasses all others.[21] "Extraordinary" means in this instance something that transcends the ordinary: a sacred body. Even in its absence, the wives preserve the memory of this body—a mummy surrounded by sacred rites. As Fatmé says, "Do not fear that your absence has made me neglect the beauty that is dear to you. Although I am seen by no one and although the finery in which I array myself is useless for your present happiness, still I attempt to maintain the habit of pleasing. I never go to bed without being perfumed with the most delicious scents" (VII, 52). To compensate for the lack of body, Fatmé literally practices idolatry. Usbek's body is incarnated in a borrowed (imaginary) body, the empty body of an idol-mummy, which nonetheless speaks, even though it lacks corporeality. The delirious "faith in love" that overtakes Fatmé's body becomes a sacred delirium toward the idol, and leads Fatmé to proclaim her faith in love as faith in the idol—the Body: "Know that I live only to adore you. My soul is completely filled with you; and your absence, far from making me forget you, would enliven my love for you if it could possibly become any more violent" (VII, 53).

Through a chain effect, this delirium communicates both its effects and the belief in the Law of the Body as a principle of obedience; as the novel advances, the delirium becomes more and more pronounced, and Zachi writes toward the end: "Nights, days, passing moments—all were for you" (CLVII, 277). The Body takes over the wives' imaginary, to such an extent that Zachi

[20] This collapse of civil and personal values onto political ones is made possible, as Montesquieu explains in Book v-14 of *The Spirit*, by the fact that in despotic government "the whole is reduced to reconciling the political and civil government with the domestic management, the officers of state with those of the seraglio" ("In what manner the laws are relative to the principles of a despotic government"), 144.

[21] All of Fatmé's Letter VII is emblematic of this transformation.

internalizes the Body's tyranny and makes herself subject to it, blaming herself for her momentary weaknesses. The result is that she conforms even more faithfully to her status of subjected wife. When the eunuch Solim takes over the seraglio to avenge Usbek's honor, and abuses her sexually,[22] her reaction is telling: "The tiger [Solim] dares to tell me that you are the perpetrator of all these cruelties.... When he pronounces the name of the man I love, I can no longer find pity for myself; I can only die" (CLVII 277). Obedience is not differentiated from Zachi's faith in love, even if it implies her death.

Thus the idealized body is the foundation of despotic politics. The despotic order selects a human body (any body will do) and then reconstitutes it into an idealized body that becomes, in turn, the Law. This second Body is the main invention of despotic order: to the exclusion of all else, despotism speaks to and about this Body, by means of its subjects' imaginary scenarios, which can attain, as we witness in the seraglio, a degree of sacred delirium. It is by this operation that the Body—the Law—dictates to each subject the conditions necessary for the harmony, sexual (love) and political (obedience), of the despotic machine, while also enunciating a method of reinforcing its authority.

Furthermore, I should explain here what I merely mentioned earlier, namely that, in the seraglio, one cannot *dissociate* an imaginary production that founds authority from one that founds submission. The imaginary operation does not function locally, but always globally. Let us reconsider, for example, the episode of the theatrical games described by Zachi, games intended to conjure up Usbek's past sexual exploits. We should note, first, that this is a *staging* of sexuality, enacted to mark Usbek's omnipotence:

Each of us had made pretense to a superiority in beauty over the others. We all appeared before you after having exhausted our imaginations in finery and ornament. *You looked with pleasure on these miracles of our art....* Happy Usbek, what charms were displayed before your eyes! We saw you wander long from one delight to the

[22] Zachi: "O Heaven! A barbarian has injured [outragée] me even in his very manner of punishing me! He inflicted upon me that chastisement which begins with shocking our modesty...that chastisement which, so to speak, brings us back to childhood" (CLVII, 276–77).

84

next; *your wavering soul remained for a long time in a state of indecision* [sans se fixer]." (III, 49, my italics)

Usbek himself is well aware of the importance attached to these theatrical games. When he describes his seduction of Roxane, his favorite wife—the only seduction that he recounts in *The Persian Letters*—he tells us that he was seduced by "the grace of her dancing and the sweetness of her voice" (XXVI, 81). This remark follows soon after a description of his "love combat" with Roxane, a combat that, although presented as highly sexualized, is actually mythologized: "Two months went by in this battle of Love and Virtue" (ibid.).[23]

What this episode brings into relief is the *theatrical nature* of seduction and not the seduction itself. Why this insistence on theatricality? Let us return, once more, to Zachi's description of the women's theatrical games and remark, this time, that this scene describes not the body of the woman but rather the *staging* of the woman's body; a theatrical staging as in the case of Roxane's alleged seduction. All of these theatrical games, performed for Usbek, communicate desire through a body that is no longer, strictly speaking, the anatomical body: it is a staged body, a theatrical or dancing body, in which sex is no longer expressed in its materiality but rather suggested metaphorically. In this sense, the seraglio is a theater that organizes a ceremonial, but not a real, sexuality. The "amorous body" speaks through the wives' dances and theatrical games, yet it speaks not of the body, but of the *lack* of a body. We witness the spectacle of an aestheticized Body, a *corporeally empty* body in which, paradoxically, the wives' bodies merge into one idealized body—the Body of the seraglio. Hence sexual activity is not Usbek's first priority. He never chooses *one* wife, for he can never choose ("Your wavering soul remained for a long time in a state of indecision"); in the single instance in which he does choose, he of course chooses the only wife who will not surrender herself physically—Roxane: "You withheld

[23] Orest Ranum has an interesting commentary on the nature of this combat. He remarks that "Montesquieu's choice of the word *immoler* [to describe Roxane's attempt to kill Usbek] suggests that he sought to convey the notion that the husband was the source of religious truth in the harem." Ranum also picks up on the theatricality involved in the sacrificial connotation of *immoler*. Cf. "Personality and Politics in the *Persian Letters*," *Political Science Quarterly* 84:4 (1969).

from me all you could of your charms and graces, and I was intoxicated with the greatest favors without having obtained the lesser" (xxvi, 81).

Moreover, Usbek advises the First Black Eunuch to instruct the wives to take part in these theatrical ceremonies: "Calm their fears [*trompe leurs inquiétudes*], divert them with music, dances, delicious drinks; persuade them to assemble together often" (ii, 48). It is imperative that the wives gather together, for it is by means of this social act that the wives become a collective, their bodies a global unit, which forms in turn the performing Body. This Body is a spectacle offered to Usbek as a social distraction, yet it upholds in still another way the seraglio's ideal of submission. The wives walk together, dance together, "theatricalize" together, and are consequently seen in the same light—literally, *regardées toutes du même oeil*. Usbek looks but never touches. He is the omniscient master who sees all, who finds satisfaction in it all—but in the mode of a civilized sexual bliss that experiences sexuality only through an aesthetic form. Hence the seraglio fulfills its function of a theater of power: there are, on the one hand, those who dance; and on the other hand, *he* who watches. The division is both sexual and political: the mastery and enjoyment *(jouissance)* of bodies through the omniscient eye, contrasted with the submission of individual bodies who dissolve into the greater Body of the seraglio.

The idealized Body of the seraglio constitutes the operation by which the despot's imaginary rules over reality. Not surprisingly, this empty Body functions for Usbek in the imaginary realm as it does for his wives. Usbek invents a Body by means of a theatrical "composition" that simulates sexual celebration in the only form that can exist in the seraglio—an imaginary one. And by continually ceremonializing sexual celebration, Usbek renders it irrefutable, "real." (Of course, Usbek's love for the ceremonial Body is nothing but the narcissistic image of his own body, projected as the perfect Body of the seraglio.) Thus we see how the despotic machine is constituted by the perfect fixation and coordination of two imaginary constructs: the image of Usbek's body as transcendent, and the ideal Body of the seraglio (the collective body of the wives). We have here two perfectly symmetrical mirror images, between which the participants *imagine* scenes of love even while reality remains, properly speaking, destitute. In the end, the seraglio is the site of a narcissistic confusion, by which these two images fuse into one.

It remains for us to show how the wives' imaginaries work out their strategies in the seraglio. From the point of view of seraglio life, the wives cling to the imaginary projection of Usbek's body as a way of protecting themselves. For any attempt, no matter how negligible, to question the transcendence of the master would automatically put into question the entire system of the seraglio. Zelis's early breach of faith in the system, which occurs about midpoint in the novel—"Even in this very prison where you hold me, I am freer than you [Usbek]. . . . Your suspicions, your jealousy, and your heartaches are all so many proofs of your dependency" (LXII, 133)—prefigures Roxane's letter, the last of the novel, which spells out her death, the collapse of the seraglio, and with it, one must assume, Usbek's annihilation. Nevertheless, and for obvious reasons, as long as they can avoid the collapse, the wives reinforce—willingly or unwillingly—the process by which the image passes for the real thing. But beyond a certain point, imaginary life cannot sustain itself anymore. And although Usbek's wives have undergone a bodily training that defies all the ruses of the imagination, the imaginary object of love (the Body) must nevertheless take form, produce itself as body, or else adultery and betrayal will ensue.[24] Things have come to pass that are no longer tolerable, writes the Chief Eunuch: "I found Zachi in bed with one of her women slaves. . . . Last evening, a young lad was found in the garden of the seraglio" (CXLVII, 270). Solim confirms the horrible news: "No longer is there to be found in the countenance of your wives that strict, vigorous virtue which was in times past enthroned there. A new sense of joyfulness, spread throughout these halls, is, to my mind, infallible proof of some new satisfaction" (CLI, 272).

---

[24] Whether the wives' betrayal is real or imagined is irrelevant. In Usbek's imaginary the distinction does not exist, as the imaginary threat of such a betrayal brings about the automatic return of the real in the form of Draconian measures against the seraglio. Montesquieu has analyzed the dire consequences of this interplay between real and imaginary in the case of jealousy: "As soon as women are placed under guard, it is natural that their guardians will seek every day to guard them even better; the effect will become the cause, and vigilance will become the most pressing reason for greater vigilance. . . . The more a man is jealous, the more he has reason to be so, and the more he must become jealous" (*Mes pensées*, 1075–76).

Suddenly the imaginary mechanism reverses itself and the process turns about: instead of sustaining Usbek's mastery, it radically undermines it.[25] The terms of this reversal are *entirely* enacted within the imaginary. Usbek, who for his wives had always stood as almighty Body *as well as* extreme sexual deprivation,[26] comes, at the end of the novel, to represent in their imaginary the second half of the equation: the almighty Body becomes, by virtue of its sexual sterility, a castrated body. This movement from an almighty to a castrated Usbek is brought about by two interrelated steps of the wives' imaginary: first, the sexual object threatens to disappear entirely and forever. As a result, they retaliate against the body that is the source of all their frustration. This retaliation takes the form of a symbolic castration inflicted on Usbek's body, a castration that finally allows the wives to come to terms with their desire within the realm of the imaginary.

Once the hold of the imaginary is broken, Usbek is condemned to be only what his wives perceive him to be: an erotic, missing body. They no longer identify him with a symbol but make him into a sexual object. Instead of denouncing the personal and social repression Usbek has been imposing on the seraglio, their only grievance is his missing body. The theme of the wives' rejected and thus devalued bodies becomes the leitmotif of their letters. Fatmé: "What do you hope will happen to a woman . . . who was used to holding you in her arms?" (vii, 52). Zachi: "Now there is nothing missing from these halls but you yourself. . . . Come back, my dear Usbek, come and make love triumphant here" (xlvii, 107).

But Usbek, whose body is spent by fatigue ("My body and my mind are depressed" [xlvii, 107]) and alienated by too much Parisian effervescence ("I have barely made a hundred paces before I am more bruised [*brisé*] than if I had gone ten leagues" [xxiv, 77]), understands less and less the orderly function that his body serves in the life of the seraglio.[27] Usbek mistakes the reason

---

[25] For an alternative interpretation, see Starobinski's "Préface," 26.

[26] Fatmé describes herself to Usbek as a "useless adornment of a seraglio, kept for the honor and not for the happiness of her husband!" (vii, 53).

[27] Nevertheless he understands perfectly well that the legitimacy of his authority depends on the state of his body. Usbek writes Nessir expressly to censure the news about his bad bodily health: "my dear Nessir, see to it that my women do

behind his wives' revolt and thus attempts to restore peace by establishing with them a new type of relationship: "I have just found out that the seraglio is in disorder and filled with quarrels and dissension. . . . I beg of you, therefore, amend your ways and do so well therein that I may, once more, reject the propositions made to me threatening your freedom and tranquillity. *For I should like to make you forget that I am your master so that I may remember only that I am your husband"* (LXV, 137). This axiom of indulgence on the part of Usbek, who pretends that his power is fundamentally good, that he understands his wives' predicament, and that he prefers to love rather than to command, makes no sense within the psychic confines of the seraglio.[28] The language of pure husbandry—the promise to forgive in the name of marital love—fails, as the wives cannot conceive of love and authority as anything but inseparable, and both are a function of Usbek's physical presence.

Usbek's ultimate blunder derives from his misconception that a letter can stand in the place of a body, that authority can forever be exercised in absentia. In response to the latest "uproar" in the seraglio, he writes to his wives: "May this letter be like unto the thunder that falls in the midst of storms and flashes of lightning!" (CLIV, 274). Far outstripping the letter's inadequacy as a medium of authority is its impotence to satiate desire. Tactfully choosing a euphemism to describe that situation, the Chief Eunuch writes him: "But all of that, magnificent lord, is nothing without the presence of the master . . . you are more absolute when you caress than when you threaten. . . . Come back then, O magnificent lord, return to these surroundings, and bring with you all the marks of your sway . . . come and calm the love that murmurs" (XCVI, 183). Only toward the end of the novel does Usbek suddenly realize that his position of mastery is not a function of familial, social, or political links, but is directly related to the very precise sexual economy of the seraglio. In a flash, as he measures the

---

not learn of the state I am in. If they love me, I want to spare their tears. If they do not love me, I do not wish to increase their boldness in any way" (XXVII, 83).

[28] Cf. Roger Kempf on this point, *Sur le corps romanesque* (Paris: Seuil, 1968), 17. Cf. also Alan J. Singerman, "Réflexions sur une métaphore: Le sérail dans *Les lettres persanes,*" *Studies on Voltaire and the Eighteenth Century* 185 (1980).

immeasurable fascination his body still exercises on some of his wives,[29] Usbek realizes his helplessness and the tragic meaning of his existence: "I am living in a barbarous climate, in the company of everything that vexes me, far removed *[absent]* from everything that interests me. A somber sadness seizes on me; I am falling into a frightful oppression. It seems to me that I am destroying myself *[je m'anéantis]*" (CLV, 274). But it is already too late for him, and the reader undoubtedly will have guessed the sinister result of Usbek's final insight: the destruction of the seraglio and, ultimately, his own death.

How does this tragic ending take place? It is the result of an imaginary crossover whereby Usbek and Solim exchange conditions. The symbolism is evident. The phallus that had been taken away from the eunuch ("when the blade *[fer]* separated you forever from your nature" [XV, 67]) is symbolically restituted to Solim ("I put my sword *[fer]* in your hand" [CLIII, 273]) and with it the impossible dream of the "second birth" comes true: "It is up to you alone to raise yourself even above your condition" (CLIII, 274).[30] The substitution is completed when Usbek, *anéanti*, finally recognizes the truth of his real condition: "Contemptible outcasts of human nature, ... you [eunuchs] would bewail your state no longer if you knew the unhappiness of my own" (CLV, 275–76). Usbek's disdain for his eunuchs, evident throughout *The Letters*, reveals at this point its hidden meaning. His disdainful judgment *(mépris)* had been founded on a misprision *(méprise)*: he was actually speaking all along of his own condition when he expressed his disdain for the eunuchs. Usbek's contempt for his eunuchs could have no other psychic source than Usbek's own disdain for himself. The satisfaction that Usbek draws throughout *The Letters* from the eunuchs' abjection would have been impossible if "someone" within him did not take a secret pleasure in being this Other, phantasmatically. This aspect of the narcissistic comedy does not escape Rica, who writes to Usbek: "It

---

[29] I have already quoted in part Zachi's final letter: "I have sustained your absence, and I have preserved my love by the very force of that love. Nights, days, passing moments—all were for you" (CLVII, 277).

[30] At this point, and for the first time in *The Letters*, a eunuch takes it upon himself to make the decisions *without* consulting the master. Solim's language is indicative of his new condition: "*I* have made my decision. . . . *I* am going to punish" (CLX, 279, my italics).

seems to me, Usbek, that we never judge of matters except by a secret return we make upon ourselves" (LIX, 128).

In the final analysis, Usbek's narcissistic truth is indeed being uttered within his own discourse, but only in the name of the Other (the eunuch). Yet paradoxically, his contempt is also a kind of refusal to forget—for Usbek, to forget his own condition. The evidence speaks for itself: by leaving the seraglio—the novel opens on this separation, a form of castration—Usbek had cut off all corporeal communication; he had closed the door of the seraglio, leaving behind the hidden secret. This is the fundamental dilemma that Usbek's departure poses for him: the interdiction against ever uncovering his own secret, the door closed on an experience that he could never *really* make his own. *The Persian Letters* speaks constantly of this secret, but in the name of the eunuch. The hermeneutic truth uncovers Usbek's secret by means of the symbolic nothingness of the eunuch. The castration that had threatened Usbek throughout the novel finally strikes: the truth about his condition is exposed without the cover of the image—*the return of the Persian real.*

The Spirit of the Body

We have derived two essential points about despotism from *The Persian Letters.* The first point concerns the role of the imaginary in the functioning of despotic politics. The seraglio's social organization is founded upon an imaginary structure that produces a model of political submission. In order to establish himself as the Law, the despot uses erotic stagings to transform the human body into a symbol through which absolute power speaks. The second point concerns the economy of political love. Political love is directed toward an image that all subjects venerate. What is it that they believe they see? Despotism consists of "faking" the body in order to transform it into the illusion of an ideal body. This is a way of legislating reality, by staging a body representing the ideal representation of a body—the Body-idol.[31] Idolatry implies that one accepts the illusion that the idol

[31] In this general perspective Suzanne Gearhart gives a perceptive commentary on the political illusions created by Louis XIV and the economic illusions created

is a full body. What is at work here is (the theory of) the simulacrum, by which one presents something that is not present in
such a way that everyone mistakenly believes in it and holds to
this belief, even though it is evident that there is nothing but an
absence. The effect of the simulacrum is nonetheless real: through
it, the love of the despot's body becomes, by substitution, love of
the Body—that is, of the institution.

This is how Montesquieu implicitly imagines the functioning
of despotism, at least according to our reading of *The Letters*.
Most of Montesquieu's critics have correctly assumed that the
seraglio fiction formulates, long before the theoretical analyses
found in *The Spirit of Laws*, the organic modalities of political
power, especially with regard to Oriental despotism. Montesquieu
himself says so in the "Réflexions" that preface the 1754 edition
of *The Persian Letters*. However, what he does not say—or could
not say—is the degree to which the enormous theoretical apparatus of *The Spirit of Laws* hinders, and even masks, the exceptional qualities of his analysis of despotic power as he *imagined*
it in the seraglio fiction. In other words, the degree to which the
imaginary scenario provided by *The Persian Letters* surpasses in
breadth and in complexity the political analyses of *The Spirit of
Laws*.[32] This will become obvious as we examine some key passages from *The Spirit*. In general, however, I shall address the
question of Montesquieu's political theory as presented in *The
Spirit* by following the same strategy I used in discussing *The
Persian Letters*: to focus not on the "objective" political history
as Montesquieu sees it,[33] but rather on the imaginary figure—the
body—around which he founds his political statements. In effect,

---

by the Law system. See her chapter "Montesquieu, the Cultural Boundaries of
History," in her *The Open Boundary of History and Fiction* (Princeton: Princeton
University Press, 1984), and esp. 122–23.

[32] In a perceptive essay that remains the best analysis of the intertwining of
eroticism and politics, Aram Vartanian emphasizes how much "Montesquieu, in
resorting as a novelist to a symbolic representation of despotism, perceived better
the deviousness of thought and the perversion of feeling that were peculiar to it,
than he succeeded in doing later by studying the same phenomena with the
analytical intelligence of the political scientist" ("Eroticism and Politics in the
Lettres persanes," *Romanic Review* 60 [1969], 25).

[33] To paraphrase Montesquieu: (political) history is defective when it gives us
anything over and above the facts, and it is defective when it gives us only the
facts (*Mes pensées*, 1339).

given that the traditional "script" of political history is punctuated by a pervasive discourse on the body, it will be necessary for us to pursue this discourse through all of its ambivalence and deficiencies in order to engage Montesquieu's political imaginary. A brief detour through Montesquieu's "scientific" work will help explain why the body occupies the cornerstone of Montesquieu's political imaginary.

What few readers of Montesquieu realize is that, before he was a "political scientist," Montesquieu was a natural scientist of sorts, and that many of his contributions to the study of human behavior and human institutions must be traced back to his earlier interest in what was then called "natural history." Certain questions fascinated Montesquieu more than others, and among these, as his work *Observations sur l'histoire naturelle* attests,[34] none intrigued him more than circulatory phenomena in both plants and animals. What the *Observations* reveals, however, is a man in search of a common set of principles that might account for as many apparently different phenomena as possible, an overall theory that would explain all plant (including the so-called mineral kingdom) and animal life in its entirety.

The "scientific" principles Montesquieu articulates for his understanding of natural history in no way prefigure modern scientific intuitions and disciplinary divisions. Try as we might to discern a distinct physiology or body chemistry, all that we find is a scheme that explains everything by purely mechanical cause and effect. Montesquieu seeks to reduce every living phenomenon to a basically physical phenomenon of displacement: of liquors in tubes, of organs relative to one another, of bodies upon one another.[35] I have shown elsewhere how Montesquieu derives two organizational models to explain the biological schemes of all life processes.[36] The first states that organization in the animal and vegetal realms consists primarily of movements of liquids in tubes. The plant, for instance, is conceived of as an entity under pressure; rising fluids push against the channels through which they travel and break out laterally to form branches or, at the tip, to carry buds into the open air. Similarly, the basic unit of or-

[34] In *Oeuvres complètes*, vol. I.
[35] See also "Essai sur les causes qui peuvent affecter les esprits et les caractères," in *Oeuvres complètes*, vol. II.
[36] "Montesquieu," in *European Writers*.

ganization in Montesquieu's description of the growth of muscle fiber is not the cell, as one would expect, but a tube or canal. Thus, for Montesquieu, circulation and changes, "whether in plants or animals, can be nothing but movements of liquid in tubes."[37]

The second model concerned with physiological descriptions and explanations depends on the transfer of motion not by the displacement of a fluid contained within a canal or a tube, but by another process that he compares to the vibrations of a spider's web or a musical instrument. Montesquieu chooses the analogy of the spider's web because it is particularly apt for expressing the pattern of movement transmitted through the nerve network of the body.[38] Impulses can pass in both directions, from the center outward or from the edge of the network to its center, but the essential factor in determining the efficiency of the system is size. If the length of the individual strand extends too far from its center, the impulse cannot be accurately transmitted. The center then will not effectively interpret the impulse, nor will it be able to send out commands efficiently. This vibration-based model is consistent with Montesquieu's conception of the circulating system of fluids: both models account for the transmission of motion within the body. In Montesquieu's conception of the general economy of the body, things circulate and push; some even push by circulating, and others circulate by being pushed. What is most important is that these various displacements *within the body never be at cross-purposes:* there must be continuity, contiguity, and most important of all, reciprocity, for that which is pushed must, perforce, also be able to push back.

Given these principles of organization and operation, anything that upsets bodily pressure ratios is bound to have a significant effect, and while the notion might strike the modern reader as charmingly literal-minded, Montesquieu viewed sexuality as just such an organic upset.[39] In effect the optimal organic system—

[37] *Mes pensées,* 1187.

[38] "Essai sur les causes," 47.

[39] It is on the basis of the human being's inflationary and deflationary sexual cycles that Montesquieu constructs his typology of the genders. In his "Essai sur les causes," Montesquieu's concept of human physiology leads him to a lengthy discussion of the effect of circulatory and pressure changes on the characters of women and eunuchs. Modern science explains the female menstrual cycle as a

the optimal system per se—is one with a hearty degree of give-and-take such that, to use a familiar formula, for every action there should be an equal and opposite reaction: "Everything is in motion, everything exerts pressure on everything else. As neighboring parts swell, those whose functions have become useless diminish, atrophy and even dry up. Everything exists in the human body at the expense of something else."[40] If one organ expands, another must shrink away, or at least shrink back, until the time comes for it to regain its former place, and more, by asserting supremacy once again.

Having seen how Montesquieu views the body, one must ask what the organizational metaphors used in a political or historical context have in common with these "scientific" principles. In his *Montesquieu: La politique et l'histoire*, Louis Althusser makes a brief but penetrating study of two of the better-known metaphors that reflect Montesquieu's understanding of the inner dynamics of a government: the image of opposing bodies used to illustrate the mechanics of power distribution in a despotic government, and the well-regulated river image, which describes the same phenomenon in a monarchy.[41] In both cases Montesquieu derives his models of government from his understanding of the phenomenal world,[42] and whereas despotism is self-destructive, monarchy is designed to emulate efficient, productive, natural laws as defined by Montesquieu: "These fundamental laws [of monarchy] necessarily suppose the intermediate channels through which the power flows" (*SL*, II-4, 112). But the similarity extends to another level of analysis. Montesquieu develops a second political model, which accounts for the interaction not within states but between states. He describes in this model a situation of give-and-take that duplicates his model of the interaction of the organs within the body. In this case, he postulates that the outward thrust of one

hormonal reaction; according to Montesquieu, it results from the mechanics of fluid buildup in the body. Because the body is made up of organs that exert pressure against each other, the buildup of fluids and their eventual outflow naturally alter the female character from day to day. By the same rationale, the eunuch, who for obvious reasons is not able to find any release for the buildup of extraneous fluids within his system, has a difficult and unnatural character (pp. 45–46).

[40] *Mes pensées*, 1189.
[41] (Paris: Presses Universitaires de France, 1969), 82–84.
[42] "Laws in their most general signification are the necessary relations derived from the nature of things" (*SL*, I-I, 98).

state against the border of its neighbor is a force that, in optimum cases, is exactly countered by the second nation's own opposition. Ultimately, Montesquieu's notion of government is sustained by the underlying concepts of integration and pressure, where all the parts of a totality are incorporated into a system such that each individual part, as in the body, is directed to the good of the whole. In addition to the models of circulation and pressure, Montesquieu also postulates that it is essential for a state to control its size and to preserve ties between the center of its power and its territorial jurisdiction. This principle is reminiscent of the emphasis placed on optimum size and centricity in his analogue of the nervous system, the spider's web. There the soul's position relative to its nerve network directly affects its ability to assert proper control over the body, in the same way that a capital's position relative to its lines of communication irrevocably determines its ability to govern.

Considerations on the Causes of the Greatness of the Romans and Their Decline is a clear example of Montesquieu's political imaginary working along the above lines. First, it would seem that Rome had broken all the rules of the body and yet—for a time at least—survived and even prospered. Ultimately, however, Rome collapsed because it had contravened too long the rules of the body-state: "When the domination of Rome was limited to Italy, the republic could easily maintain itself."[43] As soon as Rome's ambitions carried it beyond the proper boundaries imposed by the body-state, its political difficulties began: "But when the legions crossed the Alps and the sea, the warriors, who had to be left in the countries they were subjugating for the duration of several campaigns, gradually lost their citizen spirit."[44] Thus it became only a matter of time before size got the best of things: "It was the greatness [bigness] of the republic that caused all the trouble."[45] Soon it became impossible for Rome to remain actively "the center of everything."[46] It had pushed well beyond the limits of viable statehood, extended its circle of dominance outward to the point where the forward drive of expansionism would nec-

---

[43] *Considerations on the Causes of the Greatness of the Romans and Their Decline*, trans. David Lowenthal (New York: Free Press, 1965), 91.
[44] Ibid.
[45] Ibid., 93.
[46] *Mes pensées*, 1422.

essarily dissipate, for no capital can sustain such force from a distance. As long as Rome held firm, as long as its expressions of power remained constant, the meridional peoples it had pushed back to the north could be held at bay: "while the force containing them lasted, they stayed there."[47] Once Rome's power to repulse waned, what it had compressed could only recoil; a flood of people "backed against the limits of the world,"[48] as Montesquieu writes in a related context, would inundate and reconquer Europe.

Montesquieu's analysis of the fall of Rome is clear and straightforward. It is based less on historical or political facts than on Montesquieu's political imaginary as expressed by the laws of the body. Rome stretched its physical resources to the limit, and the center could no longer command; at the same time, her organs— her generals—lost the feeling of belonging to the whole: they could not or would not report back. This renunciation of the center translates itself in organic terms as a loss of vigor.[49] Rome, so ambitious in the beginning that it aspired to a corporeal takeover, meets the ignoble fate of a noncompetitive organ: it atrophies, even dries up and dwindles away—like a river that peters out.

It is well known that, in classical political thought, explanations are often based on metaphors that are elaborated into models: two such metaphors—the organism and the machine— are fundamental. Montesquieu's political analyses, which rely heavily on the structural similarities and the rules of expansion that he discerns between the state and the organism, belong to this metaphoric network. However, it is also clear that Montesquieu's designation of the state as a body is far more than just a metaphor. His political imaginary is anchored in a particular physiology of the body, which calls upon the body not as an isolated

---

[47] *Considerations*, 153.

[48] Ibid.

[49] Montesquieu carries the analogy between the state and the body a step further. He claims that a state assumes what might be characterized as an organic "life" of its own as, for example, when he suggests that the Roman Empire was devastated by its eventual division into eastern and western halves precisely because the parts of the gigantic whole had grown accustomed to one another: "Thus, although the empire was already too large, the new division ruined it because all the parts of this great body, together so long, had, so to speak, adjusted themselves to remain that way and to depend on each other" (*Considerations*, 161).

image but as a complex network that articulates the mechanics of political knowledge. Let me give a final illustration of how the body serves this function of political conceptualization in Montesquieu's imaginary. In Book xiv of *The Spirit of Laws*, Montesquieu passes from a discussion of the relationship between taxation and liberty to a study of climatic influences, even interrupting his political analyses to present the findings of his "scientific" investigations regarding a sheep's tongue submitted to temperature changes. On a certain level, this analysis seeks to demonstrate the direct effect of climate on the individual and, by extension, on institutions.[50]

There is a striking parallel between Montesquieu's findings there and the principles I have been discussing. His findings lead him to postulate two different physiological types based on climatic influence. The northern man is less vulnerable than his warmer southern counterpart, because his blood tends more toward the center, his heart is stronger, and the circulation pattern within his body makes him more able than southern types (*SL*, xiv-2, 244–45). We recall from our discussion of the Roman Empire that an essential criterion for the efficient working of an empire was a vigorous interaction between the center and its outlying domains. The hearty interaction between the peripheral surfaces of the body and its center clearly favors northern man as well as northern states. Moreover, adds Montesquieu, the patchwork of European (northern) states is in fact one great body governed by laws of territorial give-and-take, about which it is appropriate to conclude that, as in the body, "All space is filled ... everything is in motion, everything exerts pressure on everything else."[51] The idea of mutual dependence is, of course, the key to this organic notion of statehood. It is the law that prevails within the human body where, if one tissue or organ swells, its neighbors must shrink in compensation. Similarly, efficient government integrates opposing factions so that "all the parts, how-

[50] The implications of the physical relationship of climate to institutions in Montesquieu's geopolitical scheme of nations is discussed by Georges Benrekassa in *La politique et sa mémoire* (Paris: Payot, 1983).

[51] *Mes pensées*, 1189. I refer the reader to Montesquieu's conception of Europe as a large body in which the states are organs, pushing and jostling for a place of their own.

ever opposed they may appear, cooperate for the general good of society."[52] In each case, the parts are so intricately associated that a change in one component, however minute, alters the organism in its entirety.

By contrast, in the body of the southern man, just the opposite occurs. The influence of temperature causes a slow circulation between center and periphery, and the individual loses all initiative and ethical sensibility. Not coincidentally, it is in these southern climates that despotic governments are most likely to rise, and Montesquieu's description of the territorial configuration of that type of state exactly parallels his portrait of southern physiology. They have two features in common: an unwieldy mass and a center that is one in name only. The despotic state, we learn, practices a crude kind of self-protection. To buffer itself against invasion, it devastates the surrounding land, in the middle of which it then sits, isolated and *cut off* from the outside world: "Despotic governments provide [for their security] by separating ... they sacrifice a part of the country; and by ravaging and desolating the frontiers they render the [body] of the empire inaccessible" (*SL*, IX-4, 186).[53]

Let us rephrase this remark in light of our reading of *The Persian Letters*. Despotism cuts off a part of its body ("a part of the country") so that the rest of the body can function. Hence, by metonymic castration, Montesquieu shifts from the body of the despot to the body of the state. The missing body of the despot is analogous to the deserts of the body-state. The practice of "ravaging the frontiers" leads to a disembodied body *separated* from its members.[54] The themes of the sick body, the cruel treatment of the body, separation, and loneliness in Book IX bring us back

[52] *Considerations*, 93–94.

[53] This sentence reads in all English translations "they render the *heart* of the empire inaccessible." Not only does "heart" convey better the meaning intended by Montesquieu, but stylistically speaking, the French wording would be clearer from the use of *coeur*. Yet Montesquieu opted for the rather awkward formulation "le *corps* de l'empire devient inaccessible" (*Oeuvres*, vol. II, 372). Clearly something peculiar is at work in his wording, for the choice of *corps* certainly exceeds stylistic mannerism.

[54] "Despotic state preserves itself likewise by another kind of separation, which is by putting the most-distant provinces in the hands of a feudatory prince" (*SL*, IX-4, 186).

unmistakably to the figure of the eunuch. The question of the "dysfunctional" body-state becomes even more poignant when Montesquieu discusses the corrupt nature of despotic government: "The principle of despotic government is subject to a continual corruption, because it is by its very nature corrupt" (*SL*, VIII-10, 175). We recall that the principle of the seraglio was the despot's body, transformed here into the body politic. What is this corruption inherent to the nature of the despotic body politic? *Corrompu* (corrupted) comes from the Latin *cum* (together) and *rumpere* (to break into pieces); thus, by its nature, the despotic order breaks up the integrity of the body; it is literally a *corps-rompu*. Despotism mutilates bodies—that of the despot as well as that of the state—because it recognizes in the wholesome body a *structure* that threatens it; hence despotism substitutes these bodies with replacement bodies (idols or body-states) which are deformed, disfigured, or denatured—all synonymous, according to the dictionary, with "corrupted." The despotic body-state is a mutilated, diminished, lonely state, because it is intrinsically (a) *corps-rompu*.

Montesquieu writes in Book xv-19 of *The Spirit of Laws*: "In the Orient it seems that eunuchs are a necessary evil."[55] What matters here is not so much that eunuchs are evil as that they are a constitutive element of the Orient. For the eunuch, in Montesquieu's political imaginary of despotism, is omnipresent. Whereas the *heart* pumps the lifeblood of honor and virtue through monarchic and republican body-states, it is the *sexual organ* of the despot—as Usbek puts it, "this sex which moves inanimate things"—which gives life to the despotic state. But here again, as with the despot's body, whose sexual bliss is only the illusion of *jouissance,* the despotic state becomes an illusory body "inaccessible" to anyone. Like the despot, the despotic state has no interior: it reproduces the emptiness of the idol by being a "center" without periphery; its frontiers are devastated deserts that remain undefined. By the logic of the body, insofar as it can only produce separation and mutilation instead of circulation, the despotic state is destined to atrophy and perish. But there is no point in repeating it all, since the absurd economy of noncircu-

[55] "Il semble que les eunuques, en Orient, soient un mal nécessaire" (*Oeuvres,* vol. II, 508).

lation in the seraglio—the self-mutilating gesture of Usbek that leads back to the central lack of the eunuch—as described in *The Persian Letters*, prefigures every aspect of what Montesquieu says in *The Spirit of Laws* on the nature of despotism. The initial mutilation of the despotic body-state establishes despotism from the start as a *negation* of the historico-political process. Despotism does not share in the dynamics of the healthy body of history: instead, despotism exists outside of historical time, frozen in anticipation of its own annihilation, like Usbek's seraglio.

We have always been aware that there is no political order without constraints on the body. Montesquieu's original twist on this political perception is in showing that no political *theory* can exist without taking recourse to the habits, functions, and needs of the body. Montesquieu's political discourse, whose apparent object is despotism *(The Persian Letters)* or the three forms of government *(The Spirit of Laws)*, actually is a discourse on the body. All of Montesquieu's analyses of the mechanics of statehood—which later became classic categories of political analysis—are inscribed within the code of the body. The political reality he presents is meaningful only by analogy with the body; the conceptual machine behind the political real consists of images of the body; finally, the language of political analysis itself is constructed around a network of corporeal concepts and principles, which are *foreign to the reality as well as the representation of political reality*, yet which establish an "order of relationships" transferable to political analysis. Hence Montesquieu's political theory is the prototype of a "double-edged" discourse: it claims to speak about the codes that organize the functioning of political history, yet in fact inscribes all of its significations in imaginary representations of the body. To paraphrase Montesquieu's remark that "eunuchs, in the Orient, are a necessary evil," I would conclude that "the body, in political theory, is a necessary evil." The body is the (repressed) imaginary of all political reality, and as Montesquieu's case unmistakably proves, of the birth of political theory as well.

4

Man Born of Man:
Rousseau's Pedagogical Imaginary

> In my delirium I believe I can spring out of myself; I believe
> I can give my life to her [Galatea] and animate her with my
> soul.
>
> Rousseau, *Pygmalion*

Definitions

Traditionally *Emile* is studied in conjunction with Rousseau's
other works, recalling that Rousseau himself insisted upon the
unity of his *oeuvre* and described the content of his books as
constituting a profoundly interwoven system: "I have written
about various subjects, but always according to the same principles, the same morality, the same belief, the same maxims, and,
one might say, the same opinions."[1] As a consequence, Rousseauian criticism situates *Emile* within his entire work and traces

[1] Rousseau, *Lettre à Christophe de Beaumont, Archevêque de Paris*, in *Oeuvres
complètes* (Paris: Pléiade, 1969), vol. IV, 928. Several pages later in the same
pamphlet Rousseau discusses the *formal* aspect of his work in similar terms:
"When an author seeks not to repeat himself constantly...his writings come to
explain each other complementarily, and, when he is following a method, his
later writings always presuppose his earlier works. This is what I have always
tried to do, and what I have accomplished, especially in the work in question
[Emile]" (pp. 950–51).

a single line of thought from the first *Discourse* onward.[2] *Emile* is then read in a philosophical vein as a kind of reflection on the "human condition":[3] "You may very well say that it is impossible to create an *Emile*; but can you believe that this was precisely my aim, and that the book that bears that name could be a real educational treatise? This is a fairly philosophical book by virtue of the principle its author has proposed in other writings: *that man is naturally good.*"[4] Rousseau's pedagogical system is thus suspended or reinterpreted as a function of his philosophical system, with the *Profession of Faith* as the center of the work. As for the last two books of *Emile*, they are read in a social vein since they largely treat the way in which Emile and Sophie will assume their positions in society.

Since *Emile* is ostensibly a philosophical work—or a sociopolitical reflection—the reader would seem justified in ignoring any allusions the book might make to the precise meaning and nature of the pedagogical project. Rousseau specifically emphasizes this unspecific aspect of *Emile* by calling our attention to it several times: "In order not to fatten the book uselessly, I have settled for putting down the principles whose truth everyone should sense" (p. 51); "It is my design not to enter into all the details, but only to expound the general maxims" (p. 97). It is thus only the general outline of the doctrine which is of importance and which will be sketched. Rousseau is not an educator but a phi-

---

[2] Cf. for instance Jean Chateau, *Jean-Jacques Rousseau: Sa philosophie de l'éducation* (Paris: Vrin, 1962), esp. chap. 3, "Place de *l'Emile* dans l'oeuvre de Rousseau," which begins: "It would be a serious error to separate *Emile* from the rest of Rousseau's work...rather, one should analyze *Emile*, *Julie*, and the *Contract* simultaneously, and show how, from these three works, there emerges a common doctrine that represents the natural outcome of reflections that began with the first *Discourse*" (p. 91). R.J.P. Jordan, in a recent essay entitled "A New Look at Rousseau as Educator," repeats the conventional wisdom: "*Emile* is not primarily about education as such, divorced from time, place or political culture....Rousseau brought to the writing of *Emile* a theory of human relationships which he had developed in his earlier discourses, notably the *Discourse on the Origin of Inequality*" (*Studies on Voltaire and the Eighteenth Century* 182 [1979], 60, 64).

[3] "Our true study is that of the human condition" (*Emile, or On Education*, trans. Allan Bloom [New York: Basic Books, 1979]). All further page references to *Emile* will be to this translation and will appear in the body of the text.

[4] "Lettre à Philibert Cramer du 13 octobre 1764," in R. A. Leigh, ed., *Correspondance complète de Jean-Jacques Rousseau* (Oxford: Voltaire Foundation, 1965–), vol. XXI, 248–49.

losopher, and *Emile* is not written to discuss the *niaiseries* of detailed pedagogical applications: "In any case, my method [my system] is independent of my examples" (p. 192).[5]

For what reasons did Rousseau refuse as early as the preface of *Emile* to relate his system to those "particular applications" it should logically entail? What reasons indeed, since Rousseau is the first to realize that such a weakness in the composition of his book will be denounced immediately by his numerous critics: "As to what will be called the systematic part, which is here nothing but the march of nature, it is the point that will most put the reader off, and doubtless it is on this point that I will be attacked; and perhaps it will not be wrong to do so" (p. 34). Can one develop a pedagogical system—a theory of pedagogy—from principles that take no account of the relevant examples? How would such a development take place? What would be the status and signification of this theoretical system?

Before I address these questions I must clarify my working hypothesis. I do not think it is necessary, or even helpful, to derive Rousseau's pedagogical reflection from his philosophical system. To begin with this premise is to accept in its entirety his global theory of human nature; it is also to accept the theory as an infallibly constructed system where one may situate various pedagogical strategies that remain nevertheless of local importance, contingent upon the global construct. I believe the correct approach to the question is to take precisely the opposite tack: to explore the theory from the perspective of the strategy, to understand the system as a function of its applications, and hence to test the *logic* of the pedagogical reflection we might have overlooked. If it is true that one can only understand Rousseau's pedagogical project by reading it as a global system, it is equally true that this system owes its coherence to the artifices and anecdotal examples that, Rousseau to the contrary, are rigorously articulated according to the principles of the system and manifest in its nature. And if Rousseau insists upon the myth of a "philosophical" pedagogy cut off from its applications, it is perhaps because he is the first to have understood the true nature of the

---

[5] Cf. also: "My examples, good perhaps for one pupil, will be bad for countless others. If one catches the spirit of these examples, one will surely know how to vary them according to need" (*E*, 192).

pedagogical enterprise; the first to have analyzed in depth the nature of the relation between a pedagogical system and its applications, between theory and practice, and the logic that supports this relation. Or rather, I should say that Rousseau is the first to have apprehended—since he could not completely grasp—this relation, which can only be explained and understood at the level of a logic of the imaginary.

The first question to be asked is a simple one of definition: what does one mean when one speaks of pedagogy? Pedagogy presents itself as a theory of a practical order whose object is to reflect upon one or several fields of knowledge, and the processes by which this knowledge is transmitted, with a view to enlightening and directing potential educators. To extend the above definition, I will say that a pedagogical field is a space constituted by three components: (a) a measure of knowledge; (b) a measure we will call "pedagogue," that is, someone who accepts to stand before others as the representative of knowledge; (c) a measure "pupil," that is, someone who will be the recipient of this knowledge. Pedagogy thus implies a relation and a mode of functioning by which something—knowledge—passes from individual A to individual B. What remains to be specified is the way in which this knowledge passes from pedagogue to pupil; or, in other words, the way in which the knowledge-function intervenes and is transmitted in the pedagogical relation. This entails an interrogation, first, of the way in which the pedagogue's desire gives rise to and sustains knowledge in the pupil; and second, of the way in which the pupil's desire intersects the pedagogue's. It thus appears, contrary to commonly held assumptions, that a pedagogical field is not constituted as a pure relationship to knowledge. Knowledge, which normally is thought to be at the center of the pedagogical relationship, is really only in a mediated position with respect to desire; it comes into play only at the intersection, the point of crossing, of two desires. Pedagogy is thus primarily, and paradoxically, *always* a pedagogy of desire and not of knowledge.

In examining this formulation of pedagogy with respect to the radical modification Rousseau brought to the field of knowledge— and thus of desire—on the level of the pedagogical relationship, I intend to show that Rousseau was the first to have sought to formalize a pedagogical field where desire dominates knowledge and openly manipulates the characters and the knowledge-function pedagogy brings into play. It has long been recognized—and here all critics are in agreement—that Rousseau inaugurated a new type of discourse which produced a massive modification of the knowledge-function in the pedagogical field. The new pedagogical relationship circumvents knowledge altogether and becomes organized around the child—around the knowledge of the child by the pedagogue.[6] Rousseau insists, with reason, on this theoretical innovation in the preface of *Emile:* "Begin, then, by *studying your pupils better.* For most assuredly you do not know them at all" (p. 34, my italics). In sum, there is a critical displacement of the positions within the pedagogical field. The child becomes the *object* of knowledge; and the pedagogue, as the absolute knowing *subject,* comes to occupy a particular place in the pedagogical relationship, a place that will go momentarily unnamed for the purposes of my argument, but to which I will return.

The pedagogue's position as the ultimate holder and withholder of knowledge must be stressed here, for the pedagogical enterprise as Rousseau defines it only exists in a closed circuit: the enterprise finds its end in the child and its means in the master pedagogue. The tutor has no other law but the pupil to whom he will consecrate his life, and the pupil has no law but his tutor. A dual, absolute condition.[7] No third party—no one else has the right to intervene or to enter into the pedagogical circuit. The pedagogue's authority is of necessity absolute: "Emile is an orphan. It makes no difference whether he has his father or mother. Charged with their duties, I inherit all their rights. He ought to honor his parents, but he ought to obey only me. That is my first or, rather, my sole condition" (pp. 52–53).[8]

---

[6] Cf. on this point the discussion of Alain Grosrichard, "Le prince saisi par le philosophe," *Ornicar* 26–27 (1983).

[7] I will not examine here the truncated logic by which Rousseau "transforms" this dual, absolute relationship to reinstitute nature and supposedly articulate its laws through the child: "the child is at birth already a disciple, not of the governor, but of nature. The governor only studies under this first master and prevents its care from being opposed" (*E,* 61). The ruse here involves establishing a false equivalence, where the tutor's desire is given to the child (and to the reader) as the voice of nature: "I have awaited to know the one [wife] who will suit him. It is not I who make the determination, it is nature. My job is to find out the choice that nature has made" (p. 407). Several lines later, however, Rousseau gives himself away by adding: "I would have refused to raise him if I had not been the master of marrying him to the woman of his choice—that is, of my choice."

[8] The quotation continues: "This clause is essential, and I would even want

According to all educators, this massive displacement toward the child opened up the pedagogical field, which is at the origin of our modern scholastic institutions. Whence the well-worn labels applied to Rousseau: the father of modern education and the father of scientific pedagogy. Seeking in Rousseau a defender of the child's autonomy, educators have not adequately stressed the *nature* of that free development and liberty that Rousseau advocates for the child. Certainly Rousseau rediscovered the child in his specificity. Certainly Rousseau's watchword is the absence of constraint and the free play of the child's impulses—but all this takes place within the precise limits of a pedagogical field always defined by the pedagogue, and *by him alone*. Reading within our perspective, it will become clear that the modification inaugurated by Rousseau does anything but expand or renew the pedagogical enterprise. In fact, the conditions of possibility and the redistribution of the pedagogical field such as Rousseau presents them are only revolutionary insofar as they imply the impossibility of all pedagogy.

Reversals

For Rousseau the traditional pedagogical relationship is one of violence and perversion. It is the figure—and the consequence—of the perverse impulse that carries society ever farther from nature, and which the educational practices of his time promoted: "let us abandon the students living in colleges and convents to their bad morals, which will always be irremediable" (*E*, 330). In opposition to these ridiculous and dangerous establishments, where one only learns vanity and vice, Rousseau seeks to restore the pedagogical relationship to its natural truth; in so doing he hopes to re(dis)cover, step by step, the order of nature.

The pedagogical perversion as Rousseau conceives it is a perversion of the natural order, in other words, of the *order of places* each one is assigned in nature: "Nature wants children to be children before being men. If we want to pervert this order, we will produce precocious fruit which will be immature and insipid

---

the pupil and the governor to regard themselves as so inseparable that the lot of each in life is always a common object for them" (p. 53).

and will not be long in rotting" (p. 90). The order that designates man and child in their essential difference and delegates them their respective places is naturally defined by infantile weakness: "To consider childhood in itself, is there in the world a weaker being, a more miserable one, one more at the mercy of everything surrounding him, who has a greater need of pity, care, and protection than a child?" (p. 88). The pedagogical perversion is precisely the displacement, or rather, the reversal of the order imposed by the relative strength of man and child, a subtle exchange of places between commander and commanded: "What is there, then, more shocking, more contrary to order than to see an imperious and rebellious child command all that surrounds him and impudently take on the tone of the master with those who have only to abandon him to make him perish?" (p. 88).

The *apparent* hierarchy of place in traditional pedagogy is then inverted at the hands of Rousseau so that the *real* order in the positions of mastery may appear. Rousseau borrows a remark of Themistocles to illustrate his point. " 'This little boy that you see there,' said Themistocles to his friends, 'is the master of Greece, for he governs his mother, his mother governs me, I govern the Athenians, and the Athenians govern Greece.' O what little leaders [conducteurs] would often be found in the greatest empires, if from the prince one descended by degrees to the first hand which secretly sets things in motion [qui donne le branle en secret]!" (p. 84).

It is, then, this type of perversion—that makes a child the arbiter of Greece—which Rousseau wishes to ward off, first by disclosing the reality of the reversal of the natural order, then by reinstating the latter with a second reversal. Education will thus be the putting back in place of the child: "The wise man knows how to stay in his place; but the child, who does not know his place, would not be able to keep to it. Among us he is given a thousand exits by which to leave it. It is for those who govern him to keep him in his place, and this is not an easy task" (E, 84–85). Rousseau's objective is clear, the recipe simple and direct: "At the onset put him [your pupil] in his place, and hold him there so well that he no longer tries to leave it" (p. 91). But putting the child back in his place is not an easy operation; it requires an elaborate subterfuge, an artifice that is at the very heart of Rousseauian pedagogy: a system that artificially creates the necessary and sufficient conditions to produce the child—and later the man—who will remain *in place* through all displacements. The formula thus discovered will return man to a situation of natural equilibrium and assure his happiness: "O man, draw your existence up within yourself, and you will no longer be miserable. Remain in the place which nature assigns to you in the chain of being. Nothing will be able to make you leave it" (p. 83).

Rousseau's pedagogical revolution consists, as I have said, of making the system gravitate about the child. But in what way? Very specifically, by beginning with an original coercion: "Do you, then, want him to keep his original form? Preserve it from the instant he comes into the world. As soon as he is born, take hold of him and leave him no more before he is a man. You will never succeed without that" (p. 48). Why must the coercion, in order to be effective, occur at the infant's birth? Rousseau's thesis maintains that the perversion of the natural order takes place at the level of the infant's "demand." Rousseau calls it alternately *demande* and *besoin de fantaisie*, "word[s] by which I mean all desires which are not true needs *[besoins naturels]* and which can only be satisfied with another's help" (p. 84).

In a similar vein (and vocabulary), Lacan has analyzed how an individual's desire for recognition is grounded in demand, understood as one of the psychological dimensions of desire. The demand is addressed to the Other (considered as an omniscient subject) in order to fill through recognition or through love the lack one feels in oneself.[9] Hence any demand, however disguised it might be, is a wish—alternately a prayer and a command—to be recognized by the Other, *but also* to impose one's will on this Other. For if, on the one hand, a demand subjects the demander to the will of the Other, it also turns this Other into a means toward the ends of the demander. As Rousseau says, what had been a prayer becomes a command pronounced by the demander: "The first tears of children are prayers. If one is not careful, they soon become orders. Children begin by getting themselves assisted; they end by getting themselves served" (*E*, 66). In order for the tutor to prevent this reversal, it becomes crucial for him

[9] The fact that we always endow the Other with the possession of precisely that which we lack illustrates clearly that demand functions in the register of the imaginary. This is an important point, to which I shall return in the conclusion of this chapter.

"to disentangle from the earliest age the secret intention which dictates the gesture or the scream" (p. 66). Hence, by refusing from the outset to enter into the child's fight for recognition— "grant nothing to his desires because he demands it but because he needs it" (p. 85)—the tutor avoids altogether the pedogogical reversal and affirms the natural order. But to separate need from demand, one must be able to judge their difference; that is precisely the role of the tutor. Pushed to its limit, the educator's knowledge should be able to prevent and, ultimately, to annul demand. The implications of such a move for the child are obvious: his utter inability to attain recognition (as his demand is abolished) leads to his complete "takeover" by the tutor. This takeover is the essence of Rousseau's pedagogy and must above all be assured—by force or constraint if necessary, but preferably by ruse or deception. Therein lies the dilemma of Rousseauian pedagogy: not what to do with the child, but how to assume one's hold upon the child, so that the tutor's authority becomes, at the end of the educational process, a natural necessity.

In preference to brute force, Rousseau chooses deception: the violence of ruse is substituted for the violence of force. That is the great reversal Rousseau proposes. The dialectic that supports his whole pedagogical program is ruse. What he develops through ruse is an operative model that will invert the events of everyday life and the artifices of the imagination—the two registers of the real and the imaginary.[10] Rousseau sees, for example, that if the tutor makes his presence too felt, fear might lead the child to react negatively to the threat of force. Authority, if wielded with too heavy a hand, will lead to hostility and even rebellion in the child.

> Command him nothing, whatever in the world it might be, absolutely nothing. Do not even allow him to imagine that you might pretend to have authority over him. Let him know only that he is weak and you are strong, that by this condition and yours he is *necessarily* at your mercy. Let him know it, learn it, feel it.... Let him see [the heavy yoke] of necessity *in things, never in the caprice*

---

[10] It should be noted that inversion is a modus operandi that is an intrinsic part of Rousseau's epistemology: "Take the opposite of the practiced path, and you will always do well" (*E*, 94).

of men. Let the bridle that restrains him be force and not authority.
(*E*, 91, my italics)

As a result, Rousseau's psychological strategy involves trapping the child in a system where his freedom of choice is only an illusion; to this effect the pedagogue produces a series of situations that the child perceives not only as a necessary state of affairs, but also as one in which he has the initiative.

> In the most careful educations the master commands and *believes he governs.* It is actually the child who *governs.* He uses what you exact from him to obtain from you what pleases him.... At every instant pacts must be made with him. These treaties, which you propose in your fashion and he executes in his, always turn to the profit of his whims [*fantaisies*]....
>
> Take an opposite route with your pupil. *Let him always believe* he is the master, and *let it always be you* who are. There is no subject so perfect as that which keeps the appearance of freedom. Thus the will itself is made captive.... Doubtless he [the child] ought to do only what he wants, but he ought to want only what you want him to do....
>
> Thus, not seeing you eager to oppose him, not distrusting you, with nothing to hide from you ... you will be able to study him at your complete ease and arrange all around him the lessons you want to give him without his ever thinking he is receiving any. (*E*, 119–20, my italics)

It is thus a question of reversing the ordinary pedagogical relationship, of turning appearances and realities inside out. The objective: to make real power and illusion change hands so as to restore the natural order by passing the illusion to the child's side. Beyond the mere containment of the child's imaginative activity—"Put [his] nascent imagination off the track with objects which, far from inflaming, repress the activity of [his] senses" (pp. 230–31)—Rousseau's real pedagogical objective is to take over the child's imaginary. For the pedagogue the question comes down to this: how to preserve in the child a *degree zero* imaginary? Rousseau's answer is to increase the power of the imagination negatively, that is, to enclose the child in an illusory imaginary— one that undoes reality by reducing it to images that have no referent whatsoever: "By providing the imaginary object, I am the master of comparisons, and I easily prevent my young man from having illusions about real objects" (p. 329). Thus, the better to marry him, the tutor first marries Emile to an image: "I would have to be the clumsiest of men not to be able to make him passionate in advance of his knowing about whom. It is unimportant whether the object I depict for him is imaginary; it suffices that it make him disgusted with those that could tempt him" (p. 329). Rousseau's pedagogy of the imaginary reduces the child's imaginary to an image-machine, which selects images according to the tutor's desires, that is, according to the tutor's own imaginary. Hence the child, doomed to repeat the tutor's imaginary, can do no more than imagine secondhand.[11] The new art of educating—and with *Emile* Rousseau gives us a negative definition—thus consists of gaining real power and authority by censoring anything that would expose Emile to a view of the real, such that Emile is enclosed permanently within the illusory images produced by his dependent imaginary. Here, then, is the final "product" brought to its term.

> You cannot imagine how Emile can be docile at twenty? How differently we think! I cannot conceive how he could have been docile at ten, for what hold did I have on him at that age? It has taken fifteen years of care to contrive this hold for myself. I did not educate him then; I prepared him to be educated. He is now.... It is true that I leave him the appearance of independence, but he was never better subjected to me; for now he is subjected because he wants to be. As long as I was unable to make myself master of his imagination, I remained master of his person; I was never a step away from him. Now I sometimes leave him to himself, because I govern him always. (E, 332)

To prevent the risk of mastery turning into slavery, the hold must be complete: "It is important that the disciple not do anything that the master does not know about and does not want him to do" (p. 334). The pedagogical artifice, then, consists of

---

[11] Contrary to what we naively assume, the slogan "to seize the imagination" does not date from May 1968, but rather was born with Rousseau; and after him, during the French Revolution, this slogan informs an entire theory of Republican propaganda. Mirabeau's *Discours sur l'éducation publique* (1791) is a stunning illustration of such a Rousseauian strategy.

turning the child into a mechanical model, one that improves and amplifies the model in vogue among the philosophers of the time. Emile is in fact a more sophisticated version of Condillac's and La Mettrie's statues, using the tutor's will as the driving force that produces physical and psychological movements. Rousseau's choice of vocabulary leaves no doubt as to the tutor's conception of his pupil: "[my pupil,] differently *conducted* than yours, is no longer an ordinary child. He requires a *régime* special to him" (p. 51). *Régime* must be understood here in its etymological sense as a way of governing the pupil—the Latin *regimen* (government) derives from *regere*, to rule—as well as in its physical sense as the conditions and procedures defining phenomena of movement and output. When "the young brain warms up...[and] it begins to boil," efficient combustion requires letting the vapors of its "first spirits...evaporate...[and] retain, and compress the others until, over the years, all turns into heat and true force" (p. 106). The calibration of Emile's driving power consists in a perfect dosing of human "fuel"—"to put power and will in perfect equality" (p. 80) and "to prevent imagination from accelerating [the progress of nature]" (p. 316)—so as smoothly to break in the human machine and ease its transition to the state of manhood: "his body...begins to quiet down, while his mind, half developed, seeks its turn to take flight" (p. 315).

The pedagogue knows his machine, and not only on a practical level. He can also submit it to a theoretical decomposition and name each one of its aptitudes and movements: "Not a single movement takes place in his soul which his mouth or his eyes do not reveal, and often the sentiments he experiences are known to me sooner than to him" (p. 319). The pedagogue tunes into the child as one tunes one's ear to a naturally harmonious mechanism. His function is to prevent any abnormal friction or accidental misfire, in short, any unexpected change or deviation in regimen (the dangers of *écarts* are often alluded to in *Emile*). From his pupil's birth the tutor "watches over the nursling, observes him, follows him. He vigilantly spies out the first glimmer of his weak understanding" (p. 61); when the child becomes an adolescent, the tutor's task varies only slightly: "you ought to be wholly involved with the child—observing him, spying on him without letup and without appearing to do so, sensing ahead of time" (p.

461). A deft and crafty pilot, a modern Ulysses of pedagogy,[12] the tutor can rejoice in seeing his machine function to perfection, smooth-running, free from all irregularities. Here is that admirable human mechanism in all the fine precision of its functioning.

> Consider my Emile—now past twenty, well formed, well constituted in mind and body, full of sense, reason, goodness, and humanity, a man with morals and taste, loving the beautiful, doing the good, free from the empire of cruel passions, exempt from the yoke of opinion, but subject to the law of wisdom and submissive to the voice of friendship, possessing all the useful talents and some of the agreeable ones.... He brings together all the goods that can be obtained at once. (E, 418–19)

The role of pedagogical knowledge thus comes down to governing the pupil in the most *economic* way possible, by avoiding or masking the questions posed by real experience and which might curtail the maximum educational output: "One should realize that I do not resolve his questions when it pleases him, but rather when it pleases me.... While the child is still without knowledge, there is time to *prepare* everything that comes near him in order that his first glances meet only objects suitable for him to see" (p. 95, my italics). To prepare to see (or *not* to see) are the key terms of the pedagogical relationship: the theoretical knowledge of the pedagogue is conceived of by Rousseau as an administrative power whose strategy is one of stage direction.[13] As director, the pedagogue both manipulates and conceals the logic of the spectacle, which he passes off as a raw event. The pupil must not only be taken in, but hypnotized by the dimension of *necessity* implicit in these events (i.e., things must necessarily happen the way they do): "The child ought to be wholly involved with the thing, but you ought to be wholly involved with the

---

[12] "Ulysses, O wise Ulysses.... No longer leave the tiller for an instant, or all is lost" (E, 212).

[13] As Rousseau writes in the *Letter to D'Alembert:* "Theater settings provide a lesson in practical philosophy which is surely more worthy and better understood than all of the vain speculations that muddle the young minds of our school-children" (quoted by Jean Starobinski, *Jean-Jacques Rousseau: La transparence et l'obstacle* [Paris: Gallimard, 1957], 116).

child" (p. 189). The child is entirely captivated by the thing at hand precisely so that he will not see the pedagogue's actions. In Rousseau's staging the tutor holds the position of director, standing behind the floodlights, which both blind and illuminate the child-actor. The tutor blinds in the sense that he protects himself from inquisitive scrutiny—"[the child] will also not be spying on your morals with a curiosity motivated by jealousy and will not find a secret pleasure in catching you misbehaving" (p. 120)—and at the same time illuminates in the sense that he exposes the child to a total and perfect legibility. Emile can be read like an open book. "One reads in his face all the movements of his soul. By dint of spying them out, one gets to be able to *foresee* them and finally to *direct* them" (p. 226, my italics).

It is thus not enough to prepare and to see; it is also necessary to see in depth, to "foresee" so as to predict and hence direct: "He ought not to make a step without your having foreseen it; he ought not to open his mouth without your knowing what he is going to say" (p. 120). The educational hold is then complete: the pedagogical artifice envelops knowledge; it arranges scrupulously prepared lessons about the child, attributes a necessity to the sequence of life experiences, without the child ever knowing the logic of this artifice.[14]

In that respect, Rousseau, who all along seemed reluctant to give examples in support of his principles, is strangely fond of explaining in minute detail the numerous stratagems he did use (when it is a question of autobiographical episodes) or would have

[14] Paradoxically, the master's omnipotence, which is perceived by Rousseau as a "salutory dupery" in Emile's case, becomes completely suspect and sinister when it turns on Rousseau himself. Starobinski provides an insightful analysis of this reversal when he remarks that Rousseau's condemnation of his persecutors' project is broached in language that bears an uncanny resemblance to Rousseau's pedagogical advice: "Their surveillance tactics were no less efficient: they watched him [Jean Jacques] so vigilantly that every word he spoke was noted, every step he took registered, and every plan he made discovered at the very instant of its conception. They arranged everything such that, however free he might appear to be in the presence of other men, he would be unable to enter into any real exchange with them, doomed to remain alone in a crowd, and ignorant of all that was going on around him, particularly concerning himself.... They had bound him in so many ways that, amid all that feigned liberty, he could not pronounce a single word, take a single step, move a single finger, that they had not foreseen and determined" (*Dialogues* in *Oeuvres complètes* [Paris: Pléiade, 1964], vol. 1, 706).

used to break the resistance of badly brought up children. As an example of Rousseau's peculiar inclination, let us take the semi-autobiographical episode in which he recounts his relationship with Jacques-Armand Dupin de Chenonceaux, who was thirteen years old when he became Rousseau's pupil. This episode is exemplary, for we see a conflictual relationship develop between tutor and pupil, in which the former's authority is openly brought into question. In the scene where little Dupin has decided, against Rousseau's wishes, to go walking alone in order to test his tutor's authority once again, Rousseau begins to execute a plan that will teach the young man a lesson:

> He got dressed, a bit uneasy at seeing me let him go ahead and not following his example.... He began to feel his weakness ... he finally stepped out on the street, consoling himself somewhat for the harm that could happen to him by the hope that I would be made responsible for it.
>
> *This was just what I was waiting for. Everything was prepared in advance;* and since a kind of public scene was involved, I had provided myself with the father's consent. Hardly had the child taken a few steps before he heard, right and left, remarks about him.... Alone and without protection, he saw himself everybody's plaything....
>
> Meanwhile one of my friends, whom he did not know and to whom I had given the responsibility of watching over him, was following him step by step without his noticing it, and accosted him when the time was right ... he made him so well aware of the imprudence of his escapade that at the end of half an hour he brought him back to me, *tractable, embarrassed, and not daring to lift his eyes....*
>
> As for me, I received him without reproach and without ridicule, but with a bit of gravity.... The next day I saw with great pleasure that in my company he passed with a triumphant bearing before the same people who had jeered at him the day before because he was all alone when they met him. It can be well conceived that he did not threaten me anymore with going out without me.
>
> *It is by these means and others like them* that during the short time I was with the child I got to the point of being able to make him do *everything I wanted without prescribing anything to him,* without forbidding him anything, without sermons, without exhortations, without boring him with useless lessons. (*E*, 123–24, my italics)

Two lessons illustrating Rousseau's method in an exemplary manner can be gleaned from this episode. The first is a strategy of a political nature. To govern the child one must first govern his milieu and his entourage: "You will not be the child's master if you are not the master of all that surrounds him" (*E*, 95). What first appears to be a pedagogical method of indirect discipline proves to be the reflection of a profoundly political maxim. In order to govern *at all* the statesman must depersonalize his power behind the necessity of things and events; his own desire and will to power must seem to efface themselves in the name of the general will: "The greatest talent of chiefs of state is to disguise their power so as to make it less odious, and to govern the state so peaceably that it seems to require no leaders."[15]

The second lesson of the Jacques-Armand Dupin de Chenonceaux episode is of an epistemological nature, and it results from an analysis of power relations. The stage direction as pedagogical strategy has the acquisition of power for its sole object. The set of individuals who participate in Rousseau's demonstration are distributed quasi-mathematically. The demonstration is unassailable; the family, the servants, the whole village are accomplices—often even decoys—available to the tutor as much for dominating the pupil as for shielding himself from the latter's potential hold: "the first abuse that is tolerated leads to another, and this chain ends only with the overturning of all order and contempt for all law" (*E*, 334). This is why all of the pupil's knowledge must remain within a dimension of ignorance.[16] Not only is he ignorant of those ideas the tutor has determined to be beyond his grasp, but more specifically, he is ignorant of the nature of his own knowledge. The pupil must acquire all possible knowledge and savoir-faire, except the knowledge of his real position and the savoir-faire of pedagogy, which would permit him

---

[15] Rousseau, "Discours sur l'économie politique," in *Oeuvres complètes* (Paris: Pléiade, 1964), vol. III, 250. Cf. also Vincent Descombes's brilliant analysis of the "fiction" underlying Rousseau's concept of the general will which governs the political citizen in the *Social Contract*, in "La vérité du vrai," *Critique* 369 (1978), esp. 159–60.

[16] "As a somnambulist, wandering during his slumber, sleepwalks on the brink of a precipice into which he would fall if he were suddenly awakened, so my Emile, in the slumber of ignorance, escapes perils that he does not perceive" (pp. 319–20).

to understand his relationship to the tutor.[17] The pupil must remain blind to the logic with which the tutor engenders experience
in his wake. All relation of cause to effect must seem to be of
simple necessity: the pupil has nothing but things before his eyes,
and those things must appear to speak for themselves so that,
under the veil of necessity, the tutor may live out the fantasies
of his desire.

Providence

Things in nature are supposed to speak for themselves. That is
why Rousseau wanted to close all books and only consider the
text of nature. Books imitate and deform nature; they counterfeit
and corrode it by playing on children's imaginations. Hence Rousseau's well-known denunciation: "Reading is the plague of childhood" (*E*, 116). "I hate books. They only teach one to talk about
what one does not know" (p. 184). Instead of books Rousseau
favors presenting the child with "a situation where all man's
natural needs are shown in a way that a child's mind can sense,
and where the means of providing for these needs emerges suc-
cessively with equal ease" (p. 184). In other words, Rousseau
would like to find a situation where all man's natural needs would
be displayed and adapted to the child's mental universe. Suddenly,
on the same page on which we were told he hated books, Rousseau
changes tone and becomes impassioned: "Ardent philosopher . . .
do not put yourself out. This situation has been found; it has been
described and, without prejudice to you, much better than you
would describe it yourself—at least with more *truth* and simplicity" (p. 184, my italics).[18] Thus this marvelous situation ex-

---

[17] The savoir-faire of pedagogy is that which truly threatens the natural order,
for its acquisition by the child could overturn the respective positions of power
in the pedagogical relationship. Since Rousseau's sole purpose is to find a law
that would prevent the traditional movement of reversal from dependency into
domination, it is clear that the tutor's position must remain intransitive and that
his knowledge must not be transmitted to the child. Thus Emile will never be
the master of himself, nor that of anyone else, including his own children. I refer
the reader to the concluding words of Emile in the book's last paragraph: "remain
the master of the young masters. Advise us and govern us. We shall be docile. As
long as I live, I shall need you" (p. 480).

[18] *Truth* is a key word in Rousseau's vocabulary. However, in Rousseau's ar-

ists; unfortunately it exists in a book. So be it; one cannot have his cake and eat it too: "Since we absolutely must have books, there exists one which, to my view, provides the most felicitous treatise on natural education.... What, then, is this marvelous book? Is it Aristotle? Is it Pliny? Is it Buffon? No. It is *Robinson Crusoe*" (p. 184).

Emile, who is now in that period of life Rousseau called the age of force (twelve to fifteen years old) and psychologists call the imitation phase, will have a single concern and amusement: taking himself for Robinson—"I want it to make him dizzy; I want him constantly to be busy with his mansion, his goats, his plantations.... I want him to think that he is Robinson himself, to see himself dressed in skins" (p. 185). And indeed, what better means to turn Emile's head in the desired direction than to give him as an example the "natural man" par excellence, absolutely separated from society and at first glance deprived of all resources? There is certainly no better educational fiction than Robinson's daily practice of spelling out and revealing the ABC's of man's needs, which must be designated as natural and hence necessary. *Robinson Crusoe*—"castle in Spain of this happy age when one knows no other happiness than minimal necessities and *freedom*"—will allow Emile to recognize the superiority of the man of nature, who judges all things by himself according to "the true relation of things" (p. 134), over the social man, whose needs and desires have been denatured by institutions.

But in reality this novel, which seems to recount the life of an individual outside the social space, is the novel of culture itself, written under the guise of nature. Nature's simulacrum works to culture's advantage, making *Robinson Crusoe* the novel that, in effect, carries out the program of the ideological formation of culture.[19] *Robinson Crusoe* is not just any story, but the story of

---

gument truth constitutes a *functional* rather than an ontological principle. In this context, it is enlightening to see what he considers to be the *vérité* of his method in *Emile*: "When my method deals satisfactorily with all aspects of a single problem, and, *in avoiding one difficulty, prevents another,* then I judge that my method is good and that I am on the right path *[dans le vrai]*. This is what I believe I see in the *expedient* it suggests to me here" (p. 328, my italics).

[19] "In fact, this book is ... the first novel of culture, the first novel of formation—the novel of cultural apprenticeship, of culture's re-production according to a model it imposes as necessary, through the detour of a fiction—the fiction of the 'nature' of a human being who, in a state of separation, must discover what

History; the story of an investigation that begins on a desert island and which proposes to reconstruct man's origins and the rigorous order of pains and vicissitudes which governed his passage from the natural to the cultural order. But this ostensible investigation is falsified for two reasons: first, because the image of the origin in this case presupposes what it would engender—it is thus a deceptive origin seen backward from its end point; and second, because the world reproduced by Robinson is the reproduction (in the two meanings of the word, both as copy and as repetition) and not the genesis of culture. But if this is so, what will become of Emile-Robinson at this stage of Rousseau's pedagogical program?

It is not relevant to my argument to ask how much Rousseau understands—or misinterprets for his purposes—the meaning of the social and cultural constraint when he presents this fiction to Emile as the text of nature ("This state, I agree, is not that of social man; very likely it is not going to be that of Emile. But it is on the basis of this state that he ought to appraise all other states of affairs" [p. 185]). What must be noted above all is the fact that Emile can only read this fiction as the text of nature, since the stage props upon which the novel is built escape his awareness completely. In fact, he is only allowed to read one part of *Robinson*, to the exclusion of what Rousseau calls the novel's "rubbish"—"This novel, disencumbered of all its rubbish [*fatras*]" (p. 185)—that is, Robinson's story both before his shipwreck and after his departure from the island. This edited version of the novel featuring the "island Robinson" satisfies appearances at the expense of reality, in such a way as to mask the logic of culture's staging and expose it under the guise of the raw event, spontaneous and natural.

But *Robinson Crusoe* further exemplifies Rousseau's lesson. We have seen that for Rousseau the concept of an *ordered freedom* is the essence of the pedagogue's strategy. In the case of Robinson this translates into a concept of *controlled freedom*. The only ap-

---

necessity means. If one gives such a work to children, one does so—appropriately—in order to educate them, to inform them that there *do not exist* multiple ways of viewing the course of human affairs and that, as far as reworking the world is concerned, the best strategy is still to conform to the accepted model" (Hubert Damisch, *Ruptures, cultures* [Paris: Minuit, 1976], 28).

parent restriction to Robinson's actions is provided by his surroundings—the island. Robinson always perceives his constraints
as resulting from natural causes, never from culture's artifices.
Now Rousseau's garden props, which are crucial for understanding his project in *The New Eloise*, for instance, function in a homologous manner to Defoe's island. The perfection of the
gardener's art lies in making his intervention invisible; thus he
fosters the illusion of a fatherless nature. "Nowhere do I see the
slightest trace of cultivation. All is green, fresh, and vigorous and
*the gardener's hand is nowhere to be seen. Nothing contradicts
the notion of a desert island* which came to me upon entering, and
I see no human footsteps. Ah! said Monsieur de Wolmar, it is because we have taken greats pains to efface them" (my italics).[20]

We know that for Rousseau education is quite literally a garden
art: "Plants are shaped by cultivation, and men by education" (*E*,
38).[21] The tutor thus applies the gardener's artistry to his pupil:
pedagogical staging repeats point by point, within its own frame
of reference, the illusion of the artificial desert in which everything seems to be born of itself. In a most eloquent and concise
way, Julie sets forth the terms of the Rousseau-Defoe pedagogical
theorem: "It is true, she said, that nature has done everything,
but under my direction, and there is nothing here which I have
not ordered" (my italics).[22] Like desert and island gardening, pedagogy reaches perfection when the tutor manages to erase his
own traces. And yet, I believe there is in Rousseau's affinity for
Defoe's novel—"What resource this folly [the Robinson theme]

[20] *Julie, or The New Eloise*, trans. Judith H. McDowell (University Park: Pennsylvania State University Press, 1968), 311.

[21] Rousseau is hardly the first to use this horticultural metaphor, which is in
fact a leit-motif of all pedagogical discourse: human kind harbors the seed of a
healthy development, and all pedagogues—from Locke to Schreber, and not overlooking Rousseau and Kant—have sought to nurture and direct this development.

[22] Ibid., 305. Here again Julie's views are not, in themselves, particularly original.
The Elyseum letter, when juxtaposed with any history of the English garden, reads
like a compendium of opinions drawn from the landscape theories of Addison,
Shaftesbury, Pope, and others. In *The Art of Landscape Gardening* (1803), Humphry Repton sets down four requisites for perfection in landscape art: to respect
the genius of place, to imitate nature by means of well-concealed art, to disguise
the boundaries in order to give the impression of extension or freedom, and to
display natural beauties while hiding natural defects of a place. I am indebted to
Gregory Ulmer's unpublished paper "Landscape Pedagogy" for these remarks.

would be for a skillful man [Defoe? Rousseau? Or both?] who knew how to engender it solely for the sake of taking advantage of it" (*E*, 185)—something more than mere kinship of strategy. *Robinson Crusoe* occupies a very particular place in Rousseau's pedagogical enterprise, and with good reason!

It is explicitly stated in *Emile* that imitation has grave consequences because it forces one to "leave" oneself and become other; in Rousseau's words, it makes us leave our place to occupy that of another: "The foundation of imitation among us comes from the desire always to be transported out of ourselves. If I succeed in my enterprise, Emile surely will not have this desire" (p. 104).[23] Almost immediately afterward, however, an exception to this rule against imitation is made: Emile is authorized to make himself other; he is even commanded to become Robinson—the island Robinson. Emile is thus commanded to identify himself with a utopic ideal of man free from *all* relationships, those of society necessarily included. Rousseau, of course, does not see this identification/imitation as a departure from the self, since the unit of measure that the island Robinson represents approaches as closely as possible the "absolute whole": "Natural man is entirely for himself. He is a numerical integer, the absolute whole *[l'entier absolu]* which is relative only to itself or to its kind. Civil man is a fractional integer dependent on the denominator; his value is determined by his relation to the whole, which is the social body" (p. 40). Unlike the man of society who is judged from the slant of public opinion, the "numerical integer" implies the return of judgment to the self. Emile-Robinson will thus think and live like the "absolute whole," alone in the abstract universe of the island (or of the garden); alone before nature, the elements, and like Robinson, before Providence.

Let us recall here the theme of Providence, which recurs more than once in *Robinson Crusoe*. In fact, it is a theme that appears systematically, even mechanically, in the novel. It is under the sign of Providence that the story of Robinson begins, and it is under this sign that all his adventures take place and that the different episodes of the narrative find their coherence. Robinson's whole island existence is a series of miracles produced by Prov-

[23] For a discussion of the role of imitation in the corruption of "natural simplicity," see Jacques Derrida's *Of Grammatology*, 204–5.

idence for his moral edification. Once more with this providential theme we decipher the inscription of the masterful pedagogical ruse. For it should be noted that Providence appears in *Emile* as well, and it plays a very special role.

The episode in *Emile* in which Providence first manifests itself probably occurs during a trip Rousseau took to Venice in 1743. Having made the acquaintance of an English tutor who is touring Europe with his pupil Lord John, Rousseau witnesses a strange scene in which the tutor reads Lord John a letter concerning Miss Lucy, his fiancée. Miss Lucy's mother writes that her daughter spends all her time embroidering sleeve cuffs for her betrothed. Rousseau "naturally" assumes that the letter from Lucy's mother is a machination on the tutor's part to discourage Lord John from frequenting a disreputable young Venetian woman who had also given him as a gift a set of cuffs he was wearing. But to his surprise he discovers that "Monsieur John went out a moment later to put on other cuffs, and I said to his governor: 'You have a pupil with an excellent nature. But tell me the truth, wasn't the letter from Miss Lucy's mother arranged? Is it not an expedient you devised against the Lady of the cuffs?' 'No,' he answered, 'the thing is real. I have not put so much art in my efforts. I have applied myself with simplicity and zeal, and God has blessed my work' " (pp. 470–71). And Rousseau adds immediately after: "The incident involving this young man did not leave my memory. It was not apt to produce nothing in the head of a dreamer like me" (p. 471). Now we have seen how and to what extent stage direction is involved in Rousseau's pedagogy. The episode of Lord John will serve to consecrate—and one might say to justify—the pedagogical ruse; it will also help us understand better Rousseau's profound fascination with *Robinson Crusoe*.

If one sets *Emile* against Defoe's novel, one can see how the role and place of Providence in Defoe coincides exactly with that of the tutor as master of knowledge in Rousseau's pedagogical theater, except that here the master pedagogue Rousseau wishes to go even further by taking onto himself the power and omniscience of God, and thus supplant the divinity in its providential role. The substitution is simple and direct; there is a strict homology of place and function between the tutor's relationship to Emile and that of Providence to Robinson, which gives its full meaning to Rousseau's letter to the abbé Maydieu in answer to a question concerning the education of the abbé's charge, the Duc de Villequier's son: "For him, men of letters will never be anything but men of another world; I can think of only one model that could represent reality in his eyes, and this model is you, Monsieur. The position you hold is the most noble and grand position on earth. Let the common people think what it will of your station; in my mind, I see you *in the place of God*—you create a man" (my italics).[24]

Dreamlike Imaginary

What is the further meaning of this pedagogical machine, which not only excludes but replaces Providence? What is the significance of this Robinson, the model given to Emile and with whom Rousseau himself, according to his correspondence, identified? To take oneself for God or Robinson, the integral man without other—the man born of man—is to rehearse once again the classic fantasy of pure autocreation. The staging of Rousseauian knowledge is thus more than ever the staging of a birth where the deliverer *is* the delivered, both born of a single delivery. Like Pygmalion, whose admiration for his creation is deflected back onto himself, Rousseau can say: "I cannot tire of admiring my work: I adore myself in what I have done."[25] We are touching here upon the founding phantasm of the pedagogical vocation, the phantasm of autogeneration, where one gives birth and in so doing is reborn. And indeed, in *Emile* Rousseau speaks only the language of the self—a language by which the pupil is turned into a product and a projection of the imaginary rather than relating to any reality. The truth of Rousseau's pedagogical delirium is thus exposed: it is the delirium of autocreation in and by which education ceases to be centered around a relationship and becomes instead an autonomous process whose value lies in its closure. To educate thus means for Rousseau phantasmatically to produce oneself by oneself outside all begetting. *Like Emile, the pedagogue must be an orphan.* As his own father and his own mother, he

[24] "Lettre à l'abbé Jean Maydieu du 9 février 1770," in *Correspondance complète de Jean Jacques Rousseau*, vol. XXXVII, 232. And Rousseau pursues: "If you see things as I do, how this idea must exalt you within!"
[25] Rousseau, *Pygmalion*, in *Oeuvres complètes* (Paris: Pléiade, 1964), vol. II, 1226.

thus accedes to the limitless creation that escapes the other's desire.

This movement of pure creation, where self as subject coincides with self as object, unfolds outside temporal history. *Emile* never ends, or rather it ends on a repetition of the beginning.[26] To the tutor's solemn declaration, "Here my long task ends, and another's begins. Today I abdicate the authority you confided me" (p. 478), Emile replies: "As long as I live, I shall need you. I need you more than ever now that my functions as a man begin" (p. 480). Predictably then, Rousseau's pedagogy can only project itself within the time of an eternal beginning, a time of plenitude, without history and without temporality—the time of the phantasm.

This view of an imaginary pedagogy is corroborated further by Rousseau's utopic view of childhood. In Rousseau, the postulate of a preestablished harmony is contingent upon the postulate that a natural harmony has been perverted by culture. In that sense, the dream of childhood enacts the pedagogue's conviction that a golden age anterior to the repressive effects of the environment, can be retrieved by education in the state of childhood. Childhood in itself provides Rousseau with a means of skirting the progression of time and hence the ongoing corruption of human nature; it implies an evacuation of history and reality—a space above change and beyond movement. Thus Rousseau reinterprets the time of childhood as a metaphysical time when human nature finds its ideal actualization. To give oneself an imaginary child and then to identify with it in fantasy is to affirm the possibility of a pure happiness, outside time and free from the conflicts and

---

[26] For an analysis of this movement as a return to the origin, see Paul de Man's "Self and Pygmalion," in his *Allegories of Reading* (New Haven: Yale University Press, 1979) and Christie McDonald's "The Animation of Writing: *Pygmalion*," in her *The Dialogue of Writing: Essays in Eighteenth-Century French Literature* (Waterloo, Ontario: Wilfrid Laurier University Press, 1984). Both of these readings "problematize" Jean Starobinski's earlier study of Rousseau's *Pygmalion*, titled "La statue voilée," in *La transparence et l'obstacle*. In turn, Alain Grosrichard also reads *Emile*'s conclusion as a return to the origin, but, in a psychoanalytic register: "Rousseau has Emile pronounce in the end a truth that is unheard of for his day, a truth that Freud has only recently accustomed us to hear: namely, that no father . . . can come to occupy this position, or fulfill the paternal role, without straying from it, because it is always *as a son* that he is called upon to play this role" ("Le prince saisi par le philosophe," 136).

sorrows of temporal history. This is why Rousseau's education is projected in the smooth, serene time of the imaginary, without any obstacle between desire and its realization. We witness here the disproportion of a delirious pedagogy whose limitless, phantasmatic character removes the educative desire from the realm of real contingencies and places it in the register of the imaginary, where *everything becomes possible*. As Rousseau warns his reader: "It will be believed that what is being read is less an educational treatise than a visionary's dreams about education" (*E*, pref., 34).[27]

It is less important, however, to emphasize the utopic quality of education as Rousseau presents it (an emphasis that is not particularly innovative or original) than to reflect upon the *ideal* nature of the pedagogical process. Such reflection will lead us necessarily to acknowledge that pedagogy, like all ideals, is organized around a lack. For if, on the one hand, in the pedagogical relationship, the pupil's desire to know must intersect the desire of the tutor who wants his pupil to know; on the other hand, if the pupil knows, then that which might effectively sustain his desire is annulled. The pedagogical misunderstanding—and perversion!—always participates in the paradoxical nature of desire as lack, where all satisfaction can only be a function of expectation and never of realization. It follows that there is a fundamental dimension of impossibility to the pedagogical aim. That discovery is perhaps, or rather probably, Rousseau's greatest innovation: to have sought to present pedagogy for what it is—an impossibility. Thus, to the accusations leveled against him, which he reports in his preface—"Propose what can be *done*, they never stop repeating to me"—Rousseau's answer is dramatically lucid: "Such a project, in certain matters, is much more *chimerical* than is mine" (p. 34, my italics). This amounts to saying that *Emile* had been conceived from the beginning as a scenario of the imaginary, which would later become a book translating the failure and the impossibility of pedagogy in its practical import.

This further answers one of the questions I asked at the begin-

---

[27] Likewise, in his "Lettre au Professeur Jacob Vernet du 20 novembre 1760," written during the composition of *Emile*, Rousseau remarks: "I have yet to publish some sort of educational treatise, full of my usual reveries, the final fruit of my rustic walks in the fields" (*Correspondance complète de Jean Jacques Rousseau*, vol. VII, 332).

ning of this essay, on the relationship in Rousseau between pedagogical theory and practice. By now it has become clear that the great imaginary pedagogical scenario has no relationship to concrete situations, to what Rousseau called examples. In fact, theory in this instance is founded precisely upon those principles that practice disclaims. Theory, as it is phantasmatically constituted and propagated, is only theory to the extent that its unreality will confirm the imaginary educative position of the pedagogue. The truth of Rousseau's pedagogical theory does not rest upon a reality principle but upon an imaginary production; that is, a dreamlike scenario that permits the phantasm to function unencumbered, a production by which nothing could intervene and say to the phantasm: *You are false, you are not in the realm of truth.*

The delirious dimension of *Emile* guarantees Rousseau that with the expansive, dreamlike imaginary and the theoretical phantasm, nothing can be realized outside his desire. For if by chance the theory escaped its imaginary status and took form with respect to practice, it would reintroduce the bridle of reality, which must be negated if the unbounded pedagogical dream is to operate. As a result, *Emile*'s pedagogical theory will lend itself to the educative dream-scenario *without ever risking a confrontation with examples*, for otherwise Rousseau would lose his reason—which is of course his delirium—to educate.

Lacan on Rousseau's Couch

In a recent book of major importance, *Dire Mastery*, François Roustang asks the question: why does one create disciples? His answer: so as not to go crazy! For by retaining, diffusing, and transmitting the master's words, the disciple transforms the master's solitary speech into a principle of communication.[28] This is also Rousseau's concern. For fear of seeing his writings disappear, he needs an interlocutor, preferably a disciple. And what if one

---

[28] Roustang characterizes as follows the master-disciple relationship: "My disciples, who remember my words and propagate them, release me from my solitary speech, and transform it into science and a principle of communication; they are my safeguards *[garde-fous]*" (*Dire Mastery*, trans. Ned Lukacher [Baltimore: Johns Hopkins University Press, 1982], 34).

has the misfortune not to have a disciple? As Rousseau would say, one must then invent one, hallucinate one if necessary: "I have hence chosen to give myself an imaginary pupil" (*E*, 50). The result is Emile, Rousseau's imaginary interlocutory and disciple, his double. Emile is the imagined "Other as self," which will permit Rousseau to bestow upon his delirium the function of psychoanalytic cure.

Rousseau's habitual state of mind is well known. Thinking himself endlessly persecuted, different, on the brink of madness, Rousseau invents, by way of a cure, an imaginary disciple. In this manner, Rousseau, whose eternal motive is to be heard and judged by all, will in fact be heard, but on his own terms.[29] The Other that he summons, the imaginary disciple, thus liberates Rousseau from his obsessive need for recognition. Rousseau analyzes this situation quite clearly. He knows that his pedagogical thought is the outcome of a "rêverie" and he senses that it evolves through a peculiar procedure that he himself might have characterized as delirious. He is aware that although this disciple does not exist in everyday reality, he nevertheless exists virtually, that is, phantasmatically, in all of us. Rousseau recognizes this and writes to this effect: "Should this man not be found, it is at least possible that the memory of having read these pages, imprinted upon the mind of my readers, will one day awaken in one of them ... some happy effect that cannot happen during my lifetime because of the passion that moves them against me; and this is all that is necessary to begin the work of Providence."[30] Roustang comments on this quote in these terms: "This is thus the final state of the interlocutor: a person who has read without understanding, yet who retains the memory."[31] How are we to interpret such a memory devoid of understanding, especially if we suspect that Rousseau's pedagogical mystification is founded upon the figure of this imaginary interlocutor?

It is understandable, and not mystifying, that Rousseau himself should be so absorbed in his own fiction that it comes to replace

---

[29] On the subject of Rousseau's narcissistic positioning vis-à-vis society, see the two chapters "La solitude" and "La réclusion à perpétuité," in Starobinski's *La transparence et l'obstacle*.

[30] Quoted in François Roustang, "L'interlocuteur du solitaire," *Revue de l'Institut de Sociologie* 1–2 (1982), 172.

[31] Ibid.

reality. I have already argued why it is essential for him to set his pedogogical machine in motion by giving it the consistency of reality. Nonetheless, there is a mystification inherent to *Emile*, a discursive trap into which all of its readers fall so completely that, even when Rousseau reminds them that his theory is fictional, they do not hear him. What is it that allows for such a slippage, by which the theory of *Emile* passes from a personal "delirium" to the status of a pedagogical law recognized by everybody—a law that in the end imposes itself as the reality of all education? What is the secret of the ruse employed by Rousseau to transform the scenario he sought to develop in *Emile* into a discourse of truth?

The mechanism is by now fairly predictable; it consists in transposing the master-disciple relationship onto the author-reader rapport: like the disciple, the "all-mighty" reader initially occupies a position of power, albeit an illusory one, until, through a reversal, the author imposes his mastery. First, Rousseau establishes the interlocutor-reader as the holder and judge of his destiny, as when he stakes his fame on the reader's "memory of having read these pages, imprinted upon [his] mind." But what is imprinted in the reader's mind if not the story of Emile's *tutor*, that is, the story of every reader's fundamental phantasm of self-recognition? In effect, every reader of *Emile* is offered an opportunity to manifest his own irresistible desire for self-recognition through the very phantasm that he recognizes and with which he identifies in Rousseau's writing. In other words, the pedagogical trajectory of the tutor becomes the model for the phantasmatic trajectory of the reader, who thereby discovers the means *to produce through his own imaginary his own captive disciple*—trapped in a state of permanent dependency and availability. The reader-interlocutor, toward whom Rousseau was, at first, allegedly indebted for his recognition, is thus trapped in a situation of dependency within a discourse that bewitches and paralyses him.

Hence by placing the interlocutor-reader in the "providential" place that was left in abeyance in his imaginary scheme ("this is all that is necessary to begin the work of Providence"), Rousseau forces the reader to assume the pedagogical appropriation of his own delirium. The ultimate disciple—the one with memory but without understanding, according to Roustang—is every modern reader of *Emile*, all of us who have transferred onto ourselves

Rousseau's therapeutic cure. By inscribing the author-reader relationship within the pattern elaborated in the pedagogical ruse, Rousseau thus transforms his delirium into a general theory to which all pedagogues subscribe, recalling as Roustang so eloquently puts it, "Delirium is the theory of the one, whereas theory is the delirium of several, able to transmit itself."[32]

In this movement from delirium to theory, one can easily identify a contemporary institution, founded on a certain "perversion" of knowledge: the school of Lacanian psychoanalysis. One consequence of the dogma of infallibility cultivated by Lacan was to graft the analytical relationship onto a relationship of power. Lacanian psychoanalytical knowledge is rooted in a willful confusion of two registers: the registers of responsibility and of power. Like Rousseau's pedagogical knowledge, psychoanalytical knowledge is organized by Lacan along the lines of an authoritarian institutional structure—*L'Ecole Freudienne de Paris*, founded in 1964 and disbanded in 1980—which is based on a rapport of power that guarantees that the relationship between the group and its leader cannot be modified. In other words, all the answers to the questions addressed to Lacan always rest with Lacan himself, such that the apprentice-analyst always depends on the laws pronounced by the master.

In this respect, Roustang has demonstrated that Lacanian training is a form of learning without questioning, which allows at best a progress of accumulation through repetition. Its first strategy consists in engaging the disciples such that they become entirely absorbed in their efforts to understand Lacan, leaving them very little chance to criticize him. (This also explains Lacan's recourse to esoteric forms of knowledge, playing simultaneously

---

[32] *Dire Mastery*, 34. Much can be said about the parallels between psychoanalytic and pedagogical theory. On this point, both François Roustang and more recently Marie Balmary (*L'homme aux statues: Freud et la faute cachée du père*, which I discuss in Chapter 7) show convincingly that it is only through a *process of transmission* that Freud's delirious speculation (concerning his father's seduction of an unknown second wife) acquired its theoretical status and later became formalized into psychoanalytic canon. Psychoanalysis and modern pedagogy would thus have come into being as the unresolved outcome of the fantasies of two individuals. Perhaps Freud had already had this insight when he wrote in 1925: "At an early stage I had accepted the *bon mot* which holds that there are three impossible professions—educating, healing, and governing—and I was already fully occupied with the second of them" (*Standard Edition*, vol. xix, 273).

the roles of a linguist, a mathematician, a philosopher, and a psychoanalyst . . . for his fellow specialists.) The second Lacanian strategy revolves around the function of citation as a kind of spokesperson—in French *porte-parole* means literally one who carries the word of another—a function in which citation comes to constitute a law of speech through which the hidden source of authority is transformed into absolute authority.

> *In advance* and for the future, they put their trust in Lacan. Their relationship to Freud has been assimilated into *deferred action.* Nothing, however, has changed. Another transference is in the same blind spot, the transference onto Lacan. Those who understand his writings are content to repeat his words or to embroider upon his theory. Those who do not understand his writings assume that Lacan understands them and that if they are very studious, they will one day also understand. Under no circumstances do they question Lacan's sayings or presuppositions. In group discussions, for example, a quotation from Lacan acts as a concluding point or verdict, as the last word, which no one dares to criticize, analyze, or assess from a subjective viewpoint. . . . This mania for citing Lacan reveals an imaginary identification with the master.[33]

It is unnecessary to add that under these conditions any critical attitude with respect to Lacan's "theories" becomes mentally and psychically impossible. The analyst, who can never utter a single word that puts to the test either the truth or the error of the master's discourse, becomes, like Emile, a pure reflection of (the views of) the master, the only guarantee being the pseudo-oracular writings of Lacan.

Moreover, it would be easy to show how the model of Lacanian psychoanalytic training takes its inspiration from Rousseauian pedagogy. On a formal level, like Rousseau, Lacan devotes all of his writings to the establishment of the fundamental concepts that would serve to assure a scientific status to psychoanalysis; but, in fact, analytic technique proper—clinical examples—remains secondary for Lacan, as if his theory were not necessarily based on a practice. Second, on a functional level, love is a dimension of demand in Lacanian analytic vocabulary. Hence demand for Lacan, just as for Rousseau, never exists in isolation; it

---

[33] *Dire Mastery,* 21–22.

uses the pretext of "need" to emerge. As the need is satisfied, the demand becomes all the more pressing, for demand is the fundamental movement toward recognition on the part of the subject. "To demand—that is all that the subject has ever done, all that he has lived for," says Lacan, speaking of the analysand.[34] Uncanny resonances of Rousseau speaking about the child!

Now, Lacan has taught us that the analyst *must not* respond to the demand of his patient. He must frustrate the patient so as to force a restructuring of his symbolic organization by way of his imaginary.[35] We recall that, in the same way, Rousseau's pedagogue possessed the knowledge of how to separate need from demand in order to frustrate the child's demand, and ultimately to be able to prevent it altogether. The Lacanian cure proposes to frustrate the subject's demand in precisely the same terms. That there may lie in this power to frustrate—in the name of a therapeutic cure—the power to drive the subject mad or to destroy him, has become painfully obvious in recent years, within the Lacanian establishment.[36] But perhaps post-Lacanian psychoanalysis is still in the memory stage, without understanding yet. To understand the implications of Lacanian therapy might one day require a "return" to *Emile* rather than to the *Ecrits*.

[34] Jacques Lacan, "Direction de la cure," in *Ecrits* (Paris: Seuil, 1966), 617. The object of demand of the analysand as well as the infant is the same: the desire to have one's desire recognized by the other; that is why, as we have already seen in the case of the child, demand is fundamental to the coming to consciousness of the self.

[35] "By the mediation of the demand, the entire past gapes open, right down to the final depths of earliest childhood" (ibid.).

[36] Cf. Roustang, "L'illusion lacanienne," *Critique*, 456 (1985).

5

Staging the Libertine Imaginary I:
The Theoretical Scenario

> Qu'imaginer? J'avais tout fait, tout exécuté.
>
> Sade, *Nouvelle Justine*

"Moi la Vérité. . . . "

Readers who approach Sade unprepared may well find themselves abandoning the task quickly, overcome by disgust, nausea, and boredom. Almost everyone has tried to read Sade, urged on by prurient curiosity and titillated by references to his work in everything from pornographic ephemera to weighty treatises on Western culture. In most cases, however, the reader's reaction is one of bafflement: the marquis's major thrust appears to be that flagellation flags and sodomy satiates, and that to revive their waning sexual appetites his heroes and heroines require large doses of philosophizing. These, unfortunately, tend to have a soporific effect on readers, who, lacking such a stimulus, will probably dismiss what they have heard about Sade's seminal influence and depart for more accessible sources of gratification.

This situation, painful for any writer, is even more so in Sade's case because of the serious pretension he had concerning the "aesthetic" quality of his work—a pretension that perhaps helps to explain why his monumental oeuvre (at least with regard to size) encompasses all the known literary genres: philosophical dialogue, fiction, drama, poetry, political writing, the historical novel, the novella, the tale, the fabliau, the short story, along with a fairly substantial correspondence.[1] Sade's numerous comments regarding his own literary endeavors as well as his "literary criticism" are unfortunately spread throughout his works, so that a coherent picture is difficult to draw. However, there exists one text—a kind of theoretical preface to *Les crimes de l'amour*, entitled "Idée sur les romans"—which has the double merit of concisely recording Sade's literary opinions while at the same time expounding his theory of literature, in effect a theory of writing *avant la lettre*.

In this twenty-page essay, Sade gives first a short history of the novel from the Greeks to Lewis's *The Monk*. He expresses his greatest admiration for Cervantes, gives the nod of approval to Madame de Lafayette and Scarron, deems *Candide, Zadig, Manon Lescaut,* and *La nouvelle Héloïse* masterpieces, and concludes by enthusiastically acknowledging the novelistic genius of Richardson and Fielding, who, says Sade, taught the French "that only a penetrating study of the human heart, truly the most confounding maze found in nature, can inspire the novelist, whose work must reveal man...as he is when subjected to vice and jolted by all the passions" ("Idée," IV, 26–27).

---

[1] The Pauvert edition of Sade's *Oeuvres* numbers at present thirty-five volumes, twenty-one of which are novels: *Les infortunes de la vertu, Aline et Valcour (A&V), Justine (Just), La nouvelle Justine (N. Just), Histoire de Juliette (Jul),* and *Les 120 journées de Sodome (120 J).* The short stories *Les crimes de l'amour* are collected in vols. 4 to 6; the pedagogical pamphlet *La philosophie dans le boudoir (Philo)* is in vol. 25; the novellas, tales, and fabliaux are in vol. 7; the political writings in vol. 8; the historical novels in vols. 13 and 31; the plays in vols. 32–35; and finally, a limited number of Sade's letters appear in vols. 29 and 30, under the title *Lettres de Vincennes et de la Bastille.* The ten volumes of *Les journées de Florbelle* never reached us, as his son Armand de Sade and the prefect Delavan burned them right after Sade's death. I have used the following translations: *Juliette,* trans. Austryn Wainhouse (New York: Grove Press, 1976); *Justine* and *Philosophy in the Bedroom,* trans. Richard Seaver and Austryn Wainhouse (New York: Grove Press, 1965). All other translations are my own. References to *Juliette, Justine,* and *Philosophy* are to the English editions of these works and appear in the body of the text with relevant abbreviation and page reference. References to the other works of Sade will also appear in our text with the relevant abbreviation (unless the source is obvious), volume number, and page number from the Pauvert edition.

This commentary on Richardson and Fielding constitutes an oblique answer to the central theoretical question raised in "Idée sur les romans": "What is the purpose of novels?" (IV, 32). Inverting the common conception of the relationship between history and fiction, Sade attributes to history the depiction of appearances, whereas fiction embodies the essence of man. As a consequence, says he, the good novelist should closely follow all of nature's inclinations ("the novelist is the man of nature" [IV, 34]), for they mirror faithfully the heart of man. Thus, by portraying nature in its most minute details, the novelist will mark his narration with the seal of the *most exact truth.* In effect, this is the one point that Sade never stops advocating throughout his work: the novelist must always tell the truth, the whole truth, and nothing but the truth. If there is a Sadian philosophy regarding works of imagination (including his own fiction), it rests entirely on one idea, one certitude, one obsession: that of telling the truth. The arguments may be changed, the rhetoric altered, the novelistic ground rules transgressed—nevertheless the principle of truth remains. Whether it is in a short theoretical essay such as "Idée sur les romans" (note for this purpose the singular use of *idea*) or in the ten volumes of the *Justine-Juliette* sequence, we are told repeatedly that the man of letters must speak in the name of truth: "Such are the sentiments which are going to direct our labors, and it is in consideration of these intentions that we ask the reader's indulgence ... for the sometimes rather painful situations which, *out of love for truth,* we have been obliged to dress before his eyes" (*Just,* 458). And the entire sequence ends with Juliette telling Noirceuil in the last paragraph of the novel: "Why dread publishing [our adventures] when the truth itself, and the *truth alone, lays bare the secrets of Nature,* however mankind may tremble before those revelations? Philosophy must never shrink in speaking out *[La philosophie doit tout dire]*" (*Jul,* 1193).

The question that occurs at this point is one of definition: what does truth mean for Sade? What are its foundations? Its modalities? Its implications? The first answer that comes to mind is the following: truth is a form of verisimilitude, for as Sade's "Idée" makes clear, there is an unavoidable connivance between them. Ultimately, the boundaries between the *vrai* and the *vraisemblable* are so fragile that the two become indistinguishable. As Sade puts it: "You [the novelist] are asked not to be truthful *[vrai]* but merely plausible *[vraisemblable]*; to demand too much of you would detract from the pleasures that you prepare for us" ("Idée," IV, 35). Is this, then, the meaning truth acquires for Sade? We should not be surprised if this is the case, as it was traditional for eighteenth-century novelists to anchor their narratives in some type of truth-verisimilitude technique. In fact, Sade borrows two of the rhetorical procedures commonly used by his contemporaries. The first is the recourse to an "outsider's" testimonial, the cliché that says, "What I am about to tell you is not off the top of my head, I am only transcribing what was already written in such and such a letter, which was given to me." The other procedure Sade employs is the one calling for authorial intervention. At a given moment, the author intervenes and speaks in his own name in order to assure his reader of the veracity of his narrative.

The first procedure, elaborated by Diderot and Sterne with real genius, is practiced by Sade with extraordinary clumsiness. When, in *Aline et Valcour*, he is supposed to be copying a body of letters, there is one that takes up a whole volume and tells of events that the author of the letter could not have known about. And when the contradictions become so obvious as to necessitate a commentary from Sade himself, he does not hesitate to explain in a footnote that the negligences we may have noticed in this letter are a further proof of the veracity(!) of his reporting.[2]

This peculiar kind of intervention should make the reader want to pause and examine the topics or situations Sade is discussing when he feels the need to assure us personally of the truth of his narrative. One most often encounters this situation when one or another of Sade's characters is sexually aroused by the spectacle of a massacre or a disaster; then Sade cannot resist the temptation to intervene: "My intimates know that . . . everything I say relating to the voluptuous side [of my narrative] is authentic, that I have depicted nothing but the accustomed behavior and characteristic attitudes of the persons I mention, and that had they been witness to these scenes, they could not have rendered *more sin-*

---

[2] "The repetitions, the negligence evident in this letter prove Valcour's state of mind, and cannot fail to convince the reader that no one is making light of his good faith when we assure him the veracity of this correspondence" (*A&V*, XII, 124).

cere accounts of them" (*Jul*, 762).[3] This example occurs after Juliette and her Italian friends have indulged in a grandiose orgy while witnessing from a terrace in Rome a fire that burns thirty-seven hospitals and kills twenty thousand people. Another instance occurs after an extended orgy testing various sexual "recipes." Like a doctor explaining a prescription to his patient, Sade then advises his reader how to remain permanently aroused: "This care [following ejaculation] consists in having oneself sucked without delay, in having one's balls comforted and fondled, and in the application of very hot cloths. It is also helpful, after the crisis, to absorb restoratives, or spirituous liquors. The latter employed as lotions upon the testicles will also produce excellent effects" (*Jul*, 1065).

Clearly, then, although Sade never ceases to declare that he is portraying the truth, the truth function of the narrative—whatever the technique used to this effect—is asserted when its content is most lacking in both verisimilitude and veracity. So what is the meaning of this truth? One could hypothesize that since it does not concern the realistic nature of Sade's descriptions, truth may instead describe the logic of his argumentation. What the characters argue at the moment they are enacting their wildest sexual acts, the logic they use to explain or justify these acts—this is what has to be true. Veracity would thus be a function and a result of the argumentative process by which desire, murder, and violence (all of which fall under the rubric "vice") are justified. And indeed, the reader discovers with some relief that this may be the case, if he is to believe what Sade writes in "Idée sur les romans." Sade would have preferred not to narrate the perpetration of heinous acts, but unfortunately, he says, the force of truth obliges him to do so. And if he has given vice power over virtue,

---

[3] This note concludes on a further assurance of truthfulness: "I take this occasion to assure the reader that the same applies to the descriptive part of my narrative; it is scrupulously exact" (*Jul*, 762). Both Pierre Klossowski and Roland Barthes have commented on Sade's use of personal notes. Klossowski considers that they function on an ironic register (*Sade mon prochain* [Paris: Seuil, 1967], 54), whereas Barthes sees them as an intrusion of a "discursive reality" within the flow of the fiction (*Sade, Fourier, Loyola*, trans. Richard Miller [New York: Hill and Wang, 1976], 167). Whatever the interpretation of these notes, they appear often enough to let readers judge for themselves. I note in passing a few relevant ones from *Juliette*: xx, 169, 213; xxi, 177; xxii, 71–72, 311; xxiii, 138, 147, 320; xxiv, 221, 281. These references are to the Pauvert edition.

it is precisely in order to inspire pity and compassion for the sufferings of virtue, thus providing the finest eulogy for it: "Some say that I paint with too heavy a hand, that I endow vice with excessively odious traits. Do you want to know my reason? I do not wish to make vice attractive. . . . I want vice to be seen stripped to its essence and hence feared and detested; and I know of no better way to achieve this than to expose vice with all of the horror that characterizes it" ("Idée," IV, 43).

At a superficial level such an argument permits Sade to defend himself against the criticism that vice is not punished nor virtue recompensed in his novels, and this in the name not only of logic but also of the highest dramatic tradition.[4] But on a more fundamental level, Sade explains the necessity of laying bare such criminal deviations by reminding his readers that he is not addressing them because of the pleasure his narratives hold, but in spite of the obvious horror they will provoke. He is not addressing his readers' sensibility, but their reason, and only their reason. Reason dictates that man follows nature and nature dictates to man all of his criminal actions.[5] Thus following the path of reason, "as only a philosopher can do," Sade contends that he will demonstrate in an irrefutable manner *the truth of the logic by which vice is always rewarded and virtue always punished.*

It is undoubtedly dreadful to be obliged to depict, on the one hand, the horrendous woes that the heavens inflict upon a sweet, sensitive woman of impeccable virtue; and, on the other hand, the bestowal of prosperity upon those who torment or mortify that very woman. Yet the man of letters, who is *philosophical enough to speak the truth [dire le vrai]*, overcomes his distaste; and cruel by necessity, he mercilessly employs one hand to strip off the finery with which stupidity superstitiously adorns virtue, and with the other hand, boldly reveals to the ignorant fool who had been duped by appear-

---

[4] "For in the end, what are the two principal mainsprings of dramatic art? Have not all the great authors told us that they are *terror* and *pity?* Now what can provoke *terror*, if not the spectacle of crime triumphing? And what can inspire *pity* if not the sight of long-suffering virtue? One can either abandon any hope of interesting his audience, or subscribe to these principles" ("A Villeterque," VI, 214).

[5] "Nature's primary impulses are invariably criminal. . . . The individual who Nature molds for kingship . . . that royal personage, I say, will take his daily bath in the blood of his subjects; nevertheless, he will be Nature's man" (*Jul*, 966).

ances, a vision of vice flourishing amidst the charms and pleasures that unfailingly surround and accompany it.

These are the sentiments that are going to direct our labors; and it is in consideration of these intentions that we shall bring together the most cynical language and the strongest and most audacious systems ... in order to depict crime as it truly is—always triumphant and sublime, always contented and privileged—and likewise, to describe virtue in its essence, that is, always sullen and always sad, always pedantic and always afflicted by misfortune. (*N. Just*, xv, 11–12)

From this introduction to the *Justine-Juliette* sequence, it is clear that "to speak the truth" for Sade has to do with the demonstrative sequence (the reasoning process) according to which virtue (Justine) is always subjugated by vice (Juliette). There is an immediate problem, however, and in view of what we have just claimed, it is a rather troubling one.

When one follows the novels of Sade, one sees immediately that there is absolutely no logic in the rewarding of vice and the punishment of virtue. In fact, each time the virtuous Justine is punished, her punishment is never due to her having reasoned incorrectly. Justine is faultless in her calculations, but the miseries that befall her and the punishments she endures are inflicted by chance.[6] The inverse is true for Juliette, who commits the most hideous crimes. Consider for instance the episode that follows her "affair" with the pope. After Juliette has sold her charms to the pope, she robs him and leaves with her friend Sbrigani for Naples. On their way they are captured by Brisa-Testa, the greatest brigand of Italy, and condemned to death. What saves Juliette? The correctness of her calculations? Her reasoning power? Not at all. Simply the fact that Brisa-Testa turns out to be the brother of her good friend Clairwil, and so Juliette is spared and treated as a friend. It is thus obvious that for Juliette, just as for Justine, it is always chance that intervenes. Virtue is punished and vice prospers not as a result of the logical consequences of the characters' actions, but as a result of arbitrary events that Sade sets up as he wishes. Were one to redistribute these events in a different manner, the results would obviously not change. It is there-

[6] As she exclaims out of despair, at one point in her story: "incomprehensible decrees of nature, deign to explain yourselves to me" (*N. Just*, xvi, 125).

fore not the rationality or the truth of vice and virtue that are brought into question by Sade, despite his repeated assertions. But then what is it that he really is trying to accomplish when he pretends always to speak the truth, when he pretends to address only his readers' reason, whereas in fact his narrative braces itself for something else? To try to answer these questions, let us turn to two passages from *Juliette* which elaborate the question of Sadian truth.

The Theoretical Scenario

The common characteristic of major libertine discourses is that, in all of them, the libertine expounds sexual theories, or what might be better described as methodological recipes for *jouissance*.[7] I shall analyze two among many similar theoretical discourses, focusing primarily on the best-known and most illustrative text, the famous "Discours de la méthode," which Juliette propounds to Madame de Donis. These two discourses lay out the principles and causes of desire and of *jouissance*, according to leit-motifs common to all libertine discourses: (1) our pleasures must not be grounded in the senses, over which we have no control; (2) we must identify our passions and explain them according to "philosophical" principles in order to attain to the state of indifference to all things, the condition of ascetic wisdom attained by the mastery of one's drives, which the Stoics call apathy; (3) apathy constitutes for Sade the condition of a superior eroticism, a particular method that guarantees the libertine's mastery over *jouissance*. With these general considerations in mind, let us now examine the two texts.

In the first discourse, Saint-Fond speaks to Juliette about the pleasures of the imagination.

> Imitate me, Juliette, your native leanings are in this direction....
> For fleshly pleasure cannot possibly delectate save when one outsteps
> every limit in one's quest; the proof thereof is that there must be a

---

[7] For a survey of the avatars of the concept of *jouissance*, see Jane Gallop, "Beyond the *Jouissance* Principle," *Representation* 7 (1984). On a more serious note, see Octave Mannoni's chapter "Histoire de la jouissance," in *Ça n'empêche pas d'exister* (Paris: Seuil, 1982).

breaking of all restraining rules before pleasure begins to be pleasure; go farther yet, break still another and the irritation becomes more violent, and necessarily so with each ascending step; and you do not really attain to the true goal to which these pleasure-takings point until the ferment of the senses has reached the extremest pitch, until you have got to the final limit of what our human faculties can endure.... He who also would know the whole wild power and all the magic of lubricity's pleasures must thoroughly grasp that only by undergoing the greatest possible upheaval in the nervous system may he procure himself the drunken transport he must have if he is to properly enjoy himself.... Therefore, pleasure must be complete, the clash must be as violent as possible... hence, the soul must be prepared, tranquil, its serenity ensured by certain mental attitudes or certain physical postures, so that it lies *in a calm and contented state* and then the imagination's fire must set the furnace of the senses alight. From this point onward *give that imagination free rein, act its every deviation [ne lui refusez aucun écart]*, its every whim.... Indulge yourself, oh, my Juliette... to the irregularity of your caprices... may your voluptuous imagination ensure *variety* to our disorders; only by *multiplying* them will we attain happiness... never lose sight of the fact that *all human felicity lies in man's imagination*, and that he cannot think to attain it unless he heeds all his caprices. The most fortunate of persons is he who has the most means to satisfy his vagaries. (*Jul*, 340–43)

This first discourse treats imagination within a larger context, whereas the second has a more precise pedagogical objective. Juliette herself speaks here to her friend Madame de Donis, who is already mightily perverted, but not quite "enough." Madame de Donis has to undergo her final apprenticeship, to cross the last barrier into perversion. And here is the advice that Juliette gives her.

Let me impart my secret. Go a whole fortnight without lewd occupations, divert yourself, amuse yourself at other things; for the space of those two weeks rigorously bar every libertine thought from your mind. At the close of the final day retire alone to your bed, calmly and in silence; lying there, summon up all those images and ideas you banished during the fasting period just elapsed, and indolently, languidly, nonchalantly fall to performing that wanton little pollution by which nobody so cunningly arouses herself or others as do you. Next, unpent your fancy [imagination], let it freely dwell upon aberrations [égarements] of different sorts and of ascending magnitude *[par gradation]*; linger over the details of each, pass them all one by one in review; persuade yourself that you are absolute sovereign in a world groveling at your feet, that yours is the supreme and unchallengeable right to change, mutilate, destroy, annihilate any and all the living beings you like. Fear of reprisals, hindrances you have none: choose what pleases you, but leave nothing out, make no exceptions; show consideration to no one whomsoever, sever every hobbling tie, abolish every check, let nothing stand in your way; leave everything to your imagination, let it pursue its bent and content yourself to follow in its train, above all avoiding any precipitate gesture: let it be your head and not your temperament that commands your fingers. Without your noticing it, from among all the various scenes you visualize one will claim your attention more energetically than the others and will so forcefully rivet itself in your mind that you'll be unable to dislodge it or supplant it by another. The idea, acquired by the means I am outlining, will dominate you, captivate you; delirium will invade your senses, and thinking yourself actually at work, you will discharge like a Messalina. Once this is accomplished, light your bedside lamp and write out a full description of the abomination which has just inflamed you, omitting nothing that could serve to aggravate its details; and then go to sleep thinking about them.

This is only the first part of Juliette's discourse on method, for she goes on to instruct her interlocutor:

Reread your notes the next day and, as you recommence your operation, add everything your imagination, doubtless a bit weary *[blasée]* by now of an idea which has already cost you fuck, may suggest that could heighten its power to exacerbate. Now turn to the definitive shaping of this idea into a scheme *[formez maintenant un corps de cette idée]* and as you put the final touches on it *[en la mettant au net]*, once again incorporate all fresh episodes, novelties, and ramifications that occur to you. After that, perform it *[commettez ensuite]*, and you will find that this is the deviation *[écart]* which suits you best and which you will carry out with the greatest delight. My secret, I am aware, has its wicked side but it is infallible, and I would not recommend it to you if I had not tested it successfully. *Note:* Everybody who has even a mild leaning toward crime recognizes his portrait in this paragraph; may he then extract all possible benefit from what precedes and from what follows it, conceiving the way of living delightfully the kind of life to which Nature has appointed him, and may he be persuaded that the hand which gives these counsels speaks from experience. (*Jul*, 640–41)

Writing is here put to a perfectly clear use. The process described corresponds to a process of masturbation. One starts by giving free rein to the imagination; after a first *jouissance*, one writes, sleeps, then reads what has been written. There follow new imaginings, a further elaboration through writing, and then Juliette says, to finish off her recipe, "commettez ensuite"—as if the libertine could implement daily all of his imagination's fantasies.

Two preliminary remarks with respect to this last text: first, it is clear that in this case writing, far from being the instrument of rational communication described by Sade ("I am addressing myself only to the readers' reason"), appears to be merely a crutch for individual fantasizing. Writing is the instrument through which one links erotic revery with a sexual practice. The text, moreover, emphasizes that writing is a purely solitary and individual activity, since it should lead, in Juliette's recipe, to the most appropriate *écart* for each practitioner of the method. Writing is thus one stage in the constitution of a sexual practice, merely one stage leading from revery to enactment. Second, as the author's footnote suggests ("the hand which gives these counsels speaks from experience"), it is highly likely that Sade followed his own recipe for phantasmatic writing, and that this was the procedure by which he generated his novels during his long years of incarceration.

We cannot, at this point, be under any illusion about the nature of Sade's *écriture*. It is nothing more than sexual fantasizing and has little to do with reason. But then what is the reader to make of the alleged relationship Sade maintains between the writing of his fiction and truth? Let us return to Juliette's text for a more detailed reading.

The Method

Roland Barthes, with his customary flair, was the first to note in this text a kind of parody of Loyola's spiritual exercises. The libertine, in order to produce the optimal state of receptivity to the "dictates" of desire, duplicates the very conditions of space, time, and speech—"retire alone to your bed, calmly, in silence and in total darkness"—required of the practicing Ignatian disciple.[8] This is not surprising if one recalls that Sade studied with the Jesuits from the age of eleven to fifteen and that he was quite probably subjected to the exercise of meditation common in all Jesuit colleges.

For Ignatius as for Sade, it is thus the imagination that is called upon to be the medium and instrument of the spiritual/sexual operation. But as Barthes remarks, the imaginative process in Loyola is strictly disciplined in order to fulfill a function of selection.[9] This is not at all the case with the libertine imagination, which remains open to all enticements. The libertine imagination must, first, include the largest possible stock of perverse impressions (Saint-Fond: "give that imagination free rein, act its every deviation") and, second, invent a procedure that allows one to choose the strongest and most arousing image from the available spectrum. With Sade, unlike Loyola, it is not the subject that "fixates" a referent, but the referent that hallucinates the subject. It is as if by setting up a mechanism that forces the most powerful desire to manifest itself, the libertine creates the necessary conditions for becoming the designated recipient for this particular desire. Desire chooses "its" libertine, through a kind of elective affinity, and thus fixes the flux of the subject's imagination. As Juliette explains it, "Without your noticing it, from among all the various scenes you visualize one will claim your attention more energetically than the others and will so rivet itself in your mind that you'll be unable to dislodge it or supplant it by another." Juliette here describes an inscription of desire which is fundamentally passive on the subject's part. As we shall see, the elab-

---

[8] "This fantasy dictation [*dictée du fantasme*] is to be found in Ignatius Loyola, whose *Spiritual Exercises* is marked by the same protocols (retreat, darkness, imagination, repetition)" (in *Sade, Fourier, Loyola*, 164). For a philosophical reading of Juliette's lesson, see also the brilliant commentary by Marcel Hénaff in *Sade: L'invention du corps libertin* (Paris: Presses Universitaires de France, 1978), 102–11.

[9] "As voluntary action, the Ignatian imagination thus can and must have . . . the power of repulsing foreign images. . . . This negative power is what must first be recognized in the fundamental act of meditation, which is concentration: to 'contemplate,' 'fix,' 'see myself as through my imagination,' 'to see through the eyes of the imagination,' *is first to eliminate*" (*Sade, Fourier, Loyola*, 51).

oration of the "intellectual" dimension of her method confirms apathy as the cornerstone of the whole imaginative process.

The Theory

In general, libertines do not consider the sexual act as an end in itself, no matter what variations the erotic imagination may bring to it. If this were the case, libertines would not be compelled to theorize. Instead, Sadian eroticism is first and foremost dependent upon a thought exercise; sexual bliss is only an aftereffect, a concrete indication that the libertines have mastered the "science" of *jouissance.* As a result, they savor the thought of this knowledge, which triggers their long theoretical discourses. Thus, there is no corporeal eroticism for Sade; as with Clairwil, who tells Juliette that "if I am to stiffen, I must be imaginatively moved" (*Jul,* 293), the libertine libido is always placed under the government of thought.[10]

In accordance with her principles of an eroticism of the mind, Juliette puts the body under a "sexual ban." In effect, the body must be doubly neutralized: first by physical abstinence ("Go a whole fortnight without lewd occupations"), but above all by moral abstinence, brought about by apathy. For the libertine, apathy embodies the method itself, fulfilling both a practical role and a critical function. In its practical role, as Blanchot diagnosed it, apathy is the essential means for a concentration of energy. "In order to be transformed into energy, passion must be compressed and mediated by undergoing a necessary moment of insensibility; by this process passion attains its highest degree."[11] Thus, Sadian apathy, by its retentive activity, becomes the agent of the conversion of libidinal energy from minimal to maximal levels. As for its critical function, apathy permits the libertine to distinguish between good (energetic) and bad (sentimental or affective) drives. The libertine may then transform the good drives

---

[10] Cf. Barthes: "In Sade...no mythology of virility. What makes the value of sex is wit [*l'esprit*]. Wit is both an *effervescence of the head* and a guarantee of capacity [*rentabilité*], for wit orders, invents, refines" (ibid., 170).

[11] Maurice Blanchot, *Lautréamont et Sade* (Paris: Union générale d'Editions, 1967), 68.

into tableaux of the imagination whereby sexuality grafts itself onto thought.

Apathy first operates on the feelings in order to neutralize them. Juliette: "Above all avoid any precipitate gesture; let it be your head and not your temperament that commands your fingers" (*Jul*, 162). It must be emphasized here that contrary to what Klossowski has claimed in *Sade mon prochain*, the libertine is not concerned only with eliminating those feelings, such as remorse and pity, which might turn him away from libertinage. *All* feelings, even those leading to libertinage, must be neutralized. In one of the very few instances in which Juliette is strongly criticized for unacceptable behavior, Clairwil, Saint-Fond, and Noirceuil warn her to beware of the excessive sensibility she has displayed in the murder of her father.[12] In other words, libidinal drive, even if it leads to crime, remains suspect, because the libertine's passions keep him dependent on the object that incites them. In this last example, crime is only incidental to *libertinage*, whereas, as Saint-Fond remarks to Juliette, "it should always be the principal thing." True libertinage requires a break with all acts grounded in the senses, be those acts linked to a quality of the object or to the temperament (the affective drives) of the individual.[13] Because of this rupture, the libertine suffers a certain loss of identity: he can no longer recognize himself in the register of his affects, which have been radically reduced to a *tabula rasa*. From this point on, however, the libertine is in the position, by making extensive use of his imagination, to construct a true identity. Saint-Fond sums it up in the most concise way in his elab-

---

[12] "I seem still to notice the same failing in her: whenever Juliette commits a crime, it's enthusiastically; but so long as her cunt is dry she might as well be paralyzed. One must proceed *calmly, deliberately, lucidly [de sang-froid]*. Crime is the torch that should fire the passions, that is a commonplace; but I have the suspicion that with her it is the reverse, passion firing her to crime.
—The difference is enormous, Saint-Fond remarked, for in such a case *crime is but accessory, whereas it ought to have prime importance.*
—I am afraid I share Clairwil's view, my dear Juliette, said Noirceuil; you need further encouragement; this ruinous sensibility plaguing you must be dealt with" (*Jul*, 475).

[13] Sade accomplishes this freezing of sensibility on two levels: first the body is reduced to its anatomical parts with all distinguishing signs or details that would make it attractive banished; and second, the temperament is rendered insensitive by the constant obsession the libertine displays to fix, stop, organize, and reorganize sexual orgies—in other words, always to control his pleasure.

orate speech on the function of the imagination: "Hence the soul must be prepared, tranquil, its serenity ensured by certain mental attitudes or certain physical postures, so that it lies in a calm and contented state; and then the imagination's fire must set the furnace of the senses alight."

The eroticism of the mind thus recommended necessitates an active use of the intellect. Juliette: "Unpent your fancy *[imagination]*, let it freely dwell upon aberrations of different sorts and of ascending magnitude *[par gradation]*; linger over the details of each, pass them all one by one in review... reread your notes." To order, to enumerate, to review: all of these are mental activities intended to organize the phantasmatic material. It is the mind that runs the show in order to choose the scenario most apt to bring about *jouissance.* The erotic scene that follows this intellectual exercise subsequently provokes orgasm: "delirium will invade your senses, and thinking yourself actually at work, you will discharge like a Messalina." In this way, the erogenous body that had been "banished" for fifteen days is released, both completing the theoretical process and granting it a measure of reality. The orgasm is here objective proof of the effectiveness of Juliette's scenario and of her knowledge about the *jouissance* that underlies the scenario.

We should note that the eroticization of thought, as it is often experienced in sexual fantasy, is here inverted. The normal sequence begins with erogenous pleasure centered in the body, moves to the pleasure of thinking about and remembering this body and its experiences, and attains a "generalized" pleasure of thinking independent of the body. With Sade this sequence is reversed. The starting point is an affirmation that theoretical knowledge governs the logic and causes of *jouissance.* The libertine obtains pleasure by staging his science of sexual bliss in the form of a particular scenario ("the idea acquired by the means [scenario] I am outlining") which provokes, only in the *last instance,* erogenous pleasure. The libertine illustrates here what Piera Aulagnier-Spairani designates as the purest position for the perverse subject—perverse in the sense that his desire claims to find in itself the source of all law and of the real. The perverse subject affirms his sexual act in the name of a discourse of knowledge and truth. "He justifies his perversion by appealing to a surplus pleasure *[plus-de-plaisir]* which he claims to authenticate by a surplus knowledge *[plus-de-savoir]* of the truth of sexual bliss."[14]

Erogenous pleasure must therefore come at the end of the backward sequence of the libertine's phantasm since it is the proof of his science of *jouissance*. Moreover, in order to keep his theoretical mastery over *jouissance* intact and total, the libertine's phantasm of desire must be able, at a moment's notice, to be transformed into concrete sexual bliss. This process results in a curious sort of fantasy which acts out the accomplishment of desire (in the sense that it is the accomplishment that is visualized) rather than the anticipation of this accomplishment.[15] For this phantasmatic procedure to be properly carried out, however, it needs to pass through the operation of writing—an operation central to the libertine's imaginative program as presented by Juliette.

Writing

Juliette's text underlines more than once the fact that writing does not have a neutral status, nor does it play a passive role, in the working up of libertine imagination. On the contrary, writing is a very precisely determined activity: one could even say that it is of the order of a methodological necessity. First, writing does not simply fix but also intensifies sensations and acts of the imagination, absorbing and retaining the energy thus released; as a result, rewriting is further amplified by this reserve of energy, Juliette explains. Moreover, to write is to effect the passage from potentiality to performance, as the writing described by Juliette inserts the phantasm within a practice of *jouissance*. To write, as she says, is already to "perform," hence to confront reality, solely by virtue of the power of the *written* phantasm. In fact the exercise of writing participates in a dialectic that links fantasy to reality according to four distinct phases—each serving a precise function—which Juliette articulates implicitly in her lesson.

(1) Writing plays an intermediary role between the imaginary

[14] "La perversion comme structure," *L'Inconscient* 2 (1967), 14. See also the article of Jean Clavreul "Le pervers et la loi du désir" in the same issue.
[15] This explains why in Sade's novels the object of desire is always immediately and entirely open to view. The victims are always brought in naked, the immediacy characterizing the dynamic of libertine desire.

and the real. Juliette allows herself, from the very beginning, the totality of the imaginary world: "Persuade yourself that you are absolute sovereign in a world groveling at your feet." The game is to vary this imaginary world as much as possible, to extend constantly its limits. Juliette: "Yours is the supreme and un-challengeable right to change, mutilate, destroy, annihilate any and all living beings you like." Similarly, the libertine Belmor takes his imagination beyond all expectations by picturing "a thousand obscene details and episodes" until he has access to an imaginary world in which "not a single creature resists us. . . . We devastate the planet, and repeople it with new objects, and im-molate these in their turn, etc." (*Jul*, 522). It is this constant pushing back of the limits of what can be imagined that Juliette transcribes several times: "write out a full description of the abomination which has just inflamed you." Once every detail is recorded, and only then, does she fall back into reality—a reality that is reduced to an insignificant, almost nonexistent point, in-dicated by the remark "commettez ensuite." Writing is therefore the process, the moment, which leads to the real, but which at the same time, by working up the imagination, keeps repulsing the real, almost to the limits of nonexistence. Writing thus holds off reality to the point where the borderline between reality and the imagination becomes meaningless.

When Saint-Fond narrates the scene of his father's assassina-tion, he concludes his description by declaring: "parricide, incest, murder, sodomy, pimping, prostitution. . . . Oh Juliette, Juliette! never in my life had I been so happy" (*Jul*, 266). Unfortunately for Saint-Fond, he won't ever be able to murder his father again and consequently he will never again enjoy the same intense degree of bliss. All that is left is the nostalgia for an unattainable pleasure. The monk Sylvestre, however, who is more crafty than Saint-Fond and more weary of the limited pleasures afforded by reality, develops a more sophisticated system. He carefully or-chestrates the sacrifice of his daughter, forcing Justine and her friend Aurore to insult and molest him while he commits the crime; but the key to his system is that the two women must *spell out ahead of time* the blasphemies and reproaches they will utter during the ceremony, thus providing the crime with a script. "Then the two women [Aurore and Justine] seized the debauched rake . . . and as they were flagellating him, denounced him with violent invectives and reproaches, *always drawing their script from the crime which the scoundrel had envisioned"* (*N. Just,* XVII, 113).

Sylvestre's method lays bare the exigencies that govern his *jouissance:* it is impossible for him to be aroused if his fantasies are not put into words and then organized into a scenario. The text of the scenario is thus entirely ruled by the phantasm whose modalities are programmed in advance. In turn, the resulting script provides a method for the retention of the phantasm. This is why Sylvestre's universe of crime—enunciated and described in advance—can only be of the order of the imaginary. As in Juliette's recipe, the object of Sylvestre's enterprise is to suspend the real and to locate his actions within the space of writing. The real is literally evacuated by the phantasm, which is then elaborated and fixed within a script or upon the page. After that, as Juliette would say, Sylvestre can "perform."

But the relationship, mediated by writing, between the libertine and his act, is more complicated than one might conclude from the above description. When Belmor declares that reality will never compare with fantasy, he translates into his own words what Sylvestre puts into action, only he goes one step further:

> Truly, Juliette, I sometimes think the reality possessed is not worth the images we chase thereof . . . there is your ass, Juliette, there before my eyes, and beauteous is it to my contemplation; but my imagination, a more inspired architect than Nature, a more cunning artisan than she, creates other asses more beautifully still . . . *there is beauty in what you offer me there, but only beauty, what I invent is sublime.* With you I am going to do nothing that anyone else may not do, whilst with this ass my imagination has wrought, I might do things which not even the gods themselves would invent. (*Jul,* 522)

What Belmor denies here is the surplus value of pleasure that the accomplishment of the phantasm into action brings: "With you I am going to do nothing that anyone else may not do." This is because the libertine act is never anything but the imperfect and limited image of what the libertine would like to do. True pleasure is elsewhere, in the phantasmatic representation of the act, while the pleasure provided by the act itself is only a by-product. We have here another variation of Sade's eroticism of the mind: pleasure is in the act of thinking, the act itself being only the necessary and imperfect prolongation of the thought of that very act. For Belmor it is neither a question of Juliette's "real" nor of her "fantasized" behind. What arouses him is the force of the imaginative process that permits him to go beyond, as he puts it, what even "the gods themselves would invent." Thus, the fantasy, because it always has a greater value than the act, cannot be considered a simple preparation for action; instead, the phantasm fills up and eroticizes the imaginary ("all the world is ours in these enchanted moments") in order to prevent any possible recrudescence of the real.

For Belmor, as for Juliette, the act of writing, which evacuates the real and fixes its content within the phantasm, serves as a method for multiplying the phantasm by freeing it from its dependence on reality. To use a Freudian vocabulary, we can say that the first function of writing is to produce a world that will be entirely ruled by the pleasure principle and which will never again have to confront the reality principle.

(2) According to Juliette's recipe, writing must occur precisely between two moments of sexual pleasure. She explicitly states that the movement of the imagination must be gradually and skillfully guided to a first sexual pleasure; it is only after this *jouissance* has occurred that one writes. "Once this is accomplished, light your bedside lamp and write out a full description of the abomination which has just inflamed you." Then one can go to sleep, pick up by reading in the morning ("reread your notes the next day") and, as Juliette tells Madame de Donis, the whole process can begin again ("as you recommence your operation"). In other words, writing plays the role of a repetition principle (with respect to sexual fantasizing); it is writing that permits the libertine, first, to go back to what he has imagined, and second, through repetition in the imagination, to repeat the experience of sexual pleasure already obtained. Hence writing is the principle of repeated sexual pleasure, the principle of *ré-jouissance*.

It is important to emphasize here that writing not only leads to, but in effect fully constitutes, *jouissance* for the libertine. Obviously *jouissance* cannot be expressed by and in language, so that what the reader perceives of the repetition principle is the repetitive aspect of the operation *without* the pleasure that accompanies the repetition. This is not the case for the libertine, however, for whom repetition and ecstasy are two faces of the same coin. Pierre Klossowski has perceptively analyzed this aspect of the problem:

> The object of repetition is to give rise to ecstasy, an ecstasy that cannot be attained by means of language; language serves only to describe the paths and disposition that can bring ecstasy into being. But what is not immediately apparent is that ecstasy and repetition are one and the same thing. In description, the act of repeating and that of experiencing ecstasy are *two* different aspects. For the reader, all that remains is the repetition as described and the purely exterior aspect of ecstasy.... For the libertine, the accomplishment *[actualisation]* of the perverse *[aberrant]* act through writing corresponds to a repetition of the act, performed independently of its description. Accomplishing the act, writing brings about ecstasy of thought.[16]

The fact that, in the realm of writing, repetition always repeats pleasurably, not only accounts for the pleasure that Sade must have derived from writing three versions (only three?) of *Justine*. It also explains why the world of Sade's novels is the very world of repetition. The same stories are repeated indefinitely—the same figures, the same gestures, the same actions, the same speeches, the same arguments.[17] Out of writing as pure principle of repetition, everything can be perpetually and indefinitely regenerated, without fatigue, exhaustion, or even death ever showing their faces. When Sade writes at the end of *Juliette* that "the greatest successes crowned our heroes for the next ten years" (*Jul*, 1193), "ten years" could have been twenty, fifty, or one hundred years, for the activity of the libertine is outside all temporal norms. Like all of Sade's libertines, Juliette lives outside of time. Without a memory, and without a past, she has neither childhood nor future growth ahead of her, and is thus condemned to a life

---

[16] Klossowski, *Sade mon prochain*, 50–51.

[17] Regarding the pace and repetitive nature of Sade's writing, Michel Tort makes this suggestive commentary: "The choppy, repetitive unfolding of the novel corresponds exactly to the economy of the phantasm. In its very texture, the narrative mimics the phantasm, and rigorously reproduces it. It is meaningless to assert that Sade is monotonous without providing the concept that underlies this monotony...for in the final analysis, it is different in nature than that of d'Urfé" ("L'effet Sade," *Tel Quel* 28 [1967], 80).

of pure repetition within the nontemporality of the same.[18] If writing's first function is to erase the difference between the pleasure principle and the reality principle, its second function is to obliterate temporality, to erase the limits imposed by time, and to liberate repetition for its own sake.

(3) The moment of the phantasm, which is a moment of absolute plenitude, is nevertheless ephemeral; it is lacking in temporal reach, in extended duration. How then can the phantasm be kept from wearing off ? After it has been consumed once, it must be registered, inscribed in writing, so as to remain available for renewed delectation. In this way each accomplished phantasm gives birth to a new one, so that the libertine imaginary can continue its tireless unfolding. When the monk Jérôme suspects that his imaginary may be saturated, the shortage of phantasmatic material is immediately compensated for by an additional effort of the imagination. "What more was I to imagine? I have done everything, performed everything. . . . By sheer force of dreaming, this is what my scandalous imagination finally came up with" (*N. Just*, xvii, 37). The slightest variation of the imagination thus produces a whole new set of possibilities, with each deviation, each difference of detail, signifying the inventive capacity of the libertine's imaginary.[19] As in Juliette's recipe, a libertine need only add a new detail to "yesterday's" narrative, and his imagination will take off once more. Thus the role of writing is not merely to introduce the indefinite repetition of sexual pleasure; it also enables the imagination to exceed its own limits: "as you recommence your operation, add everything your imagination . . . may suggest that could heighten its *power to exacerbate.*" Ulti-

---

[18] As a consequence, says Marcel Hénaff, the Sadian novel is the *exemplum* of the anti-picaresque novel, in the sense that it can be only a novel of *repetition* and never one of *formation*. "The libertine is not the object of an evolution *[un devenir]* but rather the instrument of a timeless repetition of a proof. . . . Everything must always be done over again. . . . Thus the aim is not to expand the narrative's memory, but to mark libertine bodies" (*Sade: L'invention du corps libertin*, 161).

[19] This inventive role of the imaginary forces the notion of phantasm to undergo a radical transformation. Phantasm is no longer conceived of as the repetitive structure of a stable signifying nexus. In Sade, the logic of the phantasm is indeed repetitive, but it is a repetition that repeats only as it systematically *decenters itself* from its starting point. For every deviation that has been established must be transgressed and surpassed, hence displaced. As we shall see, this decentering of phantasm triggers a suppression of the limits of desire that is crucial for understanding the nature and mechanics of Sadian desire.

mately the libertine will reach a point where he may wonder like Delbène: "Who knows, if I have not even gone beyond what the imagination may conceive?" (*Jul*, 9).

Concerning the role of the imagination, Juliette's text also states: "Now turn to the definitive shaping of this idea *[Formez maintenant un corps de cette idée]* and as you put the final touches on it *[en la mettant au net]*, once again incorporate all fresh episodes that occur to your head." Two remarks are in order here. The first concerns the nature of the body produced by Juliette's imaginary: it is not a hallucinated body made of flesh and bone, but a body made up of ideas. The real body is here again devalued in favor of a mental substitute better suited to the libertine imagination: the body of writing. Second, the writerly body, by endlessly converting phantasms into writing and writing into phantasms, multiplies and enhances the products of the imagination. The process of writing-reading-writing again allows the imagination to exceed its limits each time. Every act of writing breaks new barriers of the imagination. I quote again part of Saint-Fond's description of this perpetual transgression of barriers: "The proof thereof is that there must be a breaking of *all* restraining rules before pleasure begins to be pleasure; go farther yet, break still another and the irritation becomes more violent, and necessarily so, with each ascending step; and you do not really attain to the true goal whither these pleasure-takings point until the ferment of the senses has reached the *extremest pitch,* until you have got to the final limit of what our human faculties can endure." Consequently writing, which frees pleasure from the limits of reality and repetition from the limits of temporal duration, is also the principle of limitlessness within the notion of limit itself, as one limit after another is posed only to be broken. Desire can thus never be the captive of a given fantasy, since there is always another fantasy to spill over into the one that precedes it; it is therefore the erasing of the very limits of fantasy that is provided by writing.[20]

[20] Philippe Roger has analyzed how the new type of orgy in the third version of *Justine* causes the object of desire to disappear in such a way that there is no longer any possibility for stabilizing the phantasm. The object of desire is chosen for libertines by lottery, while the scenarios they have to perform are specified in

Let us note, however, that the libertine who seeks to transgress the limits of fantasy through writing requires from that very writing a guarantee for all excesses of the imagination. In other words, writing must ultimately be capable of cataloguing the totality of these excesses. We have here the most insoluble of Sadian paradoxes: what procedure can guarantee the exhaustive description of a phenomenon that is defined by a mechanism of perpetual transgression? Evidently writing cannot give such a guarantee since by its very functioning it brings about a new imaginative excess.[21] The libertine's fear of missing any such excess—detail or deviation—sets off, within writing, the whole repetitive mechanism we have already traced from the standpoint of the phantasm. Whence all the narrative tics—returns, verifications, double-checks—which the libertine uses to ascertain that every detail of an argument or action has been thoroughly covered.

(4) The last function of writing is indicated in the concluding advice of Juliette's text: "After that perform [your scheme], and you will find that this is the *deviation which suits you best.*" Juliette thus encourages her "disciple" to follow her procedure of unlimited fantasizing through writing, in order to reach the maximal and most individualized transgression possible with respect to all laws and to all standards of behavior. In this way writing itself becomes the very essence of crime, or better yet, crime's finest model. This is the definition of the ultimate crime, "the moral crime, which is arrived at by means of *writing,*" which Juliette warmly recommends to Clairwil in response to her wish to discover "a crime which, even when I had left off doing it, would go on having perpetual effect . . . that even after my life was over its effect would survive in the everlasting continuation of my wickedness" (*Jul*, 525). The criminal act thus imagined— whether this act is actually performed or not is irrelevant, since writing has already nullified the pertinence of the reality principle—which is worked through and pushed to its end by writing, pushed even beyond its limits, places the individual in the most

---

an unpredictable and impersonal way in the lottery ticket that they have drawn (*Sade: La philosophie dans le pressoir* [Paris: Grasset, 1976], 218–19).

[21] In addition, writing cannot transgress the register of linguistic codes, since every deviation must be both utterable and recordable on paper. I shall discuss this question of linguistic closure in Chapter 6.

deviant state possible. From this point on, nothing can ever touch him again—neither remorse, nor regret, nor recuperation. The libertine is immune to all efforts to reform him, as he has now reached total singularity, irremediable solitude—a condition Sade terms "irregularity."

A brief detour is in order here, to clarify the central role irregularity plays in Sade's economy of the imaginary. Although noted by Sade's more important critics—Blanchot, Bataille, Klossowski, Foucault, and Barthes—irregularity has not been *operatively* related to the particularities of the libertine imagination. This is the consequence of the general interest expressed by these critics in the nature of Sadian discourse.[22] Beginning with Blanchot and Bataille, they have focused on how, in Sade's novels, discourse is completely divorced from the communicative function we see in language. Bataille expressed this view most succinctly when he remarked that Sadian discourse "is a language that denies any relation between speaker and addressees, thereby denying the very nature of language itself."[23] Indeed, Sade's discourse does not fulfill a persuasive function—neither between libertine and victim nor among libertines themselves—but instead establishes a threshold of differentiation between libertines and victims. On the one hand there are the libertines, who have the monopoly on language; on the other hand, the silent victims. What is true of discourse, however, is only the direct result of the qualitative difference between the libertine's and the victim's imaginaries. The typical richness of the libertine imaginary (which triggers the theoretical discourses as well as the descriptive scenes) is opposed to the nonexistent imaginary of the victim (Justine lives

[22] Blanchot's, Klossowski's, and Barthes's works have already been cited. Michel Foucault's treatment of Sade appears in *Histoire de la folie à l'âge classique* (Paris: Plon, 1961) and in *Les mots et les choses* (Paris: Gallimard, 1966). Bataille has written three major essays on Sade: "L'homme souverain de Sade" and "Sade et l'homme normal" in *L'érotisme* (Paris: Minuit, 1957) and "Sade" in *La littérature et le mal* (Paris: Gallimard, 1967). Of these critics, Barthes comes closest to discussing the operation of the libertine imagination, but he immediately equates it with the problematic of Sadian language. "Speech is wholly bound together with the overt mark of the libertine, which is (in Sade's vocabulary) the *imagination*. It might almost be said that *imagination* is the Sadian word for *language*" (*Sade, Fourier, Loyola*, 31).

[23] "Un langage désavouant la relation de celui qui parle avec les hommes auxquels il s'adresse, en conséquence désavouant le langage même" (in the preface to the first *Justine*, vol. II, p. xxvi of the Pauvert edition).

through three "volumes" of miseries without ever managing *to begin* to imagine the pleasures and pains that she experiences).

However, beyond the simple dichotomy—at the levels of complexity and richness—between the libertine's and the victim's imaginaries, Sade constructs a further differentiating pattern within what would appear at first as *the* typical Libertine Imaginary. That is, he introduces an original differential element: the personal *écart*, "the deviation that suits *you* best." In other words, despite the many similarities that exist among libertines, one cannot subsume them all under a single concept of Libertine Imaginary. It follows, then, that contrary to the general modern critical assumption, one should not conceive of the libertine world as a unified, homogeneous world where all the libertines are interchangeable. Of course, each libertine's imaginary is to a great extent representative of all other libertine imaginaries (by virtue of their common desires). Furthermore, each one operates according to principles identical to those that Juliette describes in her lesson. Yet it is essential to recognize, within these analogies, the most important differentiating factor: that each libertine's imaginary is individually characterized by the quantity and, especially, the quality of its *écart*, each deviation being productive of a scenario. It is precisely the difference in intensity and sophistication of these scenarios which produces, within the general world of libertinage, distinguishable, irregular individuals, irreducible to each other. This is why we often hear libertines ask one another either to explain their theories about the role of the imagination or to describe in minute detail the latest *jouissances* the other has imagined. The answer determines, according to the force and quality of one's imaginative scenarios, one's place on the absolute scale of libertinage.[24]

Early in the *Prospérités du vice*, Clairwil expresses her disdain for Juliette's libertinage in these terms: "Alack, 'tis plain to see, your mind has yet to reach full flower... and so let's end the evening with a few exercises in libidinous nastiness since we cannot close it with crimes" (*Jul*, 295). (The reader will have noticed the equivalence between the poor imaginative scenario

[24] In order to fire up his imagination, King Ferdinand keeps the archives of the imaginative feats of his predecessors—an obviously productive technique since it provokes even Clairwil's admiration. "I have never encountered an imagination so fertile as yours," says she to Ferdinand (*Jul*, 1011).

and the absence of serious criminal activity.) By the middle of the novel, however, Belmor reassures us about Juliette's libertine standing when he judges her imagination to have become productive, that is, "lascivious, rich, and diverse; I have seldom seen its equal" (p. 521). Saint-Fond confirms Juliette's ultimate superiority two "volumes" later, when he exclaims in admiration: "no one had ever imagined so much" (p. 391). But the award for optimal libertinage should no doubt go to La Durand, whose imagination transgresses the limits of the conceivable. In the course of acting out her excesses, she suddenly turns to Juliette and Clairwil: " 'Ha!' exulted the sorceress, gazing at us as we, petrified, watched these prodigies, 'are you afraid of me?' " The reply of the two friends is profound in its implications: "Afraid? No; but you are beyond conception *[nous ne te concevons pas]*" (p. 538).

One could thus establish a typology of the libertine imaginary which would act like a methodological principle of classification among libertines. It would be divided into two major categories: the first constituted by those individuals who produce *theoretical scenarios* about the functioning of the imaginary; the second constituted by "second-class" libertines who can only *describe* the excesses of their imagination. Within each class, the libertine hierarchy would be established according to the qualitative attributes—inventiveness, perversity, sophistication—of the personal scenario. Certain quantitative parameters, such as the force, intensity, and especially the steadiness of the "imaginative flow," would also enter into the final equation; then one could proceed with a libertine ranking. According to the above criteria, La Durand, Noirceuil, and Juliette, for instance, would be ranked above Saint-Fond, in the first category. They are one notch above him by virtue of the steady production of their imaginaries, whereas Saint-Fond's imaginary shows an uneven flow—good days, during which his imagination produces abominable crimes, but also bad days. "Everything that enters my imagination today [he said] falls short of my desires" (*Jul*, 271).

Consequently, La Durand, Noirceuil, and Juliette survive in the novel, whereas Saint-Fond, Bressac, Clairwil, Olympe, and Cordely—although they are major libertines—are sacrificed and die. In this way, the imaginary scenario operates methodologically, not only to provide a division between libertines and victims, but also to permit distinctions within the supposedly complicitous and unified state of libertine individuals irreducible to each other, and who *sign their irregularity by the production of personalized scenarios.* "For those with an imagination like mine," remarks Juliette to Saint-Fond, "the question is never whether this or that is repulsive; irregularity is the sole valid consideration" (*Jul*, 236). The last function of writing is thus to produce, and to lead to, the ultimate script of the libertine imaginary: the world of irregularity.

This long excursus through Juliette's lesson will now help us to understand what Sade meant when he kept declaring that he wrote in order to tell the truth. Speaking the truth, as we have seen, is neither saying something realistic according to eighteenth-century novelistic norms, nor is it arguing logically or proposing a truth that will convince the reader. From the above discussion, speaking the truth, for Sade, means specifically:

(1) The establishing of desire, fantasy, and the erotic imagination in a relation to truth such that no reality principle can be capable of undermining the former. In fact, from the moment in which writing, entirely ruled by desire, abolishes the reality principle, the verification of what is and what is not fantasy is no longer possible. Or rather, all fantasy becomes true and the imagination itself becomes its own principle of verification, since the only verification possible is to start from one fantasy in order to generate another.

(2) To the extent that writing introduces desire into the eternal world of repetition, desire is no longer just something that existed at a given moment and, having been true for that moment, will be false afterward. The suppression of temporal limits, the institution of a purely repetitive world, guarantees that desire will always be true and that nothing will invalidate it.

(3) Writing introduces desire into the world of truth, in that it never allows desire to confront anything but its own singular individuality. Writing makes it possible for desire always to be equal to its own irregularity, to be on an equal footing with its own truth, since nothing can ever stop or repress desire. Thus, as a consequence of the abolition of limits produced by the act of writing, desire becomes a law unto itself. It becomes an absolute ruler that contains its own truth, its own repetition, and its own

conditions of verification. Nothing can ever again bring into question the truth of desire, nothing can ever tell libertine desire, "you live this way, but reality is something else entirely." By virtue of the power of writing, desire has entered into the world of absolute, unlimited truth—a truth without the threat of any exterior confrontation.

(4) It should be obvious, then, why Sadian writing is in no way intended to communicate some "real" truth. It does not attempt in any way whatsoever to persuade someone of a truth that Sade would have discovered and that would be convincing to the reader in the same way that it is to its author. The writing through which Sadian fantasy passes—these signs on the page that can be read, corrected, and reread—have the function of transposing desire into a space that no objective truth can invalidate or limit. *Writing is desire become truth.* Truth has taken the form of repetitive, unlimited desire—of desire without law, restriction or exteriority. And it is precisely the suppression of exteriority with respect to desire, accomplished by writing, that allows desire to become truth. This is why Sade always talks about truth, that is, about his own desires, his own fantasies, become truth. "My secret, I am aware," says Juliette in her final remark, "has its wicked side, but it is infallible, and I would not recommend it to you if I had not tested it successfully."

6

Staging the Libertine Imaginary II: Personal and Fictional Scenarios

> Jusqu'à nos jours, l'humanité a rêvé de saisir et de fixer cet
> instant fugitif où il fut permis de croire qu'on pouvait ruser
> avec la loi d'échange, gagner sans perdre, jouir sans partager.
> Lévi-Strauss, *Les structures élémentaires de la parenté*

The Personal Scenario

Sade "signs" Juliette's last statement about the success of her
"secret" with an author's note assuring his readers that his own
experience bears witness to the truth of Juliette's advice. It is a
well-documented fact that this was indeed the case. Maurice
Heine has described the 1797 (third and last) version of *Justine*
as constituted "by scattered little sheets, attached to the margins
of various personal papers" (*N. Just*, xviii, 303). In fact, these
sheets correspond to added episodes of two sorts. "All of the
scenes recounted in these *little sheets* consist of additions to, or
developments of, the novel of 1791" (xviii, 304). Sade thus used
his own text as a springboard for his imagination, and this process
of rereading himself triggered (as in Juliette's lesson) new phantasms that he kept noting and appending to his earlier elucubra-
tions. The amplification of Sade's own writing through the
recurrence of the phantasm provides an acute form of the repetition principle we analyzed earlier, shown here at work according
to Sade's personal imaginary. In this way he "rewrote" *Justine*

three times as if the script of her adventures were indeed suscep-
tible of unlimited dilation.

Sade's method of writing has led a number of his critics (Lacan,
Béatrice Didier, Hubert Damisch, among others) to conclude that
imprisonment had become for him the necessary condition for
the production of his oeuvre.[1] Before them, however, and in an
even clearer fashion, Sade himself had explained in his correspondence the effect his isolation was having on his working
habits and, even more, on his psychological makeup. Seen in this
light, his authorial note "The hand which gives these counsels
speaks from experience" is as much a recognition of a personal
method of writing as a critical admission of the place writing
occupied in his life. The proof is in the "flesh": every time Sade
was released from prison, he created just enough commotion to
find himself incarcerated again—undoubtedly to go back to his
world of writing, "this infinity of things and details, in my view
so delicious, which serves so effectively to assuage my woes when
I allow my imagination to wander."[2]

A caveat: the real question for criticism to ask of Sade should
not concern the role writing played in his life. This is a false
question in the sense that if one has understood the function of
Sadian writing, which is to negate the difference between reality
and fiction, then there cannot be any qualitative difference between his life and his work: they both occupy the same space,
the scene of writing. What is more pertinent for us to question,
however, is what circumstances led to the slippage of the real in
Sade's case, and *how* writing came to occupy its privileged place
in the constitution of his excesses of imagination. In a sense these
are questions whose answers can come from only one source: the
text of Sade's own imaginary. Luckily, Sade's correspondence provides a kind of "autopsy" of his imaginary, an autopsy that graphs
with painstaking meticulousness the curve of Sade's psychic functioning. Sade, in his correspondence, analyzes himself as he would

---

[1] Cf. Lacan, "Kant avec Sade," in *Ecrits* (Paris: Seuil, 1966), 765; Damisch,
"L'écriture sans mesure," *Tel Quel* 28 (1967), 53; Didier, *Sade: Une écriture du
désir* (Paris: Denoël/Gonthier, 1976), 17: "Prison definitely seems for Sade to be
the necessary condition for writing."

[2] To Mme de Sade, August 1782, in *Lettres choisies du Marquis de Sade* (Paris:
Pauvert, 1963), 161. All of the letters that are cited in our text appear in this
volume.

any other object—that is, in a "scientific," objective manner. He describes first, on an operational level, the work of his psyche; and then, at a second, analytic level, he diagnoses the source of his mental illness and explains how writing came to fill a curative role.

The Operational Level

As early as 1777, one year into his second term of imprisonment, Sade warns his wife that he is on the verge of madness: "I should warn you nonetheless that it is doubtful that my mind can resist much longer to the cruel life that I lead."[3] Sade then describes the force with which his imagination is being affected by the situation. "You fancied that you were sure to work wonders ... by reducing me to an atrocious abstinence in the article of *carnal sin*. Well, you were wrong: you have produced a ferment in my brain; thanks to you phantoms have sprung forth in my imagination which I have to render real."[4] He even prescribes the remedy to his own "disease." "Had I been given *Mr. 6* [Sade] to cure ... instead of locking him up amidst cannibals, I would have cloistered him awhile with girls, I'd have supplied him girls in such good number that damn me if after these seven years there'd be a drop of oil left in the lamp! .... Thereby you might have guided Mr. 6 into the *good way*, into what they call the *honorable path*. You'd have brought an end to those *philosophical subterfuges*, to those devious practices that Nature disavows ... to those *dangerous deviations [écarts]* of a too ardent imagination, which is only too eager to substitute *illusions* for reality."[5] But for willful lack of interest on his enemies' part and lack of attention on his friends' part, "the honorable path" remains inaccessible, and as a result, the chimeras produced by his imagination multiply.

At this same period Sade writes a crucial letter to his friend Milli Rousset in which he describes both his mental alienation and the mechanics by which writing relieves him of his anxieties, hence becoming the only viable alternative to total madness. He tells Rousset, for instance, that one day, after hearing the chiming of the prison bells all morning, he had hallucinated—he uses the

[3] To Mme de Sade, 18 April 1777 (ibid., 48).
[4] To Mme de Sade, 25 June 1783 (ibid., 172).
[5] Ibid., 172–73.

terms *imaginer* and *se fourrer dans la cervelle*—a lugubrious children's poem that carried, along with the chiming, the message that he would soon be released from prison but at the price of his life. He had then been subject to a momentary fit of madness and had rushed headlong to strangle the blamable "bellringer," but having only managed to run his head against the closed prison door, he returns to his desk—*I sat down again—I took up my pen*—and I decided to respond to this rascal by giving him a taste of his own medicine . . . and I said. . . . "—and he writes the "bellringer" a poem inviting him to go get sodomized.[6] Then in the true spirit of Juliette's recipe, he transcribes what he has just fantasized. "I immediately wrote a fresh copy *[mis au net]* of this masterpiece, and I am sending it to you, so that you might see, Mademoiselle, exactly how I train myself, and how I *find new inspiration [je prends de l'esprit]*."[7] And the letter concludes on this note: "Farewell, my lovely angel, think of me from time to time, when you are lying between two sheets, with your thighs open, and your right hand busily. . . . "[8]

The scenario of the phantasmatic operation is thus complete and corroborates every phase in the elaboration of Juliette's recipe. Sequence: the phantasm precedes, has recourse to, and is then elaborated by writing. Method: one hallucinates, one writes, one recopies, but here instead of "discharging" oneself as one would expect, Sade introduces a slight variation and "hands over" the job to the girl friend. Objective: to substitute the world of writing for the persecution, real or imagined, that Sade experiences in this difficult prison situation.[9]

The Analytic Level

In a note dating from 1803 in which he discusses the system of signals he had invented to try to decipher his date of release from Vincennes, Sade examines retrospectively, but with stun-

[6] To Marie Dorothée Rousset, May 1782 (ibid., 150).

[7] Ibid., 152.

[8] Ibid., 152–53.

[9] Philippe Roger calls attention to two letters from 1783 to Mme de Sade in which the act of writing makes up for Sade's painful imprisonment: "yet further pain, my dear friend, yet another persecution, yet another *manuscript*"; and "you will be deprived of your daily promenades? Oh well! I will write verses" (quoted by Roger, *Sade*, 17).

ning lucidity, the situation that led to the breakdown of his mental faculties. This extraordinary document illuminates the process by which the Sadian imaginary becomes absolute.

> I observed that the situation wherein I was being kept and the pranks being played upon me were forcing me *to mistake true and authentic happenings for events produced* by the imbecile spitefulness of the scoundrels who had me at their mercy; the effort to render myself insensible to those events arranged by artifice had the further result of rendering me insensible to those of fate or of Nature, in such a way that for the sake of my inner peace, I preferred to give credit to nothing and *to adopt an attitude of indifference [me blaser]* toward everything. Whence there developed the terrible and dangerous situation of being ever ready to discount as a deliberate falsehood any announcement of some unpleasant truth, and in the interest of tranquility, to rank it among the lies that were multiplied in order to foster or give rise to impossible situations; nay, it may fairly be said that nothing did greater harm both to my heart and to my character....
>
> The system of signals and ciphers which those rogues utilized while I was in the Bastille and during the last of my detentions wrought yet another grave damage upon me by accustoming me *to cling to any such fantastic notion as might shore up my hope* and to any conjecture capable of nourishing it. Thus did my mind take on the *sophistical cast* I am reproached for in my writings.[10]

All of the methodological principles of Juliette's lesson find their source and their explanation in this note. The reality principle: Sade explains the reasons for his inability to differentiate between a "real" event (an event that really happened) and a "staged" event whose purpose is to exacerbate the prisoner's delirium. The jamming of the reality principle results in a confusion between reality and illusion—the first step in the subsequent takeover by the imagination. Apathy: the origin of Sade's insensibility is identified here with a kind of defense mechanism against madness that triggers his decision to become "indifferent toward everything." Truth: since reality has become as illusory as illusion has become real, truth cannot have any reference point

[10] "Note relative à ma détention [et à l'ouvrage de *Justine*]," *Lettres choisies,* 33.

in reality; consequently it establishes its own reality principle, which Sade defines as that which "shores up [his] hope," meaning, in the context of the above note, that which does not make him suffer. In other words, an event acquires a truth status according to the degree of satisfaction, and eventually of pleasure, it brings with it. We have here an embryonic version of the relationship between pleasure principle and truth that Juliette formalizes. As for Sade's "sophistical" frame of mind, it alludes to the specious logic that subtends, and the arguments that populate, his imaginary scenarios.

Hence we see that, whether in real life (imprisonment) or in his fiction, Sade had developed, to various degrees, a system by which it would be possible for him never to "drop out" of the imaginary scene, since it is only there that the phantasm is shock-proof and the scenario absolute. "This manner of thinking with which you [Mme de Sade] find fault is my sole consolation in life; it alleviates all my sufferings in prison, it composes all my pleasures in the world, *it is dearer to me than life itself.*"[11] But the space of the imaginary, as we have seen, exists only as a space of writing. The act of living according to one's imaginary then becomes an act of writing, and writing becomes the essence of Sade's being. The despair he experiences from the loss of the manuscript of the *120 journées* during the fall of the Bastille—"my manuscripts over whose loss I shed tears of blood!"[12]—these tears of blood demonstrate graphically the importance he attached to writing. The loss is irreparable, he tells Gaufridy, because "other beds, tables, chests of drawers can be found, but ideas once gone are not found again."[13] Indeed, in such a case one does not recover ideas because *ideas are inseparable from the phantasmatic scenarios that have elaborated and secured them on the page:*[14] such is Sade's investment in writing.

[11] To Mme de Sade, November 1783 (ibid., 188).

[12] To Gaufridy, May 1790 (ibid., 238).

[13] Ibid.

[14] This also explains why in the act of transcribing fantasies it is imperative not to "subtract" anything, as Sade reminds his wife when he writes her about the publication of his *feuillets:* "You can make all the corrections that you please, but nothing must be taken out *[soustraire]:* these writings may contradict, intersect, correct each other, but should never delete each other" (to Mme de Sade, June 1783 [ibid., 167]).

The Fictional Scenario

It is natural to ask at this point, from the perspective of the content of the fiction, what kind of text the Sadian imaginary has produced. Here again, Sade provides us with two complementary answers: first, the already mentioned theoretical text, "Idée sur les romans," in which he formulates the conditions of production of fiction; second, innumerable novels, short stories, and other literary works that illustrate the theory. In effect, the text of "Idée" is to fiction what the imaginary is to libertine identity: the imaginary is the theoretical seat of an eroticism of the mind which produces the libertine subject through the operation of writing, just as "Idée" comprises the set of rules by which fictional writing produces the endless narrative of desire.

The homologies, both formal and functional (insofar as writing is concerned), between the imaginary and "Idée" are striking.[15] First, at the formal level: the libertine imaginary, we recall, was determined according to the individual deviation "which suits *you* best"; "Idée" in turn defines the novel as the relation of *singular* events—"the most singular adventures in the life of men" ("Idée," IV, 11). Similarly, Juliette's original deviation/ transgression is duplicated in "Idée" by an original incest—"if [the novelist] does not become his mother's lover as soon as she brings him into this world, why then, he should never write" (IV, 34)—which inaugurates the act of novelistic writing. Finally, a theory of the evolution of narrative forms based on a transgressive model corresponds to the maximization of the imaginary *écart* necessary to affirm libertine identity: "As public taste grows more jaded *[se blase]*, as minds become corrupted, and as the reader grows weary of tales, novels, and comedies, the writer must necessarily find more striking subjects to portray" (VI, 227).

At the functional level, we also find a description of the role of writing in "Idée" identical to that of Juliette's script. First, as mentioned above, the access to writing is embodied in an original transgression—the mother-son incest. Then, having delved into

---

[15] Michel Tort has noted the structural kinship between perverse *écart* and novelistic deviation in Sade: "We find a correspondence in Sade's work between the theoretical law of maximizing the perverse deviation, and a theory of the evolution of novelistic forms and their necessary exhaustion" ("L'effet Sade," 78).

the body of his "mother-nature,"[16] the novelist probes her interior
(the metaphor is explicitly sexual: "he uncovers *[entrouvre]* with
a trembling hand the bosom of Nature in order to seek his art
and to draw his models therein" [IV, 34]) in the same way that
Juliette scrutinized her imaginary in order to produce the *tableau*
of her excesses. Having molested mother-nature, the novelist recognizes no restraints: "with no more restraints to hold you back,
feel free to exploit all of the anecdotes in history, whenever the
transgressing of this boundary seems necessary to the pleasures
that you prepare for us" (IV, 34–35). Thus, nature offers him stories, just as a mother gives pleasure to her child, but these stories
must be varied, transformed, or deformed in the manner that
Juliette recommends that the libertine manhandle his imaginary.
And Sade concludes in "Idée" that the novelist who follows his
advice will have arrived at a first draft that he must transcribe
("as soon as your first sketch is drafted" [IV, 35]), and then, but
only then: "work ardently to expand it, without confining yourself
within the limits that your sketch seems to impose on you . . .
what we ask of you are outbursts *[élans]* . . . go beyond your original outline, vary it, add to it, multiply it" (IV, 36).

This passage repeats almost word for word the "transcription-
multiplication" we had analyzed in Juliette's sexual phantas-
magory. The uses of writing in Juliette's lesson and in the text
of "Idée" are thus strictly symmetrical except for the fact that in
the former the libertine is given the freedom of the imaginary and
in the latter the novelist is given nature. This variance, which is
without theoretical significance—since both nature and the imaginary are figures of apathy which operate in the mode of excess,

---

[16] The formulation of the mother-son incest "if (the novelist) does not become
his mother's lover" is sufficiently ambiguous to leave open the possibility that
Sade is referring here to the real mother as opposed to mother-nature. In support
of such an interpretation one can cite Sade's letter to la Présidente de Montreuil
of February 1777, in which he writes her of his dream: "From the depths of her
tomb, my mother calls to me: I seem to see her uncovering *[m'ouvrir]* her bosom
once again and beckoning me to enter in it as my last remaining haven" (*Lettres
choisies*, 40). Philippe Sollers, noting the symbolic equivalence between the
mother and language (the mother tongue), argues that "Idée" relates the creation
of a new language—the language of transgression: "Of all the women that he can
reach, the mother (the mother-tongue) represents the inaccessible, burning source"
(*Logiques* [Paris: Seuil, 1968], 161).

according to a movement of perpetual self-transgression[17]—
nevertheless has a strategic importance. The recourse to nature
in the case of the fiction will necessarily direct the course of Sade's
demonstration just as it will determine the constitutive elements
and the corresponding themes of this fiction. Hence it should not
surprise the reader to discover that the scenarios produced by the
Sadian imaginary will revolve around and exploit the numerous
avatars of the concept of nature, and its distorted, false mirror
image: culture.

Sade sets out to question, by means of a transgressive fiction,
the relation between fiction in general and cultural reality. His
intent is to reveal that moment when the libertine irregular consciousness acts to transform conscious reality into fiction and
fiction into a higher form of reality. Thematically speaking, Sade's
fiction must perpetuate a primitive state where desire is freed
from the ends assigned to it by culture and brings about, by way
of imaginary excesses, pleasurable practices that would be unthinkable in a state of culture. Sade's novels and short stories are
the narrative counterpart of Juliette's theoretical imaginary—a
narrativization that permits the libertine on the one hand to dis-
mantle the cultural interdictions that are at the basis of social
rationality, and on the other hand to affirm that the phantasms
produced by nature permit the rediscovery of man's autonomous
desire.

Sade's insight is to treat the problem of nature as a problem of
the nature of desire and of language; that is, both to identify
sexuality as the privileged domain of transgression and to recognize that the transgression entails consequences that go far
beyond sexuality. In fact, Sade's use of the concept of nature
approaches that of modern anthropological theories in that it reveals and questions those sexual prohibitions that seem to found
the cultural order, most particularly the taboo against incest.

One could argue here that incest is a very common topic in the
late eighteenth-century novel and that, "ethnological erudition"
being very much in fashion at the time, it was inevitable that an

---

[17] Nature is apathetic since it tolerates life and death indifferently according to
a process of renewal whose pattern is one of permanent upheaval and self-
destruction.

author in Sade's position would tackle the subject.[18] He does so with such exceptional violence, however, that notions of "influence" or "fashion" offer only inadequate explanations. Among these is Béatrice Didier's contention that Sade represents a certain nobility and that his defense of incest is symptomatic of the general recoiling of his class from society. "The late eighteenth-century phantasm of incest reveals both a desire and a fear of self-closure on the part of a class—the nobility—which has realized that it is no longer the dominant class."[19] Didier also notes that incest provides, in structural terms, a closed situation analogous to prison confinement: "Just as he [the imprisoned Sade] is deprived of all ties to the outside world, so the incestuous couple refuses any relation that is external to itself. Yet while imprisonment is a painful source of deprivation, Sade took pleasure in imagining the solitude of incest as the supreme form of happiness."[20]

Undoubtedly, Didier's remarks shed some light on Sade's obsession with incest, yet they do not go far enough to explain either his violence concerning this subject or the painstaking and elaborate theorizing that he develops to support his characters' views on incest. I believe that the question of incest is better answered by an anthropological reading of Sade's oeuvre. We are thus to enter his work as an anthropologist enters a foreign culture; that is, to find in it configurations that embrace mankind, nature, and culture, and to learn from it other ways of thinking and feeling— a whole new language.

Sade counters those who argue for civilization with the *idea*, to use Gilles Deleuze's expression, of a primal sovereign nature: "In all of its manifestations (natural, moral, political), the law is the rule of a second nature, always linked to the demands of conservation, and which usurps true sovereignty.... Yet it is precisely this primal nature that can never be expressed: only the second nature constitutes the world of experience.... It is for this reason that primal nature is necessarily the object of an *Idea*."[21]

---

[18] See on this topic Georges Benrekassa, "Loi naturelle et loi civile: L'idéologie des lumières et la prohibition de l'inceste," in *Le concentrique et l'excentrique: Marges des lumières* (Paris: Payot, 1980), 183–209.

[19] Didier, *Sade*, 37.

[20] Ibid., 36–37.

[21] Gilles Deleuze, *Présentation de Sacher Masoch* (Paris: Minuit, 1967), 76.

But this primal nature of ours remains impenetrable, because the narrow limits of culture circumscribe the experiential world. What, then, is this nature? Sade replies that it is a primeval force "without reason or wisdom," exempt from the need to create or to preserve; it is a random violence that not only repudiates human life (*dixit* "Idées sur les romans"), but is prepared to perish as a condition of its own regeneration. When Madame de Saint-Ange points out to the philosopher Dolmancé that, according to his argument, "the total extinction of the human race would do nothing but render Nature a service," he promptly answers, "Who doubts of it, Madame?.... Wars, plagues, famines, murders would no longer be but accidents, necessary to Nature's movements" (*Philo*, 230). Hence Sade confronts us with the idea of an anarchic nature, untainted by civilization, which goes about unconcernedly mingling species. Categories, conventions, and laws— the processes by which institutions are produced and maintained—are seen to be arbitrary constructs:

> Man said "Such and such a thing will be a virtue because it is useful to me, and such and such a thing will be a vice because it does me harm": these are the futile conventions of a blinded society whose laws have no intrinsic reality.... The blind man formulates conventions in relation to the mediocre level of his faculties; and likewise, man invents laws that correspond to his meager knowledge, his narrow views, and his petty needs. *Yet there is nothing real in all of this.* ("Pensée retrouvée," viii, 70)[22]

Thus, Sade attempts to explain our identity, the essence of our nature, in terms of a more essential figuration—a figuration that would exempt desire from the limits and mediations of the social apparatus: incest. As the paradigm of transgression, incest represents the attempt to demystify our cultural foundations, and— by means of the illicit act—to liberate desire in all its integrity. In the same way that the incestuous mother-nature was at the origin of Sade's theory of the novel, in his fiction—and in particular in his short stories—he will seek to unravel the cultural fabric precisely by tracing the adventures of the incestuous family.

[22] "No, Monsieur, no, there is nothing real in the world" repeats, as a leitmotif, Eugénie de Franval to her father, concerning the diversity of moral, social, and political institutions that form the basis of civilization ("Eugénie de Franval," vi, 150).

The Family Romance

Why incest and the family? Contemporary anthropology teaches us that incest implies primarily the disappearance of familial distinctions (the intermingling of kin), which leads in turn to the breakdown of the social and institutional distinctions that are indispensable for the maintenance of social order. In the words of Bronislaw Malinowski:

> In any type of civilization in which custom, morals and law would allow incest, the family could not continue to exist. At maturity we would witness the breaking up of the family, hence complete social chaos and an impossibility of continuing cultural tradition. Incest would mean the upsetting of age distinctions, the mixing up of generations, the disorganization of sentiments and a violent exchange of rôles.... No society could exist under such conditions.[23]

It thus becomes apparent that the mechanism that underpins culture is the incest taboo. This taboo regulates what is permitted or forbidden to desire. Since it is impossible to eradicate human sexuality, society does the next best thing: it shapes and orients sexuality solely by means of cultural laws whose aims are the reduction and elimination of desire's major component: violence. This is the reason society always controls its members' sexual responsibility by subjecting their proclivities (by means of the incest taboo) to social fiats and religious ideals. The taboo drains off "excess" desire so as to protect against its consequences. Hence, by stifling desire, the interdiction transforms sexuality and channels it into a culturally viable institution: marriage, that is, the origin of the familial nucleus.

It is important to stress at this point that the phobia against incest is inadequately explained by attributing it to an innate disinclination for sexual intercourse among close kindred.[24] De-

---

[23] *Sex and Repression in Savage Society* (New York: Meridian Books, 1968), 216.

[24] This is the main thrust of Westermarck's classical thesis on incest. In his book *The History of Human Marriage* (New York: Macmillan, 1889), Westermarck affirms that persons of different sex, living together since childhood, feel an instinctive aversion to engaging in sexual intercourse with each other. I shall not discuss this thesis or the anti-incest theory that states that the mingling of blood relations would be disastrous for society. Although to my knowledge, this has

spite this purported instinct, incest is far from being a rare phenomenon, either in past or modern societies. Ethnological documentation provides us with ample proof that incest does not fill us with instinctive loathing. In fact, the very contrary is true. After all, if we were not drawn to incestuous acts, it would be both illogical and unnecessary to forbid them. There is no reason to prohibit acts that nobody wants to commit. We must therefore conclude that the aversion to incest is culturally determined. Frazer's argument on this subject remains the best:

> ...it is not easy to see why any deep human instinct should need to be reinforced by law. There is no law commanding men to eat and drink or forbidding them to put their hands in the fire. Men eat and drink and keep their hands out of the fire instinctively for fear of natural not legal penalties, which would be entailed by violence done to these instincts. The law only forbids men to do what their instincts incline them to do; what nature itself prohibits and punishes, it would be superfluous for the law to prohibit and punish. Accordingly we may always safely assume that crimes forbidden by law are crimes which many men have a natural propensity to commit. If there was no such propensity there would be no such crimes, and if no such crimes were committed what need to forbid them? Instead of assuming, therefore, from the legal prohibition of incest that there is a natural aversion to incest, we ought rather to assume that there is a natural instinct in favour of it, and that if the law represses it, as it represses other natural instincts, it does so because civilized men have come to the conclusion that the satisfaction of these natural instincts is detrimental to the general interests of society.[25]

---

never been genetically proved, even if it were true, it would not suffice to explain human aversion to incest. To say that incest has disastrous consequences is hardly to account for the fact that it may be instinctively avoided.

[25] J. G. Frazer, quoted by Freud in *Totem and Taboo* (New York: Norton Library, 1950), 123. Frazer's remarks should be corrected on one essential point, however. If it is indeed true that the incest taboo originates in the need to establish organized, permanent behavior patterns, then incest cannot be considered a *natural instinct*. Incest exists only within a culture; it assumes the notion of kinship. An animal is incapable of committing incest or abstaining from it, simply because kinship is foreign to the animal's world. Taboo, by indicating an object and making it desirable, results in the temptation to commit incest. Desire—beginning with the desire for incest—as opposed to sexual need or instinct, is always on the side of culture.

Returning to Sade, we find that on numerous occasions his characters emphasize that incestuous relationships and family feeling appear mutually exclusive to our eyes only because our culture declares them to be so. The study of other societies proves, says Eugénie de Franval in the short story of the same name, that nothing is more questionable than the notion of instinctive aversion to incest; furthermore the incest taboo is hardly a universal law, but varies from society to society and from climate to climate.

> Marriage...to my way of thinking would only lead to unhappiness. ...You clearly warned me how they [our incestuous bonds] would shock the morality of our society...but I was hardly frightened at the idea of breaking a custom which, varying from clime to clime, cannot therefore be sacred....I should deem myself the most miserable of women if I were obliged to marry...me, me married to a stranger who, unlike you, would not have double reason to love me! ("EF," vi, 115, 118–19)

In turn, M. de Franval categorically affirms that customs and mores—in short, only traditions—prohibit the union of close relatives. It was for this reason that he, "a philosopher when it came to women as he was with regard to everything else in life" (vi, 96), had decided to *reserve* his daughter Eugénie for himself, and in so doing to defy only social prejudices.

The act of incest is thus portrayed by Sade as neither inherently dangerous nor evil enough to be considered "criminal." Unable to suspect the universal character of the prohibition, Sade interprets the taboo as a purely governmental or local interdiction: "All is relative to our manners and to the climate we inhabit" (*Philo*, xxv, 62). Yet, his grasp of the taboo shows that he understands its essential function, that of inscribing man within a social and, from the point of view of nature, "fictitious" environment:

> —Because most of nature's outbursts are fatal to society, it is predictable that society considers them crimes....I am the man of nature, before being the man of society; and I must respect and follow the *infallible* laws of nature before listening to the *deceitful* laws of society.
> —In order to support Sylvestre's excellent system, says Ambroise, I

see only one recourse: we must focus on the natural man and isolate him from the social mass. (*N. Just*, xvi, 108–9)

This typically libertine scenario of regression toward a world pre-dating all law, all codification, is elaborated by Sade in some of the short stories from *Les crimes de l'amour* which I shall now analyze. My reading will confront point by point, following Sade's argument, the ethnological views expressed by Lévi-Strauss in *The Elementary Structures of Kinship*.[26]

In "Eugénie de Franval," having declared that mankind must have originated incestuously since its first protagonists were forcibly limited to an incestuous combinatorial, M. de Franval tells his daughter:

> The ties [of marriage], the fruit of usage and social convention, which I view philosophically, will never equal the ties [sexual and natural] between us.... You will always be my favorite, Eugénie.... Was it not necessary to resort to such methods to populate the world? And what was then not a sin, can it now have become one? What nonsense! You mean to say that a lovely girl cannot tempt me [would be forbidden to me] because I am guilty of having sired her?.... Ah, what sophistry!.... How totally absurd! Let fools abide by such ridiculous inhibitions, they are not made for hearts such as ours. (vi, 105, 123)

In his own way, Franval thus identifies sexuality as the site where the nature/culture transformation takes place; the passage from a "natural" order to one governed by "human conventions" hinges upon the incest interdiction. The interdict is, in other words, the basis for social order. This is the conclusion Lévi-Strauss reaches in an ethnological register. The incest taboo permits the transition from nature to culture, or to be more precise, the prohibition is the emergence point of culture: "Before the prohibition of incest, culture is still nonexistent; with it, nature's sovereignty over man is ended.... [The prohibition] is the fundamental step because of

---

[26] In *The Elementary Structures of Kinship*, trans. J. H. Bell and J. R. von Sturmer (Boston: Beacon Press, 1969), Lévi-Strauss develops a socioanthropological theory of the incest taboo; this is the reason I use him here as a basis for discussion. References to *The Elementary Structures* will appear in the text as *ESK* followed by a page number.

which, by which, but above all in which, the transition from nature to culture is accomplished" (*ESK,* 24).

The second characteristic of the incest taboo, Lévi-Strauss tells us, is that the interdiction is the basis for the transactions through which men exchange and communicate with each other. "The content of the prohibition is not exhausted by the fact of the prohibition: the latter is instituted only in order to guarantee and establish...an exchange" (*ESK,* 51). This does not mean that the taboo is in itself the means of exchange, but rather that it constitutes, by its very presence, a guarantee that the social life which will be instituted will be a system of exchange. Thus, before being a negative taboo, the incest prohibition is a positive obligation, that of the perpetuation of exchange. Before being morally culpable, incest is socially absurd. Witness this attempt by a bewildered Arapesh informant to build an imaginary case of incest with his sister—imaginary because he could not conceive of such a situation—in response to Margaret Mead's inquiry:

> Was that [incest] what I meant? That, in effect, was what I meant. No, we don't do that. What would the old men say to a young man who wished to take his sister to wife? They didn't know. No one knew. The old men never discussed the matter. So I set them to asking the old men one at a time. And the answers were the same. They came to this: "What, you would like to marry your sister! What is the matter with you anyway? Don't you want a brother-in-law? Don't you realize that if you marry another man's sister and another man marries your sister, you will have at least two brothers-in-law, while if you marry your own sister you will have none? With whom will you hunt, with whom will you garden, whom will you go visit?"[27]

Thus the essence of culture resides in the activity of exchange. The woman whom one denies to oneself is for that very reason made available; it is the taboo that makes her an "object of exchange" and which brings about her change of status from that of daughter or sister to that of another's wife. For Lévi-Strauss the incest taboo is purely social in nature, subordinated from its

[27] Margaret Mead, *Sex and Temperament in Three Primitive Societies* (New York: Laurel Edition, 1968), 93–94.

beginning to the survival of society.[28] Furthermore, Lévi-Strauss does not attach much importance to the negative aspect of the incest taboo, which he believes *to derive from the primordial need to establish cycles of exchange.*[29] These cycles may be quite complex, but ultimately they result in a balance between wives gained and sisters or daughters lost. In the Lévi-Straussian dialectic of exchange, the incestuous situation of marrying a woman from within one's own group is considered an offense against the equity of the exchange cycle. This sort of marriage rarely occurs, for it tends to create profound social upheavals. As Pierre Clastres remarks: "Social life is therefore a combat that *excludes any possibility of disequilibrium,* for any victory implies that the victor is outside the realm of combat (the realm of exchange), that is, outside of social life."[30] Lévi-Strauss's hypothesis is highly rewarding, since it is indeed true in effect that society is founded on the prescription of exchange (exogamy). It is not without interest, however, to examine closely the nature of the law of exchange, for even if the incest taboo in its positive aspect is advantageous for individuals, it is nevertheless possible that men may not adjust well to exchange. This approach to exogamy, unexplored by Lévi-Strauss, seems to me to be that of Sade.

Close scrutiny shows the laws of exchange to be a repetition of *lex talionis,* for the essential trait of exchange is reciprocity. But what kind of reciprocity? Except in the last two pages of his book where he brings up the possibility that men may after all

[28] "The prohibition of incest is less a rule prohibiting marriage with the mother, sister, or daughter, than a rule obliging the mother, sister, or daughter to be given to another" (*ESK*, 552).

[29] In a chapter of *Violence and the Sacred* (trans. Patrick Gregory [Baltimore: Johns Hopkins University Press, 1977]) entitled "Lévi-Strauss, Structuralism, and Marriage Laws," René Girard stresses the extent to which Lévi-Strauss underplays the importance of the negative aspect of the taboo. Discussing the two faces of the prohibition, Girard comes to a conclusion opposite that of Lévi-Strauss—it is the taboo that comes first: "Positive exchanges are merely the reverse of prohibitions, the results of a series of maneuvers or avoidance taboos designed to ward off outbreaks of rivalry among the males. Terrified by the fearful consequences of endogamic reciprocity, men have created the beneficial reciprocity of exogamic exchange. It is only natural that in a smoothly functioning system, positive regulations should move to the forefront as the awareness of danger grows dim" (p. 239). This is a key point that will help us understand Sade's antagonistic view of exchange.

[30] Pierre Clastres, "L'arc et le panier," *L'Homme* 6:2 (1966), 28.

resent having to exchange their women, Lévi-Strauss sees this reciprocity as a positive, fairly peaceful activity, a respectable arrangement between men, of which it might be said, in a biblical perspective, that everyone has "propheted" from time immemorial. "Then will we give our daughter unto you, and will take your daughters to us, and we will dwell with you, and we will become one people" (Genesis 34:16).

Sade, on the other hand, conceives of exogamy as a process that masks an underlying violence, which all libertines will try to bring back to the surface by denouncing the false nature of exchange.

> Let us cease to be blind concerning a brother's feelings for his sister, a father's for his daughter: in vain does one or the other disguise his feelings behind a mask of legitimate tenderness: the most violent love is the unique sentiment ablaze in them, the only one that Nature has inscribed in their hearts! Hence, let us double, triple, these delicious incests, fearlessly multiply them.... however singular they may appear to fools who, shocked and alarmed by everything, stupidly confuse social institutions for Nature's divine ordinations. (*Philo*, 236–37)

Exchange is thus perceived as a social artifice, designed to conceal the hostility caused by the loss of a personal possession: a woman. As M. de Franval clearly states, "A man does not enjoy seeing another usurp his natural rights" ("EF," vi, 96). For the libertine, a man who yields a woman to another man—especially if the woman is his sister or his daughter—not only renounces a source of pleasure, but renounces it in favor of a stranger. The one who yields is thus doubly robbed. We are in the presence of a conflict that, if expressed in terms of behavior, threatens the entire social system. Society therefore resorts to this system of reciprocal prestation: the exchange of women, marriage, etc., the intent and meaning of which are to deny the hostility that the loss of a woman engenders. The marriage ritual, besides permitting what is forbidden and legitimating what is illegitimate (the free expression of sexuality), does not primarily aim at the creation of an alliance between husband and wife, nor even at the establishment of a political alliance between families. The main function, both of marriage and exchange, is to hide hostility in the guise of alliance, to substitute apparent benevolence for real hostility, to affirm friendship so as to avoid enmity, to substitute peace for war.

Seen from this perspective, it becomes clear to what extent exogamy, by its very nature, is for Sade the fundamental obstacle to be surmounted. The act of exchange, the giving and receiving of a woman, depends on the generosity of the giver. At first glance, the gift seems to entail renunciation, the loss of the pleasure one might have obtained from the woman given to another. However, in a sociocultural context, and seen from a positive angle, the gift takes on the meaning of an acquisition. In his important work "Essai sur le don,"[31] Marcel Mauss was the first to show how the recipient feels constrained by the gift, and how he is obliged not only to accept it, but also to return it with interest. Thus the exchange value of the gift comes from the fact that the giver will eventually receive a greater gift in return. To quote Georges Bataille: "The gift would be meaningless, and we would consequently never think of giving, if it did not take on the sense of an acquisition. Thus the act of giving must come to represent the acquisition of a power.... The gift is therefore the opposite of what it appears to be: obviously to give is to lose, but the loss apparently benefits the person who incurs it."[32] Through the action of giving, says Bataille, one attains a *dépassement*. In the social context, he who gives loses a woman but gains prestige. However, to gain by losing is predicated upon the existence of the other: "the action exerted on another is exactly what *constitutes* the power of the gift, which one acquires in return for one's loss."[33] The libertine, however, does not admit reciprocity. He sees himself as solitary. He denies the existence of the other, for the essence of sexual attraction can be wholly attained only by disregarding that other, who would paralyze the movement of desire: "Superiority is necessary in the act of sexual bliss; he of the two who shares his pleasure, or who obeys, is certainly excluded from pleasure" (*Jul*, 513).

It becomes easy to understand, then, why Sade can only perceive the gift from a negative angle. To be the beneficiary of someone,

---

[31] "Essai sur le don: Forme et raison de l'échange dans les sociétés archaïques," in his *Sociologie et anthropologie* (Paris: Presses Universitaires de France, 1950), 143–279.

[32] *La part maudite* (Paris: Minuit, 1967), 129. For a philosophico-anthropological discussion of this question see Michèle Richman, *Reading Georges Bataille: Beyond the Gift* (Baltimore: Johns Hopkins University Press, 1982), pp. 30–39 and 121–22.

[33] Ibid., 129.

or of something, means losing in the act of gaining, in fact losing twice. First, if the libertine is obliged to recognize the existence of another, he will be indebted to that other; and second, adding insult to injury, he will have to repay the debt with interest, which is to say that one's loss will be another's gain. This, by definition, is contrary to the libertine's conception of his relationship to others: "This sacred law [of nature], which constantly moves and inspires us, does not instill within us the love of our neighbor as a sentiment antecedent to the love we owe ourselves.... First ourselves, and then the others, this is Nature's order of progression. Consequently, we must show no respect, no quarter for others" ("EF," VI, 186). As a result, the libertine who understands the nature of the gift will feel hatred, not gratitude, toward his benefactor. "Nothing is more burdensome than a kindness one has received. No middle ground, no compromise: you must repay it or ready yourself for abuse. Upon proud spirits a good deed sits very heavily: it weighs upon them with such violence that the one feeling they exhale is hatred for their benefactors" (*Philo*, 287). Considering the gift from the giver's point of view, the results are not qualitatively different. To give or to exchange a woman (I am thinking here of M. de Franval's arguments in favor of paternal incest) cannot but be deemed by a libertine as a loss of pleasure without hope of any other compensation.

The same reasoning applies to marriage. Marriage is less the concern of the couple involved than it is of the giver, who exchanges the possibility of sexual satisfaction for a little *dépassement*, for social respect. Seen from this angle, marriage is not only a loss of potential pleasure with a daughter or a sister, it is also an acceptable compromise between sexuality and respectability—hence Sade's hatred and horror of this hoax: "among all the bonds to be broken, I would surely recommend that the very first bonds destroyed be those of wedlock" (*Philo*, 222). He clearly sees that the father as giver is at the very heart of the cultural mechanism of exchange, that the giver's existence guarantees that exchange will function properly.[34] Consequently, with a mind to disrupting

---

[34] To defend this point one might cite innumerable examples in primitive as well as contemporary society. One need only remember that one obtains a young woman by asking her father for her hand (which is not the same thing as telling her that one wishes to marry her). And the final decision—traditionally at least—

exogamy, Sade makes incest the main attribute of exemplary pa-
ternity. The father is the *nongiver* who must break the familial
ties that hinder him from enjoying his children freely; no natural
law restrains him. "How is it that reasonable men are able to
carry absurdity to the point of believing that the enjoyment of
one's mother, sister, or daughter could ever be criminal? Is it not,
I ask, an abominable view wherein it is made to appear a crime
for a man to place higher value on the enjoyment of an object to
which natural feeling draws him close?" (*Philo,* 324–25).

It would seem, then, that the short stories of *Les crimes de
l'amour* recount the phantasm of the primitive father who represents nature in all its primal power and anarchy: "The authority
of a father over his children—the only real authority, which has
served as the foundation and model for all other forms—is dictated
to us by the voice of nature" (*N. Just,* xv, 317). The father is thus
the founder of a new order in which the act of incest determines
the libertine's sexual relation with the other and, at the same
time, negates the other: "The foremost of the laws Nature decrees
to me is to enjoy myself, *no matter at whose expense*" (*Jul,* 99).
Thus a kind of "anti-order," free from prohibition, is founded; it
is this order that permits the constitution of an individual subject
outside the circle of exchange, whose only activity is the fulfill-
ment of individual desire.

The Endogamic Challenge

In keeping with this view, *Les crimes de l'amour* presents exemplary fathers who affirm most emphatically and most often
that nothing must stand in the way of paternal omnipotence.
Franval delivers such a message to his daughter Eugénie; in the
tale "Laurence et Antonio" (v, 171–246), Charles Strozzi (although
only godfather to his future daughter-in-law, Laurence, whose real
father died when she was twelve) fulfills his fatherly function
perfectly. His first concern is to withhold rather than to exchange
his inherited daughter. In fact Strozzi plots against his own son
to prevent the latter from marrying Laurence in order to exercise

---

is for the father to make, just as, in primitive Australian tribes, the prospective
father-in-law circumcises his future son-in-law.

"properly" his paternal instinct on her. In another short story "Florville et Courval" (v, 59–140), the heroine, Florville, faces the same incestuous dilemma. This narrative treats anew the theme of Oedipal *méconnaissance*, with the result that Florville unwittingly commits three incestuous acts (with her father, brother, and son) as well as matricide and infanticide. However, what makes this narrative particularly interesting is the fact that it confronts the question of incest in terms of a linguistic problematic.

Let us observe, parenthetically, that Sade's unfailing punishment of his incestuous characters—Strozzi, M. de Franval, Eugénie, and Florville all die—is generally attributed to the fact that he is writing for a society that demands a discharge of the moral debt. Sade solves the dilemma of writing for the same society he denounces by tacking fake endings onto his stories; thus the criminals are perfunctorily done away with. This observation is certainly justified, but the discerning reader will sense that "something else" besides pure performance is involved in Sade's ending. From the standpoint of exchange, what does it mean for a character to remain in a closed incestuous situation? What is Florville's alternative, for instance, when she discovers that she has never been exchanged in an open circuit?

> Look at me, Seneval. Look at your sister, the person who seduced you in Nancy, the person who murdered your son, the wife of your father, and the infamous creature who dragged your mother to the scaffold. Yes, those are my crimes. No matter which one of you I look at, *I see an object of horror; I see either my lover in my brother or my husband in my father.* And if I look upon myself, I see only the *execrable monster* who stabbed her son and caused the death of her mother. ("Florville," v, 138–39, my italics)

A monster by virtue of her misdeeds, Florville also raises—as do all of Sade's incestuous characters—the problem of the linguistic monster. This is an important issue for Sade, who is always confronted with the necessity of moderating his "incestuous acrobatics" because he lacks a linguistic combinatorial capable of sustaining them. No kinship terminology could express Florville's position in society. To recapitulate, she is the wife and daughter of her father, M. de Courval; she is structural grandmother (being the wife of M. de Courval) and structural mother-wife (lover) and murderess of her son, Saint-Ange, who is also her structural nephew (for he was born of Florville's liaison with her brother). Finally, she is the murderess of the child she bears her father, which child is therefore a structural grandchild. I leave it to mathematicians to calculate the possible classifications open to Florville in occidental genealogies.

What should be emphasized here is the fact that there exists no kinship term that could locate Florville in any genealogical field without generating a confusion of categories which would result in the collapse of that field. Our kinship system is based on a system of oppositions between terms (father/husband/son, mother/wife/daughter, etc.). These oppositions must be sustained; that is, the terms must not overlap, or the closed system of kinship will not function.[35] The mixing of categories, the impossibility of systematization or serialization, would lead to the destruction of social order, since no one could be called father, son, brother, or sister; no one could identify himself nor recognize others by means of the kinship position occupied by each individual. Let us note here that an individual's social status should not be confused with his biological status. We know that biologically an individual cannot be more than one person at a time. But we also know that, for society, if an individual is not located by means of a kinship term, that person is nothing at all, for if one lacks a social reference point, one can have no identity. It is only once fixed within a genealogical field that the subject achieves singularity and can enter into the circuit of exchange.

It is apparent from the foregoing that the incest taboo is a

---

[35] The following article appeared in the *International Herald Tribune*, December 10–11, 1977: "WIFE AND GRANDMOTHER DON'T GO TOGETHER IN U.K. (Associated Press) Mark Goodman, 20, has announced plans in London to become his own grandfather—or almost. He wants to marry his 77-year-old step-grandmother, Mrs. Ray Goodman, a former chorus girl. But a London marriage registry office says that it can't be done.... 'It's not on. They asked us for a license but we had to tell them it was illegal. We checked to make sure but the answer was that English law prohibits it,' a spokesman for the Paddington Registry office said. 'The law specifically states that a man cannot marry his father's father's wife. It does not distinguish between its being his first wife, second, third or fourth. The closest you can be and still get married is first cousin,' he said. In Los Angeles, Goodman's mother, Selma, said that she was shocked."

problem confronting language. Language duplicates reality, reflecting and masking it at the same time. To be the daughter-wife-sister-aunt-grandmother of the same person is possible only if there is a linguistic nomenclature to support that state of being. Sade seems to have grasped that it is in language that incest uncovers its modalities; however, inasmuch as incest submits to language, it is also destined to fail. Barthes has described how the transgression of the taboo results, on the level of language, in the destruction of terminological distinctions: "To make one signified receive simultaneously several signifiers that are traditionally distinct.... The crime consists in transgressing the semantic rule, in creating homonymy: the act *contra-naturum* is exhausted in an utterance of counter-language.... To transgress is to *name outside the lexical division.*"[36] For Barthes, the significance of Sade's text lies in the nature of its performance; more specifically, in its ability to transform impossibilities of social reference ("the act *contra-naturum*") into possibilities *by way of discourse:* "The combinative (here parental) presents itself, in sum, as a complicated detour... starting with various actors, that is, from an unintelligible reality, we emerge through a trick of the sentence, *and precisely owing to that sentence,* onto a condensation of incest, i.e., onto a meaning."[37]

Obviously Barthes is correct in thinking that Sadian incest exists only because language can construct it, and that consequently, it is through language that Sade implements the fiction of an incestuous social order. But there is more to Sade than the simple contrast between discursive intelligibility and social reality. Barthes's criticism—which illustrates the strengths and weaknesses of a semiotic approach—develops according to the axiom "Sade is a text"; that is, a linguistic complex whose constitutive

---

[36] *Sade, Fourier, Loyola,* 137–38.

[37] Ibid., 33. Barthes gives as an example of a linguistic "condensation" of incest the following passage: "He says he knew a man who had fucked three children he had had with his mother, whence he had a daughter he had married to his son, so that by fucking her he was fucking his sister, his daughter, and his daughter-in-law, and he was making his son fuck his sister and his stepmother" (quoted by Barthes, 32–33). This is by no means an unusual example. Every libertine has, perforce, a version of this linguistic condensation. Jérôme: "I impregnated my first cousin; I fucked this child, who was my niece, and from this niece I had this one [Olympe], who is thereby my grand-niece, my daughter and my grand-daughter, because she is the daughter of my daughter" (*N. Just,* XVI, 227).

laws and constraints must be taken apart in order to expose its original figures. The semiotic considerations that characterize Barthes's approach lead him to resolve the problem of incest in purely formal, linguistic terms,[38] whereas, in fact, the real force of Sade's fictionalization of an incestuous social setting derives from his attempt to test the sexual, the familial (social), and only as a consequence, the linguistic logic such a situation entails. In singling out the issue of linguistic intelligibility, Barthes chooses to ignore here (although he analyzes it elsewhere in his book) the peculiar nature of Sadian narrative which actively participates— since discourse and desire occupy the same space—in the realization of the violence it advocates. To have chosen to write the narrative of incest is not an innocent, but a carefully premeditated act on Sade's part, for it means not only to inscribe the phantasm in language's sociality, and thus to give it a "concrete" status, but most important, it is to transform and to activate the phantasm of incest into a practice. Since transgression is neither operative nor satisfying in the register of the real, *the crime of writing* becomes the only significant crime for the libertine.

Thus for Sade the narrative of incest ultimately *founds* incest to the extent that for him violence is engendered through the mediation of writing. We have always known that sexuality went hand in hand with violence; the novelty of Sade's demonstration lies in its giving the same significance to discourse.[39] This is why it would be a fundamental misreading of Sade were one to take his attempt to construct incest within the limits of language as mere linguistic wordplay. It is clear that even though Sade succeeds in producing an intelligible "condensation of incest" and meaningful phrases (*dixit* Barthes), nevertheless all of his at-

[38] In this respect Barthes is very good at analyzing Sade's contamination of the "sexual syntax" both at the syntactical and semantic levels. For instance, Barthes notes how in libertine sexual practices all positions are utilized and exchanged in such a way that each character plays three or four roles *simultaneously.* One also understands Saint-Fond's "semantic bliss" at being able to conceive of six transgressions in one act: "parricide, incest, murder, sodomy, pimping, prostitution" (*Jul*, 266).

[39] Deleuze makes a similar point when discussing the demonstrative function of Sade's language: "His language is the highest realization of a demonstrative function in the relation between violence and sexuality" (in *Présentation de Sacher Masoch*, 19).

tempts at contaminating the linguistic kinship network are doomed to failure, because our kinship vocabulary does not possess constitutive elements that can support the category of the monstrous. What incest does introduce into everyday language is the "nonlanguage" of monstrosity which can result only in expulsion and death: *exit* Franval and his daughter, Strozzi, Florville; as for M. de Courval and Senneval (incestuous father and brother), "They decided to withdraw from the world. The harshest of solitudes kept them forever out of the sight of their friends" ("Florville," v, 139–40). This is the sense of Sade's tragic endings: the task of his narratives is as violent as it is impossible—the impossibility of pursuing to its ultimate conclusion an incestuous problematic in the world of discourse.

But Sade's narrative of incest touches on an even broader problematic, an epistemological problematic that every writer or philosopher who has ever reflected upon the relationship between desire and language has encountered: how can one expound a new philosophy using the language of an older one, especially if the former requires a far more radical treatment? How to produce, paradoxically, a discourse impossible and senseless by its nature (because incestuous) but which would impel the mind to imagine new configurations of desire, irreducible to those imposed by culture? Sade's passion for incest is precisely that: a phantasmatic attempt to go beyond the incest taboo. But the paradox then becomes unresolvable, for the more libertines transgress the taboo, the closer they come to nature (undifferentiation) and the more they crumble away and disappear as individual subjects. To think of reaching a natural state beyond the incest taboo is to fantasize about attaining the unthinkable. And the unthinkable can neither be thought nor fantasized.

How, then, can one identify a condition before the existence of language and translate it into an intelligible scenario? Richer in experience than Sade by two centuries, Lévi-Strauss has formulated Sade's phantasm (only as a speculative hypothesis), as well as its unresolvable contradiction: "Natural man did not precede society, nor is he outside it. Our task is to rediscover his form as it is immanent in the social state, mankind being inconceivable outside society; this means working out a programme of the experiments which would be necessary in order to arrive at a knowledge of natural man and determining the means whereby these experiments can be made within society."[40]

The Hidden Text of the Imaginary

We have analyzed the relationships between desire, truth, and the Sadian erotic imaginary on two levels: first, in the very existence of writing, where the phantasm that privileges the viability of desire over that of the real is elaborated; and second, in the inscription of the desiring subject within a fiction produced by the libertine imaginary. We must now examine the relationship desire-truth-imaginary from the standpoint of the content— allegedly philosophical—of libertine discourse.

"Philosophical" disquisitions play a crucial role in Sade's work: the mere fact of engaging in theoretical discourse leads the libertine to extreme sexual excitement, which culminates in an act of sexual violence; and this in turn incites further theorizing. The alternation between moments of philosophizing and acts of violence thus continues indefinitely. A first hypothesis would explain this alternation as one between sexuality in explanation (theory) and sexuality in action (practice): the theoretical discourses would then represent and elucidate the erotic acts that either follow or precede them. This type of hypothesis has led many critics to a "Freudian" reading of Sade, situating his theories within a speculative history of desire that would extend from libertinage in the eighteenth century to psychoanalysis in the twentieth.[41] Thus Sade is said to have announced various "truths" concerning desire that Freud later confirmed or rediscovered. For example, Sade's notion of apathy recalls the Freudian mechanisms of sublimation, just as the eroticization of the libertine imaginary resembles Freud's description of the eroticization of thought in the obsessive individual.

---

[40] *Tristes Tropiques*, 392.
[41] See Marcel Hénaff, *Sade*, 48–53, and esp. the chapter entitled "Les dépenses du corps," 209–42; Bernard Sichère, "Pour en finir avec le 'sadisme' et sa haine," *Obliques* 12–13 (1977), 70–71; Sophie Mellor-Picault, "Le corps savant et l'érotisme de tête," *Topique* 27 (1981), 5–36; and Piera Aulagnier-Spairani's "La perversion comme structure," *L'Inconscient* 2(1967).

Other possible connections between Freud and Sade include: Sade's program of excess, in which every detail of the libertine's passions is articulated so as to bring them all out in the open, anticipates the Freudian procedure of bringing the repressed into consciousness.[42] Attention to detail is as important to Sade's elaboration of the concept of writing as to the analyst's practice of listening. The Sadian obsession with staging every erotic act within *a descriptive narrative* finds an echo in Freud's own view of psychoanalysis, when he remarked that if literature did not exist, psychoanalysis would have had to invent it. Undoubtedly one could establish even more connections—the Sadian concept of nature and Freud's unconscious,[43] the relationships between pain and the pleasure principle, etc.—which would reinforce the generally accepted view that Sade "is the first to elaborate a discourse on desire in a modern sense (in a Freudian sense)... that is, a radical discourse on sexuality, on sexual desire."[44]

It is curious, however, if we concur with the description of Sade as theoretician of sexual perversions, that nowhere in his voluminous oeuvre can one find an explanation of sexuality. How and why, for example, does one libertine end up desiring his mother or sister instead of someone else who is much prettier and younger? Why does another libertine take pleasure only in parricide rather than in any other kind of murder? Sade never offers a psychology or physiology of desire which would explain or at-

---

[42] We should emphasize the similarities between the text of *Juliette*, which was analyzed in the preceding chapter, and the so-called analytic technique of "free association." See on this point the comments made by Roustang regarding Freud's appropriation of an essay by Börne entitled "The Art of Becoming an Original Writer in Three Days." Börne writes: "And here follows the practical application that was promised. Take a few sheets of paper and for three days on end write down, without fabrication or hypocrisy, everything that comes into your head. Write down what you think of yourself, of your wife, of the Turkish War, of Goethe, of Fonk's trial, of the Last Judgment, of your superiors—and when three days have passed you will be quite out of your senses with astonishment at the new and unheard-of thoughts you have had. This is the art of becoming an original writer in three days" (quoted by Roustang in *Psychoanalysis Never Lets Go*, trans. Ned Lukacher [Baltimore: Johns Hopkins University Press, 1983], 135).

[43] Cf. Marcel Hénaff, *Sade*, 150: "In a naive mode, Nature plays the role that is played in a critical mode by Freud's unconscious—the role of a *topos* of primary processes in which the demand for sexual bliss is affirmed beyond the reality principle."

[44] Bernard Sichère, "Pour en finir," 70–71.

tribute motives to his characters' behavior. Although libertine disquisitions are wide-ranging, desire and sexuality per se are never the object of these disquisitions. And yet it should be remarked that between desire—which is not present as an object of discourse—and discourse itself, there exists a quasi-physiological space where the two intersect. We have already noted the pendular nature of Sadian narrative, whereby discourse activates desire, which in turn sustains and revives discourse. We can only then conclude that the goal of these "philosophical" discourses is not to justify a certain view of sexuality through logical demonstration, but, as Barthes remarks, to arouse sexuality: "The dissertation 'seduces,' 'animates'... in the series of orgies, it indubitably functions as a rest period, but during this rest erotic energy is renewed. The libertine body, *of which language is an integral part*, is a homeostatic apparatus that maintains itself."[45] The "homeostatic apparatus" is of course the discursive machine that serves as motor to the mechanics of desire, and vice versa; the libertine body (that is, the locus of desire) "*of which language is an integral part*" (Barthes's italics) signifies that desire and discourse both occupy the same space within narrative. But if this is true, then Sadian narrative is not a discourse *about* desire, but a discourse *with* desire—discourse occupying desire's place before the latter has appeared and after its disappearance, and conversely, desire taking discourse's place when discourse falls silent.

To return to our first hypothesis, it should now be clear that the role of libertine discourse is not to enunciate truths with respect to desire and sexuality. Sadian discourse exists on an equal footing with desire: both move within a single spiral, with one constantly opposed to the other, but with neither in a position to dominate or to comment on the other. Thus, if we understand the objective of Freud's discourse to be the elaboration of certain truths—whether natural, psychological, or physiological—about desire, then Freudian and Sadian discourses are fundamentally incompatible.

Given this incompatibility, how then is one to interpret the intricate articulation of desire and discourse in Sade? The question may be asked in another way: if the discourses do not speak of

---

[45] *Sade, Fourier, Loyola,* 146.

desire, what do they speak of ? They do, in fact, treat several privileged subjects—God, the soul, the law, nature—and consistently use the same argument. These arguments derive from four basic axioms of inexistence: God does not exist; the soul does not exist; crime does not exist (since there is no law, there is no crime); nature, as regulated order of phenomena, does not exist (or exists in a contradictory mode; that is, a mode of destruction by which it cancels itself out).[46]

These four negative theses define the world of irregularity: the irregular individual is one who recognizes no norm—neither religious (God), nor personal (the soul), nor social (the law), nor natural. He is bound to no notion of immortality, of eternity, of obligation, or of duration which would exceed that of his desire. In these circumstances, if one were to give a positive formulation of such a state of being, the irregular existence would be one in which the individual recognizes no impossibility. If constraints no longer exist, there is no longer any distinction between the possible and the impossible: everything becomes possible. Thus, what we have already observed from the standpoint of writing is confirmed here by the function that these discourses with their four negative theses fulfill: they posit desire as the only viable absolute by enabling libertines to maintain all their desires, without sacrificing a single one in the name of some other absolute.

There is more, however, to these libertine discourses that Sade calls (justifiably?) philosophical. A close examination reveals that the four negative theses constitute a point-by-point refutation of our classical philosophico-religious discourse. From the time of its birth in ancient Greece, the tenets of this discourse have been approximately as follows: "You will only be yourself to the extent that you renounce a part of yourself; you will only be recognized by God if you renounce the world; you will only have a place in society if you renounce your body and your desires, etc." Thus, by a simple displacement of negation, Sadian discourse denies that which occidental metaphysics has always affirmed: God, the soul, the law, nature. But on the basis of these assertions, metaphysical discourse institutes a negative order of prescription: in the name of God, one must abstain from certain things; in the

---

[46] Cf. my article "D'une raison à l'autre: Le dispositif Sade," *Studies on Voltaire and the Eighteenth Century* 230 (1985).

name of the immortality of the soul, one must renounce certain desires; in the name of society, one must not commit certain acts. In other words, occidental metaphysics is only affirmative on the ontological level *in order* to be negative on the prescriptive level. Inversely, Sadian discourse is ontologically negative *in order* to be affirmative in the order of prescription. Whereas classical discourse valorizes the order of truth (things exist as a function of an ultimate truth) over that of desire (therefore, thou shalt renounce), Sadian discourse claims the contrary: nothing really exists, therefore everything is possible, therefore desire desires, and this is what constitutes the order of truth. Sade's contribution to the history and philosophy of thought lies in his having liberated desire from the ascendancy of truth by producing a discourse in which there is no truth without desire; in which the two are no longer separated, but are engaged in a free-playing relationship where they are both opposed and indissociable.[47]

The conviction that unbounded desire and truth are incompatible is undoubtedly one of the most venerable tenets of Western ethics and metaphysics. But to say that truth is accessible if and only if it liberates itself from desire is tantamount to recognizing that the sole function of truth is to master desire in order to exclude and replace it. From this perspective, it is no surprise that Western ethics has come to define its will to truth by its function of exclusion: truth is that which suppresses desire and thus assures access to the metaphysical position characteristic of occidental philosophy, that of being *a pure consciousness*—that moment of consciousness at which desire constitutes itself as a pure desire for knowledge, whereby the quest for knowledge becomes a closed, self-sustained enterprise. Sade's discourse is carefully constructed so as to overturn this metaphysical position, which Foucault calls the sovereignty of the philosophical subject:

[47] Schematically, one could say that we have known four types of discourses in the history of occidental knowledge. At one extreme is the discourse of the unconscious, which according to Freud is entirely affirmative (at the level both of consciousness and of desire). At the other extreme, we have the schizophrenic discourse, which is entirely negative (the world does not exist, I do not exist, others do not exist, and consequently I desire nothing—the negation of self and of desire). And in between, is located the couple composed of metaphysical discourse (which affirms within the order of truth and denies within the order of desire) and its obverse, libertine, or perverse discourse.

This experience forms the exact reversal of the movement which has sustained the wisdom of the West at least since the time of Socrates, that is, the wisdom to which philosophical language promised the serene unity of a subjectivity which would triumph in it, having been fully constituted by it and through it. But if the language of philosophy is one in which the philosopher's ... subjectivity is discarded, then not only is wisdom meaningless as the philosopher's form of composition and reward, but in the expiration of philosophical language a possibility inevitably arises ... the possibility of the mad philosopher.[48]

Sade's text realizes the figure of the "mad philosopher," alienated in language, by investing his libertine characters with a "limitless" discourse—a discourse that is perpetually transgressive by virtue of its attempts both to restore the truth function of desire and to reactivate the desiring function of truth.

Thus, contrary to what is often said, Sade's work does not provoke criminal behavior; it provokes instead the elaboration of phantasms that have long remained excluded from our—ascetic and incorrigibly ethical—occidental imaginary. And since writing is for Sade the repository for those phantasms that society represses in order to function, it is writing that provides the starting point of the Sadian imaginary—which in turn will acquire an unlimited hold upon the subject and produce the irregular individual. It should be emphasized that even if the "criminal" actions figured within writing remain without effect (since they exist only on the level of the phantasm), the integrity of the occidental imaginary is nevertheless put into question by the new space of thought Sade inaugurates with his work.

It is within this framework that the phantasmatic scenarios in Juliette's lesson and in Sade's fiction acquire their fullest meaning: to bring out the hidden text of one's imaginary. A little like Belmor—that statistician of sensual delight who calculates that a *voluptueux* can corrupt three hundred children a year, nine thousand in thirty years, and that if each child, in the course of his lifetime, did a quarter as much, then this *voluptueux* would

---

[48] Michel Foucault, "Preface to Transgression," in his *Language, Counter-Memory, Practice*, trans. D. Bouchard and Sherry Simon (Ithaca: Cornell University Press, 1977), 43–44.

have more than nine million corrupt individuals around him in the space of two generations (*Jul,* 525–26)—one can imagine Sade fantasizing the constitution of a "liberated" imaginary at a similar rate. Fortunately, the copious lucubrations that worked so well for him have still to affect his readers' imaginaries.

7

"You Are Requested to Close the Eyes": Out of the Barbershop, into the Académie Française

> If in the end [the] hypothesis bears a highly improbable appearance, that need be no argument against the possibility of its approximating more or less closely the reality which it is so hard to reconstruct.
>
> Freud, preface to *Totem and Taboo*

Psychoanalyzing Psychoanalysis

In her recent book *L'homme aux statues: Freud et la faute cachée du père*,[1] French psychoanalyst Marie Balmary attempts to reset psychoanalytic theory along the lines I have been developing here. That is, she rereads psychoanalytic theory in the context of Freud's own psychohistory—more precisely, with regard to the effect that Freud's neurosis about his father's life-style (translated in terms of a personal scenario) may have had in shaping his work, and later, psychoanalytic theory in general.

Balmary's interpretation is guided by the story of Oedipus, except that she traces it in reverse, backward in time from his birth. She unravels the story of the father, Laios, in order to interpret the son's destiny correctly. When Labdacos, Laios's father, died,

[1] Paris: Grasset, 1979; published in English under the title *Psychoanalyzing Psychoanalysis*, trans. Ned Lukacher (Baltimore: Johns Hopkins University Press, 1982).

194

Laios took refuge with King Pelops, whose son, Chrysippus, he seduced and later abducted. Chrysippus committed suicide, and as a result, Laios was cursed by Pelops. This is the origin of the curse on the Labdacides, a curse that forbade Laios from ever procreating at the risk of being murdered by his own son. In summing up the Laios-Oedipus story, Balmary diagnoses three "transgressions." In all three cases, Laios is the transgressor. First, he is responsible for the death of his host's son; second, he engenders a child in spite of the oracle's admonition; and finally, in order to cancel out his transgression, he tries to kill his son.

Why insist here on this banal, backward reading of the Oedipus myth? How does this reading relate to Freud's life? According to Balmary this relationship is the key to understanding Freud. We know that the myth version is quite different from Freud's rendition: Freud ignores the multiple links between the lives of the father and the son, and furthermore, he picks up only the part of the tragedy that denounces the son's guilt. Freud's silence on the subject of the father's guilt is complete. Why, asks Balmary, has Freud retained only the part of the myth relating to Oedipus's guilt, hence excluding everything else, despite definite homologies between the lives of Laios and Oedipus? How did such a tragedy become the foundation of a theory of psychoanalysis— the Oedipus complex—where only the son is in question?

The scene (of the crime?) shifts suddenly to Freiberg, the birthplace of Freud. There, in 1968, Josef Sajner discovered that according to the town registry Freud's father did not marry twice, as is generally believed, but rather three times.[2] Sajner found that, between Jakob Freud's marriage to Sally Kanner in 1831 and his marriage to Sigmund's mother, Amalia, in July 1855, Jakob had been married in 1852 to a woman named Rebecca. However, by 1854, this Rebecca Freud, about whom nothing more is known, disappears from the Freiberg registry. Did Jakob's second wife die, or did the marriage end in divorce? Did young Sigmund know about his father's second wife and/or about Jakob's amorous adventures? Before taking up these questions, let us first return to Greek mythology.

A father rejects his son and attempts to blur his origins: Laios/

---

[2] "Sigmund Freuds Beziehungen zu seinem Geburtsort Freiberg (Pribor) und zu Mähren," *Clio Medica* 3 (1968), 167–80.

Oedipus; a father accepts his son but hides from him the equivocal family circumstances preceding his birth: Jakob/Sigmund. If Freud were to follow the example of the myth to formalize the father-son relationship, it would incite him to develop a theory of the hidden crime of the father, but Freud envisions a different outcome. The modern Oedipus goes on the road to question the oracle, *but on his way to the truth he has a dream;* as a result, something funny happens to Sigmund in particular and to psychoanalytic theory in general.

I shall not develop the full details of Balmary's analytic work; it suffices for my purposes to say that her interpretation derives much of its force from the homology between the two fathers' stories. Freud's "forgetting" Laios becomes all the more significant when his "forgetfulness" is analyzed in a psychoanalytic key: Freud ignores what Laios had done to Oedipus only in order to be able to ignore what Jakob had done to him, Sigmund. One would have to agree with Balmary that, most likely, Freud did not consciously know about his father's second wife, but this does not exclude—as an early manifestation of the laws of the unconscious—his entertaining lingering doubts about his father's amorous life. To doubt the secret existence of Rebecca and the subsequent sin of Jakob, and to repress this knowledge, is not the same as to be ignorant about it. An event unconsciously repressed, which exists only in a dimension of suspicious ignorance, is not an event ignored. Although vague and imprecise, doubt, as a form of knowledge, remains and manifests itself in the patient's symptoms.

Cognizant of this law of the unconscious, Balmary's search for revelatory symptoms and traces in Freud's life takes her through a series of figures and events known to have fascinated Freud: Mozart's *Don Giovanni* (in which the guest statue punishes Don Juan's sexual excesses), Michelangelo's *Moses,* Jensen's *Gradiva;* and on another register, the frequent occurrence of the name Rebecca in Freud's writing, especially in the letter to Fliess in which Freud announces that he has abandoned his early theory of seduction. All of these elements seemingly point to a secret story—phantasmatic or real, the question remains—between Jakob Freud the father/seducer, Rebecca the victim, and Sigmund the son.

The novel contribution of Balmary's book derives precisely

from this reconstituted seduction story. It is from the association of Jakob with the Don Juan (seducer) figure that the author develops the theory of the hidden sin of the father in opposition to Freud's theory of the Oedipus complex, which is grounded in the hidden desires of the son. For Balmary, the Oedipus complex is a late development of psychoanalytic theory which simultaneously covers and uncovers, in the form of symptoms and traces, Freud's real discovery: that the origin of hysterical symptoms can be traced to a *real* experience of seduction by a family member, often the father—*not excluding one's own!*

Balmary backs her thesis with plenty of ammunition, but what concerns me here is less to determine whether or not the founding event in psychoanalytic theory is real or mythic—that is, whether or not Freud's reversal with regard to his early seduction theory is the result of clinical conclusions (reality) or of his obsession with the sin of his father (fantasy)—than to unravel the pattern with which we are familiar; that is, to identify the turning point, the *imaginary scenario,* that permits Freud to shunt psychoanalytic theory from clinical evidence to phantasmatic speculation. To this effect I shall focus on Freud's letters to Fliess in which he discusses first the seduction theory, and then the discovery of the Oedipus complex.

"I must tell you about a very pretty dream."

Freud's early work, based on clinical experience, leaves no room for doubt as to the veracity of the seduction theory. His letters of 1895 to Wilhelm Fliess make this point abundantly clear: "I suspect the following: that hysteria is conditioned by a primary sexual experience (before puberty) accompanied by revulsion and fright; and that obsessional neurosis is conditioned by the same accompanied by pleasure" (Letter 29, 10/8/1895).[3] This letter is followed shortly thereafter by a more enthusiastic one: "Have I revealed the great clinical secret to you, either in writing or by word of mouth? Hysteria is the consequence of a presexual *sexual*

---

[3] *The Origins of Psychoanalysis: Letters to Wilhelm Fliess,* ed. Marie Bonaparte, Anna Freud, and Ernst Kris (New York: Basic Books, 1977). All references to the letters will be given in the text according to their number and date. Whenever pertinent, I have added within brackets literal translations of sentences or words.

shock. Obsessional neurosis is the consequence of presexual *sexual pleasure* later transformed into guilt [self-reproach]" (Letter 30, 10/15/1895). Some two weeks later Freud writes triumphantly: "To-day I am able to add that one of the two cases has given me what I was waiting for (sexual shock, i.e., infantile abuse in a case of male hysteria!) and at the same time some further working through the doubtful material has strengthened my confidence in the correctness of my psychological assumptions. I am enjoying a moment of real satisfaction" (Letter 34, 11/2/1895).

Freud's research culminates in his "Aetiology of Hysteria," published in May 1896, in which he formally connects the genesis of the neuroses to experiences of seduction perpetrated upon children by their fathers. Yet, approximately six months later, at the time of his father's death, Freud suddenly experiences doubts about this same theory that he had announced with such confidence in his earlier letters:

> My aged father is in Baden in a very shaky condition.... Waiting for news, going to see him, etc., have been the only things to count in the last fortnight....I am in a rather gloomy state [I feel a pall has been cast over me]....I have run into some doubts about my repression theory...perhaps you may supply me with solid ground on which I shall be able to give up explaining things psychologically and start finding a firm basis in physiology! (Letter 48, 6/30/1896)

His next two letters to Fliess announce his father's death and Freud's depressed state of mind:

> The old man died on the night of the 23rd, and we buried him yesterday. He bore himself bravely up to the end, like the remarkable man he was.... It all happened in my critical period, and I am really [quite] down because of it. (Letter 49, 10/26/1896)

> By one of the obscure routes behind the official consciousness the old man's death affected me deeply.... By the time he died his life had long been over, but at death the whole past stirs within one [in my inner self the whole past has been reawakened by this event]. *I feel now as if I had been torn up by the roots.* (Letter 50, 11/2/1896)

In conjunction with this last remark, Letter 50 goes on to describe a dream Freud had shortly after the funeral:

198

I must tell you [Fliess] about a very pretty dream I had on the night after the funeral. I found myself in a shop where there was a notice up saying:

> You are requested
> to close the eyes

I recognized the place as the barber's to which I go every day. On the day of the funeral I was kept waiting, and therefore arrived at the house of mourning rather late. The family was displeased with me, because I had arranged for the funeral to be quiet and simple. They also took my lateness in rather bad part.

Freud interprets this dream as requiring from him an apology toward the dead father: "The phrase on the notice-board has a double meaning. It means 'one should do one's duty towards the dead' in two senses—*an apology, as though I had not done my duty and my conduct needed overlooking,* and the actual duty itself" (ibid., my italics). Clearly, Freud cannot avoid diagnosing the need for an apology. However, rather than pursuing his interpretation, he seems content to conclude rather casually that his dream was "an outlet for the feeling of self-reproach which a death generally leaves among the survivors" (ibid.). Indeed, the expression "you are requested to close the eyes" has a double meaning, but not the one Freud chooses to elaborate on. Taken literally, the phrase means: you are requested not to look at, or else not to see what there is to see, which we can translate without forcing the terms of our interpretation into *close the eyes in order not to uncover the secret of the father.* As for its figurative meaning, "to close one's eyes to something" is used generally when someone is at fault and when the witnesses of this fault decide to ignore what has happened. Taken in this sense, Freud is thus "requested to close the eyes" to a situation that, we must assume, hides a past mistake on the part of the father—Rebecca seduced and abandoned? It remains to be seen.

Curiously, or shall we say predictably, Freud returns to this dream a few years later in *The Interpretation of Dreams,* but he describes it in slightly different terms: "During the night before my father's funeral I had a dream of a printed notice, placard or poster—rather like the notices forbidding one to smoke in railway waiting-rooms."[4] The substitution of the railway waiting room for the barbershop is significant in that it transforms the nature

---

[4] *The Interpretation of Dreams,* in the *Standard Edition,* 4: 317.

and content of the notice: what was just a request "to close the eyes" in the barbershop dream becomes an *injunction* in the railway waiting room dream, "like the notices forbidding one to smoke." Furthermore, little notice has been paid to a rather gross transposition that could only be explained, to apply Freud's own remark himself, "by one of the obscure routes behind the official consciousness." That same dream that took place "on the night *after* the funeral" in Fliess's letter of 1896 occurs "during the night *before* my father's funeral" in the text of *The Interpretation* published in 1899. Hence, consciously or unconsciously (it matters little here) Freud transforms the dream content into an imperative, not toward the dead father but toward the dead father still in need of being buried, the father who has still not settled his account with the living.[5] The remark "one should do one's duty toward the dead" as interpreted by Freud, as well as the demanded "apology" and "the conduct [that] needs overlooking," have clearly less to do with Freud's physical lateness at the funeral home or with the simplicity of the funeral than with a symbolic exigency toward the "living-dead"—a symbolic exigency that will assure Jakob a fair hearing on the day of final reckoning.[6] The dream thus proposes the terms of an imaginary contract with the still unburied father, according to which Freud commits himself to "closing the eyes" at the father's request, that is, commits himself to burying the secret sin of the father as the *precondition* for his physical burial. Then, and only then, can the "actual duty" of both burials proceed.

Eleven months later, one month before the first anniversary of Jakob's death (an important date both in symbolic and religious terms) the stipulations of the contract are fulfilled by Freud. "Disturbed about matters concerning fathers" (Letter 60, 4/28/1897), tortured all along "with grave doubts about [my theory of] the neuroses" and "having a fit of gloom" (Letter 67, 8/14/1897), Freud

---

[5] It would be relevant here to cite what Freud wrote in the preface to the second edition of *The Interpretation of Dreams*: "This book has a further subjective significance for me personally—a significance which I only grasped after I had completed it. It was, I found, a portion of my own self-analysis, my reaction to my father's death—that is to say, to the most important, even the most poignant, loss of a man's life" (ibid., 4: xxvi).

[6] "God does not present the reckoning at the end of every week" (Letter 51, 12/4/1896).

announces triumphantly to Fliess that he has taken the decisive step of abandoning the idea of the traumatic role of seduction. On September 21, 1897, in the famous Letter 69, Freud writes: "Let me tell you straight away the great secret which has been slowly dawning on me in recent months. I no longer believe in my *neurotica.*" Freud gives four reasons for rejecting the seduction theory. The first two are of particular relevance: "The first group of factors were the continual disappointment of my attempts to bring my analyses to a real conclusion. . . . Then there was the astonishing thing that in *every case* . . . [elision in text] blame was laid on perverse acts by the *father,* and realization of the unexpected frequency of hysteria, in every case of which the same thing applied, though it was hardly credible that perverted acts against children were so general." In other words, having concluded that there *is* a sinful father behind every hysteric, that the seduction by the father is the *real* clue to hysteria, Freud, in keeping with the text of his imaginary contract with Jakob, obeys the injunction to "close the eyes" and concludes that the seduction theory, although supported by clinical evidence, derives from an unverifiable hypothesis.

I shall focus here on the implications of a significant omission in Letter 69 which occurs in all German editions prior to 1975, and as a result in all current French and English translations. This omission, which according to the editors is dictated by a strict policy of excluding all remarks of a personal nature, takes place when Freud explains to Fliess his second reason for abandoning the seduction theory: "Then there was the astonishing thing that in every case, *not excluding my own [mein eigener nicht ausgeschlossen],* blame was laid on perverse acts by the father.'"[7] Reading this fuller personal explanation not only confirms our

---

[7] My book was completed before Jeffrey Masson's uncensored edition of the complete Freud-Fliess correspondence was published. Masson's own translation of this passage reads: "in all cases, the *father,* not excluding my own, had to be accused of being perverse" (*The Complete Letters of Sigmund Freud to Wilhelm Fliess, 1887–1904* [Cambridge: Harvard University Press, 1985], 264). Most of the unpublished letters by Freud which Masson makes available for the first time confirm the direction of my reading. For instance, many months after his father's death, Freud was still defending his belief in the seduction theory: "A second important piece of insight tells me that the psychic structures which, in hysteria, are affected by repression are not in reality memories . . . but impulses that derive from primal scenes" (5/2/1897; p. 239). It is worth noting, however, that Freud

interpretation of the apology demanded by the father in the dream letter, but it also gives us a better feel for the frame of mind in which Freud develops the sense of having personally faulted—and failed—his father, and the ensuing feeling that his conduct stood to be corrected. Freud's state of mind resulting from the guilt-dream conforms point by point to the movement that led him to his "second breakthrough," from which psychoanalysis originated. Letter 71, written twenty-four days after Letter 69, shows that his insight into the structure of the Oedipus complex was not only the result of self-analysis, but even more precisely the direct consequence of a personal situation involving the father and in which Freud is playing once again the role of the culprit: "I have found love of the mother [being in love with my mother] and jealousy of [my] father *in my own case too,* and now believe it to be a general phenomenon of early childhood, even if it does not always occur so early as in children who have been made hysterics" (10/15/1897; my italics).

Is it conceivable that, three weeks after rejecting the seduction theory, Freud would have developed a "new" theory? Or does this theory represent the other side of the same coin? Only now the Oedipus myth is substituted for Freud's family romance: "The Greek myth seizes on a compulsion which everyone recognizes because he has felt traces of it in himself. Every member of the audience was once a budding Oedipus in phantasy, and this dream-fulfilment played out in reality causes everyone to recoil in horror, with the full measure of repression which separates his infantile from his present state" (ibid.). In effect, it is the repressed desires of the son toward the mother that makes him the murderous rival of the father. Thus, Freud can conclude that there is never any real sin on the part of fathers, including his own; there are only imaginary ones on the part of sons. As a consequence, Jakob's sin toward Rebecca is forever buried in the same way that Laios's sin is edited out of Freud's retelling of the Oedipus myth. The transfer of culpability from father to son that the myth implements is a classic case of scapegoating. Hence we can read the shift from the seduction theory to the Oedipal sexuality as an

---

also seemed to be moving toward a more moral, as opposed to psychological, explanation of the seduction theory. "Another presentiment tells me, as though I already knew—but I know nothing at all—that I shall very soon uncover the source of morality" (5/31/1897; p. 249).

instance of self-victimization by which Freud constitutes himself as the willing culprit. From then on the guilty party is no longer the father, forever protected by psychoanalysis, but the son—and with him all sons.

To recapitulate, the constitution of Freudian theory can be seen to involve three moments: first, the elaboration of the theory of seduction by the father, "not excluding my own"; second, Freud's imaginary scenario centered around the injunction "to close the eyes" in the dream encounter with the dead father; and third, the ensuing theoretical shift from the seduction theory to another theoretical scenario, that of Oedipal sexuality. Curiously, this shift, which amounts to rejecting prolonged years of clinical work, is mirrored on the personal plane not by depression, but by a great sense of relief on Freud's part—literally by a sense of victory that is even more remarkable than the theoretical reversal itself!

> It is curious that I feel not in the least disgraced, though the occasion might seem to require it. Certainly I shall not tell it in Gath, or publish it in the streets of Askalon, in the land of the Philistines— but between ourselves I have a feeling more of triumph than of defeat (which is surely not right).
>
> Were I depressed, jaded, unclear in my mind, such doubts might be taken for signs of weakness. But I am just in the opposite state. ...I am proud that after penetrating so far I am still capable of such criticism. (Letter 69, 9/21/1897)

This criticism constitutes in effect Freud's formal "apology" to Jakob, an apology by which he rejects the seduction (of Rebecca) by the father as the source of his own neurosis:

> Outwardly very little is happening to me, but inside me something very interesting is happening. For the last four days my self-analysis, which I regard as indispensable for clearing up the whole problem, has been making progress in dreams and yielding the most valuable conclusions and evidence.... To describe it in writing is more dif- ficult than anything else, and besides it is far too extensive. I can only say that in my case my father [old man] played no active role, though I certainly projected onto him an analogy from myself. (Letter 70, 3/10/97)

203

It is true that, factually, the father did not play an "active role" in Freud's neurosis. Nevertheless, as Balmary correctly argues, he played a mediated role in the sense that, as we can assume, Freud's neurosis stemmed from a woman seduced and abandoned by the father: "His father would not have played an active role *toward him*. Thus little Sigmund would not have been the object of seduction, but he would be the witness of what his father had done: causing a woman's disappearance."[8] Coincidentally, the name Rebecca appears in Letter 69 at the precise moment Freud renounces the theory that had shown the father(s) to be the guilty party: "Now I can be quiet and modest again and go on worrying and saving, and one of the stories from my collection occurs to me: 'Rebecca, you can take off your wedding-gown, you're not a bride any longer.' " *By one of the obscure routes behind the official consciousness* the repressed truth comes out fully, but only in the form of an innocuous Jewish anecdote that duplicates the gesture through which Freud "divorces" Rebecca from his father's past. With this insurance clause added, the terms of the contract between Sigmund and Jakob are now sealed forever. Freud can finally return peacefully to his self-analysis in order to consolidate his findings regarding psychoanalytic theory, a theory whose founding event is an imaginary dream injunction, and whose very expression—the Oedipal fiction—is itself another imaginary scenario.

We have just seen how Freud succeeds in theorizing his phantasm, by incorporating it into a discourse that uses "real" concepts. Hence the scenario of the Oedipal complex allows Freud to remain in a phantasmic proximity to his dead father, at the same time that it establishes in "reality" a formal rupture between them. Freud is perfectly conscious that the difference between his "delirium" and the theory he produces out of it is tenuous. In this sense, Freud himself perceives the theory of the Oedipal complex as a kind of delirium, but a delirium through which he manages to escape from madness and anguish. By assuming the form of a constituted and transmissible science,[9] the

---

[8] Balmary, *L'homme aux statues*, 149.

[9] François Roustang has decisively proven that it is the process of transmission which has endowed Freud's psychoanalytic speculations (fantasies) with their theoretical status: "The difference between theory and delirium is undecidable at any given moment and at the time of their production.... Perhaps the difference

theory becomes the means by which Freud can submit to paternal authority, all the while that he is constructing a system of defense against such authority. Thus it becomes apparent that, contrary to our general belief, psychoanalytic theory is not the founding act and the point of departure for analysis; instead, the theory is first and foremost a symptom, in psychoanalytic terms, of the fantasy of a single individual: Freud.

At this point, let us consider another founder of a subdivision of the field of human sciences: Lévi-Strauss, the founder of structural anthropology. It would be interesting, in light of what we have learned about Freud, to analyze the founding scenario of structural anthropology not in terms of Lévi-Strauss's personal problems, but rather as a function of the struggle he undergoes— just as Freud does—in his relationship with the theory that he builds. To this end, I shall attempt to undo structuralist theory as one would diagnose a symptom; that is, to trace back, and unravel, the generative phantasms in which structural anthropology is rooted.

The Unconscious Does Fieldwork

"I hate traveling and explorers. Yet here I am proposing to tell the story of my expeditions. But how long it has taken me to make up my mind to do so! It has been fifteen years since I left Brazil for the last time."[10] From the start of *Tristes Tropiques* Lévi-Strauss takes us straight to the heart of the problems that confront ethnology and structuralism. Lévi-Strauss "hates travel," for it uncovers the impossible dilemma facing the ethnologist: either he is a child of his culture and consequently cannot really grasp the otherness he is studying (because his mode of understanding is governed by the mental categories of his social context), or else he is so close to the object-culture that there is no possibility of otherness for him:

---

is that the theory is delirium of several, while delirium is the theory of one person alone.... The passage from delirium to theory or to analytic discourse is the turning point in the analysis of a psychotic. Which is to say that the only way to get through analysis when one is psychotic is to be a theoretician" (*Dire Mastery*, 154). See also my remarks in the Rousseau chapter.

[10] *Tristes Tropiques*, 17. All further references will appear in the text using the abbreviation *TT* (unless the source is obvious), followed by the page number.

And so I am caught within a circle from which there is no escape: the less human societies were able to communicate with each other and therefore to corrupt each other through contact, the less their respective emissaries were able to perceive the wealth and significance of their diversity. In short, I have only two possibilities: either I can be like some traveller of the olden days, who was faced with a stupendous spectacle, all, or almost all, of which eluded him ... or I can be a modern traveller, chasing after the vestiges of a vanished reality. I lose on both counts. (p. 43)

In either case, concludes Lévi-Strauss, ethnologists are bound to lose, for their awareness of lived experience *(le vécu)* is always falsified in relation to its real content and the order that governs it.

How then to resolve the dilemma? *Tristes Tropiques* is Lévi-Strauss's attempt at a first answer, and let us note immediately that one important factor in favor of a resolution is that at least "fifteen years" have elapsed between Lévi-Strauss's Brazilian explorations and the time of autobiographical writing. As a result of this time lag, the sequence of events which the ethnologist's consciousness was at first unable to organize into a meaningful whole acquires, as the years go by, a global coherence:

For a long time I was paralyzed by this dilemma, but I have the feeling that the cloudy liquid is now beginning to settle. Evanescent forms are becoming clearer, and confusion is being slowly dispelled. What has happened is that time has passed. Forgetfulness, by rolling my memories along in its tide, has done more than merely wear them down or consign them to oblivion. The profound structure it has created out of the fragments allows me to achieve a more stable equilibrium and to see a clearer pattern. *One order has been replaced by another.* (pp. 43–44, my italics)

What is the meaning of this new order, and how does Lévi-Strauss describe, under these conditions, the nature of anthropological knowledge and of truth?

In the crucial chapter "The Making of an Anthropologist," in which Lévi-Strauss explains his choice of a profession, he describes the role that his "three mistresses," as he calls them— Freud, Marx, and geology—played in shaping structuralism's fundamental objective:

206

All three demonstrate that understanding consists in reducing one type of reality to another; that the true reality is never the most obvious; and that the nature of truth is already indicated by the care it takes to remain elusive. In all cases, the same problem arises, the problem of the relationship between feeling *[le sensible]* and reason *[le rationnel]*, and the aim is the same: to achieve a kind of super-rationalism, which will integrate the first with the second, without sacrificing any of its properties. (*TT*, 57–58)

But beyond this new definition of knowledge, the three mistresses raise the same problem. All three disciplines begin with situations of disorder—the human psyche, social upheaval, a rugged land-scape—and yet the astute observer will recognize that beneath those surface incoherencies there is an intelligible order that is neither arbitrary nor contingent, but rather the result of a different kind of knowledge: "It was a quest which would have seemed incoherent to some uninitiated observer, but which I look upon as the very image of knowledge" (p. 56). This new order of knowl-edge is attained in all three disciplines through a logical model independent of reality: "The object is to construct a model and to study its property and its different reactions under laboratory conditions in order later to apply the observations to the inter-pretation of empirical happenings, which may be far removed from what had been forecast" (p. 57).[11]

Thus for Lévi-Strauss intelligibility is not given at the level of per-ception or of daily experience; the meaning that must be abandoned is precisely that which is immediately experienced or perceived at the phenomenal level. The meaning retained is that which reveals the essential and invariable properties of phenomena, their underly-

[11] For Lévi-Strauss it is never a question of having the model correspond to reality, but only of determining if the model available is the best one for ap-proaching reality. For instance, when discussing the notion of social structure, he does not hesitate to ignore social customs, facts, and relationships, to the benefit of the conceptual coherence of the model: "It is hopeless to expect a structural analysis to change our way of perceiving concrete social relations. It will only explain them better.... But, if a distinction is made between the level of obser-vation and symbols to be substituted to it, I fail to see why an algebraic treatment of, let us say, symbols for marriage rules could not teach us, when aptly manip-ulated, something about the way a given marriage system actually works and bring out properties not immediately apparent to the empirical observer" ("The Meaning and Use of the Notion of Model," in *Structural Anthropology*, vol. II, trans. M. Layton [New York: Basic Books, 1976], 80).

ing structure. In opposition to phenomenology, which postulates "a kind of continuity between lived experience *[le vécu]* and reality *[le réel]*" *(TT,* 57), Lévi-Strauss affirms that "the transition between one order and the other is discontinuous; that to reach reality one has first to reject experience, and then subsequently to reintegrate it into an objective synthesis devoid of any sentimentality" (p. 58). By rejecting the phenomenological approach, Lévi-Strauss is arguing philosophically against the notion of self or subject that was prevalent in the fifties in existentialism, in order to privilege instead Saussurian linguistics, which offered at the time the most systematic way of approaching human phenomena from the standpoint of the real, but independently of the experiential. The Saussurian dichotomy of *langue/parole* (which is homologous to the Lévi-Straussian opposition of *réel/vécu*) leads to a philosophy that differs from that of the cogito—of conscious reason—because it demonstrates that the signifier is subject to an order *independent* of anything that the individual wishes to say or not to say.[12] It is for these same reasons that Lévi-Strauss takes an interest in Freud's theory of the unconscious, which is likewise governed by laws that exist outside of subjective experience.

What I will be discussing here is not how anthropology as a discipline has been redefined by Lévi-Strauss in the light of the Freudian unconscious—this work has already been done, and it is well known that structural anthropology aims to show, through the relations of opposition that it uncovers, the reality of the unconscious structures that determine human behavior.[13] Rather,

---

[12] "Language *[langue]* is the social side of speech *[langage]*, outside the individual who can never create nor modify it by himself. . . . Speech *[parole]*, on the contrary, is an individual act. It is willful and intellectual" (F. de Saussure, *Course in General Linguistics*, trans. Wade Baskin [New York: McGraw-Hill, 1966], 14). By separating *langue* from *parole*, Saussure draws a line between the two orders. The order of *langue* is perceived to be primary and independent at all times from the individual's *parole*: "Language *[langue]* is such a distinct thing that a man deprived of the use of speaking *[parole]* retains it *[langue]*" (ibid.).

[13] "Thus, anthropology cannot remain indifferent to historical processes and to the most highly conscious expressions of social phenomena. But if the anthropologist brings to them the same scrupulous attention as the historian, it is in order to eliminate, by a kind of backward course, all that they owe to the historical process and to conscious thought. His goal is to grasp, beyond the conscious and always shifting images which men hold, the complete range of unconscious possibilities. These are not unlimited, and the relationships of compatibility or incompatibility which each maintains with all the others provide a logical

I will analyze how, at a theoretical level, when the most unsolvable problem concerning the nature of structuralist knowledge abruptly confronts Lévi-Strauss, it is only by means of an imaginary production that he succeeds in resolving it. In other words, structuralism, or rather structural anthropology, has its point of departure neither in anthropological reality, nor in anthropological experience, but rather in a particular production of the Lévi-Straussian unconscious—an imaginary scenario that I shall attempt to bring to light through a reading of one chapter of *Tristes Tropiques*, "The Apotheosis of Augustus." In it, the cornerstone of the structuralist operation is put into place at the very moment that Lévi-Strauss grants total license to the imaginary signifier.

Ruffled Feathers

Readers of *Tristes Tropiques* undoubtedly remember "The Apotheosis of Augustus," the dramatic fable that concludes the final section ("The Return") of the book. The setting at Campos-Novos is worth recalling. Lévi-Strauss is tired, discouraged, openly depressed. He finds himself separated from his companions (who have been immobilized by an epidemic), alone in the midst of two enemy Indian tribes who are fighting each other and who "were not particularly well-disposed towards me. I had to keep a sharp look-out and all anthropological work became virtually impossible" (p. 375).

He is about to put into question the entire anthropological edifice: does one become an ethnologist as a result of one's profound incompatibility with one's own social group, or is this nothing but a maneuver aimed at advancing one's career by exotic means? Is anthropology the product of an existential choice or of a vocation? Or is it a ruse by which one marks and flaunts one's difference from one's fellow citizens?[14] The internal crisis pro-

---

framework for historical developments, which, while perhaps unpredictable, are never arbitrary. In this sense, the famous statement by Marx, 'Men make their own history, but they do not know that they are making it,' justifies, first, history and, second, anthropology. At the same time, it shows that the two approaches are inseparable" (*Structural Anthropology*, vol. I, trans. Claire Jacobson and Brooks Grundfest Schoepf [New York: Basic Books, 1963], 23).

[14] "It was now nearly five years since I had left France and interrupted my

vokes in Lévi-Strauss a state of corporeal trance that is coupled with sharp intellectual acuity. He is kept awake by this mental activity; images of paintings, sentences swarm in his head; he is in the grip of great instability and mental anguish. Suddenly, one afternoon, amid the horrendous heat and all-encompassing silence of the Mato Grosso, "crouched in my hammock under the mosquito net, which protected me from 'pests' but because of the fineness of the weave made the air even less breathable" (p. 378), the imaginary scenario propels itself onto the scene of his unconscious: "I had the idea that the problems bothering me could provide the subject-matter of a play. It was as clear in my mind as if it had already been written" (ibid.). The scenario occurs here as the final outcome of an intense preparatory work that bears the marks of a partial and temporary dissociation (in contrast to a more global dissociation, which would lead, for example, to mental disorder). Without fully attempting to understand the meaning of the psychodrama he is experiencing, Lévi-Strauss transcribes its content. The finished product is so clearly defined in his unconscious that he knows the whole play before writing it, "as if it had already been written." Thus he goes on transcribing, transcribing, and transcribing: "for six days, I wrote from morning till night on the backs of sheets of paper covered with word lists, sketches and genealogical tables. After which, inspiration abandoned me before the work was completed, and has never returned since" (p. 378).[15]

What is remarkable during this whole episode is that the type

---

university career. Meanwhile, the more prudent of my former colleagues were beginning to climb the academic ladder: those with political leanings, such as I had once had, were already members of parliament and would soon be ministers. And here was I, trekking across the desert wastes in pursuit of a few pathetic human remnants. By whom or by what had I been impelled to disrupt the normal course of my existence? Was it a trick on my part, a clever diversion, which would allow me to resume my career with additional advantages for which I would be given credit? Or did my decision express a deep-seated incompatibility with my social setting so that, whatever happened, I would inevitably live in a state of ever greater estrangement from it?" (*TT*, 376).

[15] The reader undoubtedly will have noticed that the "creation" of structural anthropology, like that of God's universe, is accomplished in six days. On a more important register, however, given how careful a reader of Saussure Lévi-Strauss was, it is worth noting that the Saussurian image of the sheet of paper uniting two independent entities back to back applies here *literally:* the imaginary scenario constituted by the play grafting itself on the obverse of the ethnological material (reality). I am indebted to Pierre St Amand for this remark.

of quasi-hallucinatory delirium that Lévi-Strauss undergoes does not bring about any disturbance in his thinking. He enters a state of self-observation, becoming a doubled personality even more acutely conscious than one would normally be of all that is going through his mind. This sharp awareness of the text of his own unconscious exemplifies the Lévi-Straussian imaginary scenario and distinguishes it from either a dream situation, or plain delirium. In any event, the episode concludes, to Lévi-Strauss's great surprise—is it really a surprise?—on a particularly pleasing note: "On rereading my scribblings, I don't think there is any cause for regret" (ibid.). Of course, Lévi-Strauss only means at this juncture that he has no regrets about the esthetic quality of the play produced by his unconscious. Yet, in fact, he should have no regrets in retrospect about "The Apotheosis" on more than mere esthetic grounds; for, as we shall see, this play constitutes the *manuel de défense et illustration* of structuralism in anthropology.

The play, which is offered as a new version of *Cinna*, presents two childhood friends, Augustus and Cinna, who each personify one aspect of the unresolved "anthropological" dilemma that confronts Lévi-Strauss—and anthropology in general. Cinna is a social renegade, "who thought he had opted out of civilization, and who discovers that he has used a complicated means of returning to it, but by a method destructive of the meaning and value of the choice which he had originally believed himself to be faced" (ibid.). Augustus is the representative of society, who understands that "all of his efforts have been strained towards an end which dooms them to oblivion" (ibid.).

The play opens on a decree from the Roman senate to elevate Augustus to the rank of God. Soon thereafter Camille, Augustus's sister, announces the return of Cinna after ten years of life in the jungle. While pondering the meaning of the honor that is about to be bestowed upon him, Augustus is torn over whether or not to see his childhood friend once again. Camille, who is in love with Cinna, urges Augustus to do so, "since she hoped that Cinna's wayward and poetic disposition, which had always been in evidence, would prevent Augustus from opting irrevocably for conventional *social regimentation [verser du côté de l'ordre]*" (*TT*, 379). Lydia, Augustus's wife, is against such a meeting, for Cinna has always spelled trouble for her husband: "Cinna had always exercised a *disruptive influence [un élément de désordre]*

Scenarios of the Imaginary

on Augustus' career" (ibid.). Let us keep in mind this opposition—Cinna/Augustus equals disorder/order—for our interpretation of the play will hinge upon the transformation that this opposition undergoes.

Throughout the course of these discussions, Augustus has a tête-à-tête with a mythological eagle who explains to him the meaning of his impending divinity:

> Augustus would realize that he had become a god, not by some radiant sensation or the power to work miracles, but by his ability to tolerate the proximity of a wild beast without a sensation of disgust, to put up with its stench and the excrement with which it would cover him. Carrion, decay and organic secretions would become familiar to him: "Butterflies will come and copulate on your neck and any kind of ground will seem good enough to sleep on; you will not see it, as you do now, bristling with thorns, and swarming with insects and infection." (*TT*, 379–80)

One can justifiably consider the eagle's speech one of several variants on the great narrative of nature. The eagle affirms the impure and antisocial aspect, the inherent ambivalence, of the sacred, which can just as easily be malevolent as benevolent. In this light, filth and impurity (the central elements of the eagle's discourse) designate more than something dirty or disgusting. Rather, they embody nature's anarchic qualities—its variable and unpredictable manifestations, its web of incoherencies, its confusionism—in sum, the fundamental undifferentiation that characterizes nature. Thus Augustus will enter into the domain of the sacred not as an individual, that is, as *difference*, but rather as a supplement of impurity which will add itself to all of the other natural impurities: "Carrion, decay and organic secretion [will] become familiar to [you]: 'Butterflies will come and copulate on your neck.' " Natural processes render all beings uniform, abolish that which differentiates them, and eliminate that which distinguishes them; all this occurs not in order to achieve "structuralist harmony," but rather to create a natural indistinction in which the very idea of difference is stripped of meaning: " 'any kind of ground will seem good enough to sleep on; you will not see it, as you do now, bristling with thorns, and swarming with insects and infection.' "

Let me make a brief methodological digression. At every step

212

of the way, structural anthropology seeks relations of opposition and differences. As I mentioned earlier, its fundamental postulate is that meaning is provided by the structure. It follows that to meet structuralism's demands for order, the raw material under observation must adhere to rules of combination and permutation. Unfortunately for structural anthropology—and for Lévi-Strauss—nature offers raw material in which one can find neither the possibility of systematization nor the transposition of a model. Any comparison or opposition, however sophisticated, which structuralism might offer us becomes meaningless in the face of the most unforeseen natural juxtapositions, by which the signifying (culturally speaking) phenomena lose their specificity and their meaning. Whether or not the binary oppositions so dear to structuralism have a role to play, the interpenetration of opposite terms and the mixing of genres which are produced by natural indistinction reduce to nothing the separation that is crucial to structural dichotomies. Thus the eagle's speech is essentially an explanation to Augustus of the confusional role played by the sacred—a role that structuralism is not prepared to admit. However, Augustus/Lévi-Strauss recognizes immediately the crux of the issue—"Augustus, having been made aware of the problem of the relationship between nature and society through his conversation with the eagle" (*TT*, 380)—and consequently he will seek to resolve this "theoretical" problem with most notable eagerness and promptness.

First, Augustus grasps the fact that the sacred of which the eagle speaks is not antisocial, but rather a divinity that belongs to the realm of nature: the discourse of the eagle is *antithetical* to society, and not *anti*social. This is the true source of Augustus's fear: any identification with the divinity would not only be incompatible with his social being, but would also result in his expulsion into nature. His terror intensifies with the appearance of the sacred in the city: "The third act opened in an atmosphere of crisis; on the eve of the ceremony, Rome was swamped by an onrush of the divine: the walls of the imperial palace cracked and it was invaded by plants and animals. The city was returning to the state of nature as if it had been destroyed by a cataclysm" (*TT*, 381). Under these conditions, one can only sympathize with Augustus in his decision to accept, even to choose, to be assassinated by Cinna and thereby to gain the *social* immortality to which he aspires, rather than to join the gods and find himself turned into a lizard, an insect, or a plant! Accordingly, there follows a complicated assassination plot through which, in the murder of Augustus by Cinna, each will preserve the meaning of his past and gain some form of immortality: "Thus they would both win the immortality they dreamed of: Augustus would enjoy the official immortality of books, statues and worship; and Cinna the black immortality of the regicide, and would thus be reintegrated into society while continuing to oppose it" (p. 380). Nevertheless, all is not yet entirely lost for Augustus, and before he has to fix his choice between the two godly options that are before him—the social and the natural—he will attempt one final effort to overcome the naturalist problematic: the political solution.

Let us return for a moment to the passage that follows the eagle's discourse. The text in its entirety reads as follows: "In the second act, Augustus, having been made aware of the problem of the relationship between nature and society, decided to see Cinna again; *the latter had in the past preferred nature to society*, the opposite choice to the one which had led Augustus to imperial dignity" (ibid., my italics). We detect here a not so subtle shift in Augustus's thinking. Whereas, at first, he was against the idea of meeting with Cinna, upon further reflection he decides to see his old friend. Worth noting as well is the fact that Cinna now stands as the symbol of nature in Augustus's mind. This new symbolic association is confirmed later in the play when, in response to Cinna's description of his foray into nature, Augustus is quick to recognize the eagle's speech: "I [Cinna] have eaten lizards, snakes and grasshoppers; and I approached these foods, the mere thought which is enough to turn your stomach, with the emotion of one about to be initiated and the conviction that I was going to establish a new link between the universe and myself.... [Augustus] recognized with alarm that Cinna was saying the same as the eagle" (*TT*, 381).

Cinna, however, as we recall, is neither a savage nor a primitive nor under any circumstances a man from nature, as Augustus would like us to believe. He is only a social renegade who longs for a return to society, provided that it be on his own terms:

During his ten years of adventure, he had done nothing but think of Camille, the sister of his childhood friend, and whom he could have married had he said the word. Augustus would have been delighted to give her to him. But it would have been intolerable for him to obtain her according to the rules of the social code; he had to win her in defiance of the established order, not through it. Hence his effort to acquire an heretical prestige which would allow him to force society's hand and make it grant him that which it was, in any case, prepared to accord. (*TT*, 380)

The gratuitous aspect of Cinna's challenge shows that, in his case, we are only dealing with a symbolic exigency. And although at times Cinna had been reduced to eating "lizards, snakes and grasshoppers," he nevertheless remains, even at the height of his depression (probably caused by indigestion!), the most social of human beings. In contrast to Lévi-Strauss, who was obsessed with a Chopin melody throughout his stay at Campos-Novos, Cinna chooses a more "classical" route: "To fill the emptiness of the endless days I would recite Aeschylus and Sophocles to myself" (ibid.). In this respect, the antisocial character of Cinna is clearly marked in the text—he rebels against society, against order, etc.—and it is only to put this more in evidence that the binary opposition *order/disorder* keeps surfacing throughout the play.

Yet in order to reach any possible resolution of the problem posed by the (sacred) eagle, it will be necessary, for Augustus, to find a "discreet" way to bypass it. Hence in contrast to Augustus, who represents all along the social order, Cinna will come to symbolize nature instead of the negation of society. Transposed into the personal register, this shift is best explained as a Lévi-Straussian vision of the world which is totally social, and which leaves no place, be it philosophical or methodological, for nature. It follows that, within such a vision, the opposite of society can never be nature but only that which negates society—for instance, those who violate the interdictions that uphold its order. It is for this reason that the purely social and cultural opposition *disorder/order* is, for Augustus's purposes, usefully substituted for the fundamental *nature/culture* opposition. Ethnological reality is replaced by a structural necessity. For the same reason, it does not take much for Camille to persuade Augustus/Lévi-Strauss "that he had misinterpreted the situation, and that Cinna, rather than the eagle, was the messenger of the gods" (*TT*, 381).

Hence Cinna assumes the function of mediator in the unfriendly exchange between the impure eagle and society's representative. And ethnology becomes an affair between the two complementary poles of the social order, which proceed to join forces precisely in order to exclude the intruding eagle: "If this were true, Augustus saw the possibility of a political solution. He had only to trick Cinna for the gods to be deceived at the same time" (ibid.). It is thus by virtue of the intervention of the social misfit, under the guise of a counterfeit nature, that the sacred (the gods) will be taken in hand by the representative of the social order, which had not previously possessed nature. This line of reasoning, by which Augustus is fooling the gods in duping Cinna, is a rationalization intended to conjure away the true representative of nature, that is, the eagle.

In view of the resolution of the play, this turn of events provides for an interesting commentary. Having disposed of the problem of the eagle, Augustus is no longer anxious to join the ranks of the gods. He thus backs out of his deal with Cinna without, of course, telling him so: "It was agreed between them that the guards would be withdrawn and then Augustus would offer himself as a defenseless victim to Cinna's dagger. But instead, Augustus secretly arranged for the bodyguard to be doubled so that Cinna did not even get near him. Confirming the course of their respective careers, Augustus was to succeed in his last undertaking; he would be a god, but a god among men, and he would pardon Cinna" (*TT*, 382). By such a scheme, Augustus attains a divinity that will spare him both the unpleasantness of impurity and the risks of assassination. Only one piece of the puzzle remains to be fitted in for us to properly conclude our reading: we need only substitute, for the foiled murder of Augustus, the symbolic murder of the eagle—Lévi-Strauss's *necessary* oversight.

Interpreted in this light, the apotheosis of Augustus is fully achieved. Lévi-Strauss need not even provide a conclusion to the imaginary scenario depicted by the play: "I cannot quite remember how it was all supposed to end, as the last scenes remained unfinished" (p. 381).[16] Paradoxically, Lévi-Strauss's forgetfulness

[16] For a suggestive reading of the nonconclusion of "The Apotheosis," see Jeffrey Mehlman's "Punctuation in *Tristes Tropiques*," in *A Structural Study of Autobiography: Proust, Leiris, Sartre, Lévi-Strauss* (Ithaca, N.Y.: Cornell University Press, 1974), 216–20. Mehlman interprets Lévi-Strauss's decision not to conclude as a commentary on the nature of anthropological activity: "The rudiments of

stems from an excess of knowledge: he cannot recall the conclusion only because he knows "too much." But, in fact, the conclusion to the play had been disclosed earlier, albeit offhandedly, by Livia: "the apotheosis was the crowning point of Augustus' career: 'It was exactly what he deserved,' in other words, the Académie Française" (p. 379).

Some thirty years after Lévi-Strauss imagined Augustus's crowning at the Académie Française, Lévi-Strauss himself was indeed elected to this august body. The interview he subsequently gave to the magazine *Lire* provides a suitable ending to the missing conclusion of his alter-ego's apotheosis:

> *Interviewer:* Is your presence in the Académie a mere anecdote, or does it symbolize your respect for that which lasts throughout the years?
> *Lévi-Strauss:* It is unquestionably the sign of my respect for institutions, for all that endures. I did not try to enter the Académie Française. But when I was asked with insistence, I accepted, for I believe myself to be bound by a sort of duty to participate in the preservation of a value system and of an institution which go back fairly far into history.... I consider the Académie an historical monument that we should try to preserve.[17]

The Consequences of Theory

"The study of these savages leads to something other than the revelation of a Utopian state of nature or the discovery of the perfect society in the depths of the forest; it helps us to build *a theoretical model of human society, which does not correspond to any observable reality*" (*TT*, 392, my italics). The reader will undoubtedly recognize this passage, cited earlier, in which Lévi-Strauss invokes Rousseau's teachings and which constitutes, in its own terms, structural anthropology's own *profession de foi.* It is in this sense that we must understand Lévi-Strauss's often-repeated claim that structuralism reconciles nature and man un-

---

this absence of a (happy) end may be sensed in *The Apotheosis of Augustus:* 'The final stage will never be reached ... the file is never closed.' What is the end of anthropological activity? Lévi-Strauss has asked. The answer must again be: to have no end" (p. 220).

[17] *Lire* 93 (1983), 106.

der the aegis of structuralist science. Lévi-Strauss must consequently assert at all costs that the structuralist model takes priority over all of the relations that it sets up; in other words, he must see not so much a description of the real in the model, as a description of the model in the advent of the real. Ultimately, the confrontation with reality—in this case, with nature—becomes impossible, because reality is elided by the model, which serves as reality's only truth. In order for the model to function, one must eliminate anything that draws attention to the empirical character of facts, especially if those facts belong to "the big book of nature." That is, Lévi-Strauss refuses to consider relations between nature and culture in any way that is not purely *formal*. It is evidently false to think that the oppositions sought by structural anthropology may not exist in the ethnographic material uncovered by the ethnographer. Such oppositions do, of course, exist, and sometimes play a key structuring role in the constitution of social organization.

It remains nonetheless true that every aspect of the social life studied by structural anthropology must, in keeping with methodological necessity, eliminate any trace of nature. Thus, for example, the passage from nature to culture is either a *false* problem that this school ignores—only myths deal with this chaotic relation, and no true structuralist science would deign to consider it[18] —or a problem that structuralist anthropology circumvents, by resorting to the ideological and methodological ruse that consists in the kind of metonymic substitution (natural/sacred/impure equals antisocial equals disorderly) I have just analyzed.

Futhermore, from a methodological point of view, Lévi-Strauss insists throughout his work on the well-ordered logic that is proper to the unconscious: all justifications must refer back to the unconscious in order to discover what makes such explanations intelligible. This rule applies even more rigorously in the case of Lévi-Strauss. His unconscious successfully calls upon the imaginary psychodrama it has produced in order to dispose of any ethnographic knowledge that would be troublesome for the abstract systematizations upon which Lévi-Strauss will found a structuralist theory of culture. What Lévi-Strauss expresses through the voice of the eagle is merely the formulation of a

---

[18] Cf. on this point René Girard's *Violence and the Sacred*, 55–57, 241–44.

discourse that he is unable to conceptualize, yet which he senses to be incompatible with the discourse that he intends to undertake. Hence the eagle is invoked in order that the sacred disease it embodies might be dispelled and consequently replaced by a healthier structuralist sacred, one assimilated to society. Lévi-Strauss's unconscious produces the imaginary scenario required to act as the laboratory model that is so necessary to his general endeavor. Thus, as a crucial preliminary step in approaching empirical reality, Lévi-Strauss must first live the real according to the modality of the imaginary, for only in this manner, and in this mode, can he resolve the theoretical conflict facing ethnological structuralism.

The imaginary scenario provided by "The Apotheosis" clearly illustrates that professional and methodological preoccupations play, for Lévi-Strauss, a central role in activating a powerful theoretical production that excludes ethnographic reality. For even while "The Apotheosis" founds in a systematic and complete manner the theory of structural anthropology, the play "deconstructs" and exceeds the limits of meaning and structure that are produced by structuralist knowledge. This paradox is evident from the play's own structuration. At first we are presented with a variety of differential signs which encourage us to divide the plot elements of "The Apotheosis" into two different camps. Yet, as the play progresses, what becomes most striking is not how Augustus and Cinna differ, but rather how they are similar; in fact, they emerge as characters who have almost everything in common. In the end, the only difference that remains between them is *nondifference:* Cinna is an Augustus who, by chance, is of modest birth; and Augustus is a Cinna who is falsely convinced that he lords over the "bestiary of the city." The plague of undifferentiation which hits the city is, to use Girardian terminology, also symbolic of the impending crisis between the two enemy brothers—a crisis in which the eagle comes to constitute a convenient scapegoat.

From a methodological standpoint, "The Apotheosis" calls for the kind of structuralist analysis I have strategically adopted for the purpose of my demonstration; yet in its very structure, the play exceeds and deconstructs structuralist formalism. Thus despite Lévi-Strauss's effort to do away with natural (ethnographic) undifferentiation, the imaginary scenario produces precisely the

Postscript: Anguish

> Although we are unable to think of the real proper, it remains the essential reference point of our thinking.
>
> Clément Rosset, interview in *Le Monde.*

In the end, what is the link between the theoretical knowledge provided by imaginary productions and reality? Let us focus for a moment on the two authors discussed in the preceding chapter. For both Freud and Lévi-Strauss, theory is conceived as a relationship to a "subject supposed to know" (*dixit* Lacan) in a situation in which knowledge only exists as a lack. For both authors, theoretical knowledge, whether analytical or anthropological, is made possible only by a willful misprision of the truth. Finally, for both of them, it is a real crisis (the death of a father, the reconsideration of one's vocation) that unleashes theory—which constitutes itself as such by working through an unbearable recollection. The memory (the father's injunction, the eagle's speech) which founds the theory is unbearable because it involves, in each case, a *murder*, albeit one that is indirect and one that is symbolic (to do away with Rebecca and the eagle, respectively). To say, for example, that Freud fought off the phantom of his father by debating theory with Fliess would be insufficient. Something else underlies the theory. The death of the father would be nothing and could lead to nothing were it not for the pact "to close the eyes."[1] By this pact, Freud pledges to sacrifice Rebecca once

[1] This pact resembles the pact between the brothers in *Totem and Taboo.* We are all familiar with the thesis espoused by Freud in *Civilization and Its Discon-*

221

and for all in order to eliminate any possibility that the "bad" reality might return. Freud needs the pact, so that he may theorize the discourse of the unconscious. Similarly, Lévi-Strauss needs to "close the eyes" on the eagle's sacrifice in order to theorize the discourse of structural anthropology. *In both cases, the truth of the theory materializes against a backdrop of death:* sacrifice or symbolic murder.

This same backdrop of death reappears in Rousseau's, Montesquieu's, and Sade's attempts at theory. It would perhaps be useful to review, however briefly, the parallels. It is no accident that Rousseau chooses to erect the theoretical fiction of *Emile* upon a sort of symbolic murder of the biological parents, by which nature becomes the infant's mother and the real father is done away with to cede his place to the tutor. Similarly, the two key episodes of *The Persian Letters*—when Rica and Usbek apprehend the hidden secret of despotism—are both intimately linked to death. That is, in formulating his theory of despotism as a form of castration, Montesquieu must subject both Rica and Usbek to experiences of symbolic death: first, Rica faces the loss of his image in the world ("I fell into a frightful nothingness") and then, at the end of the *Letters*, Usbek confronts his sexual nothingness. For Sade, it is his imprisonment—another form of mental and physical separation, or death—that triggers his mental breakdown and the resulting slippage of his reality principle, which is at the origin of his theory of writing. Thus Rousseau, Montesquieu, and Sade provide corroboration for the conclusion we had reached in the cases of Freud and Lévi-Strauss: death looms behind the constitution of the theories of each of these authors. But who, or

---

tents in which he argues that anguish is the fantasized repetition (since the father is dead) of an anguish inspired by the real threat posed by the father to the sons, when he wants to keep all of the women for himself. It remains to be determined why, having killed the father, the sons renounce reaping the benefits of their murder. Thus the question comes down to questioning the nature of the reality that leads to such a renunciation and that remains a source of anguish and guilt for the sons. To schematize—and to avoid anticipating on my general conclusions—let me say that, insofar as it represents murder of the father and desire for the mother, the Oedipus complex is the Freudian theorization of the anguish of castration, that is, the anguish of facing the real, given that for the sons castration is the fundamental threat posed by the real (father). See on this point Jean Laplanche's book, *Problématiques*, vol. 1: *L'angoisse* (Paris: Presses Universitaires de France, 1980).

rather what, is *really* being sacrificed in the end, in order for theory to come into its own?

I shall pursue this question by returning to the examples of Freud and Lévi-Strauss. Their respective imaginary scenarios clearly indicate that theory begins to take shape right after the injunction of the father and the speech of the eagle; that is, at the very moment that each one is suffering extreme anguish. Freud says that anguish is always anguish in the face of something *(vor etwas)*; in these cases, in the face of what? Obviously, each feels anguish at the possible return of the particular thing—Rebecca or the eagle—that he does not want to see: the repressed reality. It should be emphasized that for Freud, as for Lévi-Strauss, anguish is *simultaneous* with their apprehension of the real. If one were to conjecture that, when the real is far away, there is no reason to fear it, and that after it has "arrived" there is nothing more to fear from it (as the dreaded event has already occurred), it becomes clear that anguish attains its culminating point when the real is "on its way." For both Freud and Lévi-Strauss, anguish is the sign of the imminence of a reality that must be eliminated at all costs. In other words, anguish is directly linked to a reality so unbearable that, to protect themselves, those who must endure it reach desperately for a figuration—a theory—which will allow them to bracket this reality before it contaminates their imaginary.

The truth of theory rests therefore upon a "founding murder," as René Girard would say: not the murder of Rebecca, of the eagle, or of anyone in particular, but more fundamentally, the murder of the real.[2] "To close the eyes" is the insurance clause that grants to theory, be it analytical or anthropological, a willful misprision of the real: a misprision that continues to govern and protect us from the anguish of the real—that of real fathers and eagles—and from the knowledge of its proximity.

The above conclusion should not come as a surprise, for it derives from theory's global strategy to impose its version(s) of reality. As I remarked in the preface of this book, the modern

---

[2] See Girard's *Violence and the Sacred.* For a reading of the origin of mathematics, and of geometry in particular, as grounded in a sacrificial murder, cf. also Michel Serres's two essays "Mathematics and Philosophy" and "The Origin of Geometry," in *Hermes: Literature, Science, Philosophy,* ed. Josué Harari and David Bell (Baltimore: Johns Hopkins University Press, 1982).

critical enterprise is characterized by a divorce from the real, whose existence is defined negatively, whereas absence is a privileged notion. If we keep in mind the overall aim of theory's break with the real, we can begin to understand the reasons for our present infatuation with theory in general, and even more so with theories of desire, of lack, and of absence.

First, in passing itself off as a simulation of reality, theory reaffirms the critic's conviction that it is impossible to represent the real in itself. Second, by conceiving of theory as an anticipated or already accomplished representation of the real, always tangential to it, the critic is able to avoid the real per se: the more sensitive one is to theory, the less sensitive one becomes to reality. Third, to confound even further the possible effects of the real, modern criticism has recourse to various theories of lack. In effect, a theory of desire as lack, which proclaims the merits of absence[3] —and the formulations are indeed striking: "desire only lasts the time of its unsatisfaction," "the object of desire is always the Other"—asserts in essence that desire never implicates real objects, so that in the end we should not expect anything from reality. Critics of lack, of desire, and of absence hold the real to be undesirable in and of itself: if desire has a natural affinity for what *is not*, it is because that which *is* is considered undesirable. Our modern fascination with a philosophy, a psychoanalysis, and a literary criticism that are all theories of lack can therefore be explained by the fact that they all accomplish a double bracketing of the real. Double, in the sense that the function of theory proper is to suppress the real, and that a theory that centers on reality's lack of real, suppresses it even more so.

Perhaps this also helps explain why the ultimate winners in the contemporary theoretical sweepstakes are not Foucault, Lévi-Strauss, Deleuze, or Serres, but rather the theorists of lack—Derrida, Girard, Lacan. Their theories reign over our critical scene

---

[3] A remark concerning the concept of absence to which I refer here: as the reader may have suspected, what is fundamentally feared in the real is the degree of absence implied by the fact of death. The essential characteristic of this absence is to be quite real; it could even be considered the condition of possibility for the real to exist. On the other hand, the absence implied in the desire for an absent object is an unreal absence, that is, a phantasmatic substitute for something that actually does not exist—a substitution whose principal function is to protect us from the real experience of absence. For an elaboration of the concept of absence, see Clément Rosset, *Le philosophe et les sortilèges*, 108–10.

because, by being situated at the *vulnerable* point of the real, they dominate it better than any other theory. Indeed, this domination of the real is a part of the great illusion—the modern phantasm— of theory: to convince us that the only existing reality is the one that theory claims to provide through its interpretive grid, outside of which no other reality can exist. And yet for all of its efforts to master the real, theory only succeeds in affirming its presence. For before the intervention of theory, we could only grasp the real through approximations, whereas by ostensibly subscribing to theory—especially to those modern theories that consider the real insufficient—yet using it as a negative foil, we begin finally to apprehend the real.

Bibliography

Althusser, Louis. *Montesquieu: La politique et l'histoire.* Paris: Presses Universitaires de France, 1969.

Anderson, Wilda C. *Between the Library and the Laboratory: The Language of Chemistry in Eighteenth-Century France.* Baltimore: Johns Hopkins University Press, 1984.

Aron, Raymond. *Les étapes de la pensée sociologique: Montesquieu, Comte, Marx, Tocqueville, Durkheim, Pareto, Weber.* Paris: Gallimard, 1967.

Aulagnier-Spairani, Piera. "La perversion comme structure." *L'Inconscient* 2 (1967).

Balmary, Marie. *L'homme aux statues: Freud et la faute cachée du père.* Paris: Grasset, 1979. Trans. Ned Lukacher, *Psychoanalyzing Psychoanalysis.* Baltimore: Johns Hopkins University Press, 1982.

Barthes, Roland. "Ecrivains, intellectuels, professeurs." *Tel Quel* 47 (1971).

——. *Critical Essays.* Evanston, Ill.: Northwestern University Press, 1972.

——. *S/Z.* Trans. Richard Miller. New York: Hill and Wang, 1974.

——. *Sade, Fourier, Loyola.* Trans. Richard Miller. New York: Hill and Wang, 1976.

Bataille, Georges. *L'érotisme.* Paris: Minuit, 1957.

——. *La littérature et le mal.* Paris: Gallimard, 1967.

——. *La part maudite.* Paris: Minuit, 1967.

Benrekassa, Georges. "Montesquieu et le roman comme genre littéraire." *Roman et lumières au 18ᵉ siècle*. Paris: Editions sociales, 1970.

———. *Le concentrique et l'excentrique: Marges des lumières*. Paris: Payot, 1980.

———. *La politique et sa mémoire*. Paris: Payot, 1983.

Blanchot, Maurice. *Lautréamont et Sade*. Paris: Union générale d'Editions, 1967.

Brooks, Peter. *The Novel of Worldliness*. Princeton, N.J.: Princeton University Press, 1969.

Burgelin, Pierre. *La philosophie de l'existence de Jean-Jacques Rousseau*. Paris: Presses Universitaires de France, 1951.

Caillois, Roger. "Montesquieu ou la révolution sociologique." *Cahiers de la Pléiade* 18 (1949).

Callot, Emile. *La philosophie de la vie au xvıııᵉ siècle*. Paris: Marcel Rivière, 1965.

Chateau, Jean. *Jean-Jacques Rousseau: Sa philosophie de l'éducation*. Paris: Vrin, 1962.

Clastres, Pierre. "L'arc et le panier." *L'Homme* 6:2 (1966).

Clavreul, Jean. "Le pervers et la loi du désir." *L'Inconscient* 2 (1967).

Coleman, Patrick. "Characterizing Rousseau's *Emile*." *MLN* 92:4 (1976).

Condillac, Abbé de. *Essai sur l'origine des connaissances humaines*. Paris: Galilée, 1973.

Critique. "La traversée de l'Atlantique." Special issue, 456 (1985).

Damisch, Hubert. "L'écriture sans mesure." *Tel Quel* 28 (1967).

———. *Ruptures, cultures*. Paris: Minuit, 1976.

DeJean, Joan. *Literary Fortifications: Rousseau, Laclos, Sade*. Princeton, N.J.: Princeton University Press, 1984.

Deleuze, Gilles. *Présentation de Sacher Masoch*. Paris: Minuit, 1967.

De Man, Paul. *Allegories of Reading*. New Haven, Conn.: Yale University Press, 1979.

Derrida, Jacques. *De la grammatologie*. Paris: Minuit, 1967. Trans. G. Spivak, *Of Grammatology*. Baltimore: Johns Hopkins University Press, 1976.

Descombes, Vincent. *L'inconscient malgré lui*. Paris: Minuit, 1977.

———. "La vérité du vrai." *Critique* 369 (1978).

———. "Les mots de la tribu." *Critique* 456 (1985).

Didier, Béatrice. *Sade: Une écriture du désir*. Paris: Denoël/Gonthier, 1976.

Donato, Eugenio. "*Tristes Tropiques*: The Endless Journey." *MLN* 81:3 (1966).

———. "Lévi-Strauss and the Protocols of Distance." *Diacritics* 5:3 (1975).

———. "The Ruins of Memory: Archeological Fragments and Textual Artifacts." *MLN* 93:4 (1978).

Durand, Gilbert. *Les structures anthropologiques de l'imaginaire.* Grenoble: Imprimerie Allier, 1960.

Durkheim, Emile. *Montesquieu et Rousseau: Précurseurs de la sociologie.* Paris: Marcel Rivière, 1966.

L'Ecrit du temps. "Constructions de la réalité." Special issue, 8/9 (1985).

Ehrard, Jean. "Le despotisme dans *Les lettres persanes.*" *Archives des Lettres Modernes* 116 (1970).

Einstein, Albert. "Physics and Reality." In *Ideas and Opinions of Albert Einstein,* trans. S. Bargmann. New York: Crown, 1954.

——. "Autobiographical Notes." In P. A. Schilpp, ed., *Albert Einstein: Philosopher-Scientist.* New York: Harper, 1959.

Feynman, Richard P. "What Is Science?" *The Physics Teacher* 7:6 (1969).

——. *Surely You're Joking, Mr. Feynman.* New York: Norton, 1985.

Fish, Stanley. "Consequences." *Critical Inquiry* 11:3 (1985).

Foucault, Michel. *Les mots et les choses.* Paris: Gallimard, 1966.

——. *Surveiller et punir.* Paris: Gallimard, 1976.

——. *Language, Counter-Memory, Practice: Selected Essays and Interviews by Michel Foucault,* ed. D. Bouchard, trans. D. Bouchard and Sherry Simon. Ithaca, N.Y.: Cornell University Press, 1977.

——. "What Is an Author?" In J. Harari, ed., *Textual Strategies.* Ithaca, N.Y.: Cornell University Press, 1979.

Freud, Sigmund. *The Standard Edition of the Complete Psychological Works of Sigmund Freud.* Ed. James Strachey. London: Hogarth Press, 1953–74.

——. *The Origins of Psychoanalysis: Letters to Wilhelm Fliess.* Ed. Marie Bonaparte, Anna Freud, and Ernst Kris. New York: Basic Books, 1977.

——. *The Complete Letters of Sigmund Freud to Wilhelm Fliess, 1887–1904.* Ed. Jeffrey Masson. Cambridge, Mass.: Harvard University Press, 1985.

Gearhart, Suzanne. *The Open Boundary of History and Fiction: A Critical Approach to the French Enlightenment.* Princeton, N.J.: Princeton University Press, 1984.

Geertz, Clifford. *The Interpretation of Cultures.* New York: Basic Books, 1973.

Girard, René. "Marivaudage and Hypocrisy." *American Society Legion of Honor Magazine* 34:3 (1963).

——. *La violence et le sacré.* Paris: Grasset, 1971. Trans. Patrick Gregory, *Violence and the Sacred.* Baltimore: Johns Hopkins University Press, 1977.

——. *Des choses cachées depuis la fondation du monde.* Paris: Grasset, 1978.

——. "Narcissism: The Freudian Myth Demystified by Proust." In Alan

Bibliography

Roland, ed., *Psychoanalysis, Creativity, and Literature: A French-American Inquiry.* New York: Columbia University Press, 1978.

Gossman, Lionel. "Literature and Society in the Early Enlightenment: The Case of Marivaux." *MLN* 82:4 (1967).

Grimsley, Ronald. "The Idea of Nature in the *Lettres persanes.*" *French Studies* 5 (1951).

Grosrichard, Alain. *Structure du sérail: La fiction du despotisme asiatique dans l'Occident classique.* Paris: Seuil, 1979.

——. "Le prince saisi par le philosophe." *Ornicar* 26–27 (1983).

Harari, Josué. "D'une raison à l'autre: Le dispositif Sade." *Studies on Voltaire and the Eighteenth Century* 230 (1985).

——, ed. *Textual Strategies.* Ithaca, N.Y.: Cornell University Press, 1979.

Harari, Josué, and Jane McLelland. "Montesquieu." In George Stade, ed., *European Writers: The Age of Reason and the Enlightenment.* New York: Scribner's, 1984.

Hénaff, Marcel. *Sade: L'invention du corps libertin.* Paris: Presses Universitaires de France, 1978.

Holton, Gerald. *Thematic Origins of Scientific Thought: Kepler to Einstein.* Cambridge, Mass.: Harvard University Press, 1973.

——. *The Scientific Imagination: Case Studies.* London and New York: Cambridge University Press, 1978.

Huet, Marie-Hélène. *Rehearsing the Revolution: The Staging of Marat's Death.* Berkeley and Los Angeles: University of California Press, 1982.

Jimack, Peter. *La Genèse et la rédaction de* L'Emile *de Jean-Jacques Rousseau. Studies on Voltaire and the Eighteenth Century* 13 (1960).

——. "Rousseau and the Primacy of the Self." *Studies on Voltaire and the Eighteenth Century* 32 (1965).

Juranville, Alain. *Lacan et la philosophie.* Paris: Presses Universitaires de France, 1984.

Kempf, Roger. *Sur le corps romanesque.* Paris: Seuil, 1968.

Klossowski, Pierre. *Sade mon prochain.* Paris: Seuil, 1967.

Lacan, Jacques. *Ecrits.* Paris: Seuil, 1966.

——. *Séminaire* XI. Paris: Seuil, 1973.

Laplanche, Jean. *Problématiques,* Vol. I, *L'angoisse.* Paris: Presses Universitaires de France, 1980.

Lévi-Strauss, Claude. *Les structures élémentaires de la parenté.* Paris, The Hague: Mouton, 1967. Trans. J. H. Bell and J. R. von Sturmer, *The Elementary Structures of Kinship.* Boston: Beacon Press, 1969.

——. *Tristes Tropiques.* Paris: Plon, 1955. Trans. John and Doreen Weightman. New York: Atheneum, 1974.

——. *Anthropologie structurale,* I and II. Paris: Plon, 1958, 1973. Trans. Claire Jacobson and Brooks Grundfest Schoepf, *Structural Anthropology,* I and M. Layton for S.A. II. New York: Basic Books, 1963, 1976.

Lire 93 (1983).

Lotringer, Sylvère. "Le roman impossible." *Poétique* 3 (1970).

Loy, J. Robert. *Montesquieu.* New York: Twayne, 1968.

McDonald, Christie. *The Dialogue of Writing: Essays in Eighteenth-Century French Literature.* Waterloo, Ontario: Wilfrid Laurier University Press, 1984.

McLelland, Jane. "Metaphor in Montesquieu's Theoretical Writings." *Studies on Voltaire and the Eighteenth Century* 199 (1981).

Malinowski, Bronislaw. *Sex and Repression in Savage Society.* New York: Meridian Books, 1968.

Mannoni, Octave. *Clefs pour l'imaginaire ou l'autre scène.* Paris: Seuil, 1970.

———. *Ça n'empêche pas d'exister.* Paris: Seuil, 1982.

Marivaux, Pierre Carlet de Chamblain de. *La vie de Marianne. Romans.* Paris: Pléiade, 1949. Trans. W. H. McBurney and M. F. Shugrue, *The Virtuous Orphan.* Carbondale, Ill.: Southern Illinois University Press, 1965.

Mauss, Marcel. *Sociologie et anthropologie.* Paris: Presses Universitaires de France, 1950.

May, Georges. *Le dilemme du roman au XVIIIᵉ siècle.* Paris: Presses Universitaires de France, 1963.

Mead, Margaret. *Sex and Temperament in Three Primitive Societies.* New York: Laurel Edition, 1968.

Mehlman, Jeffrey. *A Structural Study of Autobiography: Proust, Leiris, Sartre, Lévi-Strauss.* Ithaca, N.Y.: Cornell University Press, 1974.

Mellor-Picault, Sophie. "Le corps savant et l'érotisme de tête." *Topique* 27 (1981).

Miller, Nancy K. *The Heroine's Text: Readings in the French and English Novel, 1722–1782.* New York: Columbia University Press, 1980.

Montesquieu, Charles-Louis de Secondat, Baron de la Brède et de. *Discours sur l'usage des glandes rénales; Observations sur l'histoire naturelle; Mes pensées; Oeuvres complètes,* vol. I. Paris: Pléiade, 1951.

———. *Les lettres persanes. Oeuvres complètes,* vol. I. Paris: Pléiade, 1951. Trans. J. Robert Loy, *The Persian Letters.* New York: Meridian Books, 1961.

———. *Considérations sur les causes de la grandeur des Romains et de leur décadence. Oeuvres complétes,* vol. II. Paris: Pléiade, 1951. Trans. David Lowenthal, *Considerations on the Causes of the Greatness of the Romans and Their Decline.* New York: Free Press, 1965.

———. *De l'esprit des lois. Oeuvres complètes,* vol. II. Paris: Pléiade, 1951. Trans. David Wallace Carrithers, *The Spirit of Laws.* A Compendium of the First English Edition. Berkeley: University of California Press, 1977.

Oppenheimer, Robert. *Robert Oppenheimer: Letters and Recollections.* Ed. Alice Kimball Smith and Charles Weiner. Cambridge, Mass.: Harvard University Press, 1980.

Ortigues, Edmond. *L'Oedipe africain.* Paris: Plon, 1966.

Poulet, Georges. "Marivaux." In *La distance intérieure.* Paris: Plon, 1952.

Ranum, Orest. "Personality and Politics in the *Persian Letters.*" *Political Science Quarterly* 84:4 (1969).

Richman, Michèle. *Reading Georges Bataille: Beyond the Gift.* Baltimore: Johns Hopkins University Press, 1982.

Robert, Marthe. *Roman des origines et origines du roman.* Paris: Grasset, 1972.

Roger, Jacques. *Les sciences de la vie dans la pensée française du* xviii*e siècle.* Paris: Armand Colin, 1963.

Roger, Philippe. *Sade: La philosophie dans le pressoir.* Paris: Grasset, 1976.

Rosbottom, Ronald. *Marivaux's Novels.* Rutherford, N.J.: Fairleigh Dickinson University Press, 1974.

Rosset, Clément. *Le réel: Traité de l'idiotie.* Paris: Minuit, 1977.

———. *Le philosophe et les sortilèges.* Paris: Minuit, 1985.

Rousseau, Jean-Jacques. *Les confessions. Oeuvres complètes,* vol. i. Paris: Pléiade, 1964. Trans. Ernest Rhys, *Confessions.* London: J. M. Dent, 1931.

———. *La nouvelle Héloïse. Oeuvres complètes,* vol. ii. Paris: Pléiade, 1964. Trans. Judith H. McDowell, *Julie, or The New Eloise.* University Park: Pennsylvania State University Press, 1968.

———. *Pygmalion. Oeuvres complètes,* vol. ii. Paris: Pléiade, 1964.

———. *Correspondance complète de Jean Jacques Rousseau.* Ed. R. A. Leigh. Oxford: Voltaire Foundation, 1965–.

———. *Emile. Oeuvres complètes,* vol. iv. Paris: Pléiade, 1969. Trans. Allan Bloom *Emile, or On Education.* New York: Basic Books, 1979.

Rousset, Jean. "Marivaux ou la structure du double registre." In *Forme et signification.* Paris: José Corti, 1962.

———. *Narcisse romancier.* Paris: José Corti, 1973.

Roustang, François. *Un destin si funeste.* Paris: Minuit, 1976. Trans. Ned Lukacher, *Dire Mastery: Discipleship from Freud to Lacan.* Baltimore: Johns Hopkins University Press, 1982.

———. "L'interlocuteur du solitaire." *Revue de l'Institut de Sociologie* 1–2 (1982).

———. *Elle ne le lâche plus...* Paris: Minuit, 1980. Trans. Ned Lukacher, *Psychoanalysis Never Lets Go.* Baltimore: Johns Hopkins University Press, 1983.

———. "L'illusion lacanienne." *Critique* 456 (1985).

Sade, Donatien Alphonse François Xavier, le Marquis de. *Lettres choisies du Marquis de Sade*. Paris: Pauvert, 1963.

——. *Oeuvres complètes.* 35 volumes. Paris: Pauvert, 1956–70. Trans. Richard Seaver and Anstryn Wainhouse, *Justine* and *Philosophy in the Bedroom*. New York: Grove Press, 1965. Trans. Austryn Wainhouse, *Juliette.* New York: Grove Press, 1976.

Sade, écrire la crise. Ed. Michel Camus and Philippe Roger. (Colloque de Cerisy 1981). Paris: Belfond, 1983.

Safouan, Moustafa. *Jacques Lacan et la question de la formation des analystes.* Paris: Seuil, 1983.

Saïd, Edward. *Beginnings: Intentions and Method*. New York: Basic Books, 1975.

——. *Orientalism.* New York: Pantheon, 1978.

——. *The World, the Text, and the Critic.* Cambridge, Mass.: Harvard University Press, 1983.

Sartre, Jean-Paul. *L'imagination.* Paris: Felix Alcan, 1936.

——. *L'imaginaire.* Paris: Gallimard, 1940.

——. *L'être et le néant.* Paris: Gallimard, 1943. Trans. Hazel E. Barnes, *Being and Nothingness: An Essay in Phenomenological Ontology.* New York: Philosophical Library, 1956.

Saussure, Ferdinand de. *Cours de linguistique générale.* Paris: Payot, 1972. Trans. Wade Baskin, *Course in General Linguistics.* New York: McGraw-Hill, 1966.

Schlanger, Judith. *L'invention intellectuelle.* Paris: Fayard, 1983.

Schwartz, Joel. *The Sexual Politics of Jean-Jacques Rousseau.* Chicago: University of Chicago Press, 1984.

Serres, Michel. *Hermes: Literature, Science, Philosophy.* Ed. Josué Harari and David Bell. Baltimore: Johns Hopkins University Press, 1982.

Sichère, Bernard. "Pour en finir avec le 'sadisme' et sa haine." *Obliques* 12–13 (1977).

Singerman, Alan J. "Réflexions sur une métaphore: Le sérail dans *Les lettres persanes.*" *Studies on Voltaire and the Eighteenth Century* 185 (1980).

Sollers, Philippe. *Logiques.* Paris: Seuil, 1968.

Spitzer, Leo. "A propos de *La vie de Marianne.* (Lettre à M. Georges Poulet)." *Romanic Review* 44:2 (1953).

——. *Linguistics and Literary History: Essays in Stylistics.* Princeton, N.J.: Princeton University Press, 1967.

Starobinski, Jean. *Montesquieu par lui-même.* Paris: Seuil, 1953.

——. *Jean-Jacques Rousseau: La transparence et l'obstacle.* Paris: Gallimard, 1957.

——. *L'oeil vivant* II: *La relation critique.* Paris: Gallimard, 1970.

——. "*Les lettres persanes:* Apparence et essence." *Neohelicon* 2 (1974). Reprinted as the preface to the Gallimard edition of *Les lettres persanes.*

——. "La littérature, le texte et l'interprète." In Jacques Le Goff and Pierre Nora, eds., *Faire de l'histoire: Nouvelles approches.* Paris: Gallimard, 1974.

Todorov, Tzvetan. "Réflexions sur *Les lettres persanes.*" *Romanic Review* 74:3 (1983).

Tort, Michel. "L'effet Sade." *Tel Quel* 28 (1967).

Valéry, Paul. "Préface aux *Lettres persanes.*" *Variété* II. Paris: Gallimard, 1930.

Varney, M., ed. *Abrégé de toutes les sciences à l'usage des enfants.* Nouvelle édition. Paris: chez Volland, 1790.

Vartanian, Aram. "Eroticism and Politics in the *Lettres persanes.*" *Romanic Review* 60 (1969).

Voltaire, Jean-Marie Arouet, dit de. *Mélanges.* Paris: Pléiade, 1961.

Wahl, François, ed. *Qu'est-ce que le structuralisme?* Paris: Seuil, 1968.

White, Hayden. *Tropics of Discourse: Essays in Cultural Criticism.* Baltimore: Johns Hopkins University Press, 1978.

Name Index

Name Index

Gearhart, Suzanne, 91n
Geertz, Clifford, 35n
Girard, René, 19, 28n, 34n, 177n, 218n, 219, 223–224
Gossman, Lionel, 28n, 70n
Grosrichard, Alain, 73n, 106n, 125n

Heine, Maurice, 161
Hénaff, Marcel, 144n, 153n, 187n, 188
Holton, Gerald, 39–40, 41n
Huet, Marie Hélène, 63n

International Herald Tribune, 183n

Jordan, R. J. P., 103n

Kempf, Roger, 89n
Klossowski, Pierre, 137n, 146, 152, 156

Lacan, Jacques, 19–20, 36n, 59n, 109, 127, 130–132, 162, 221, 224; Ecole Freudienne de Paris, 130
Lafayette, Madame de, 134
La Mettrie, J. O. de, 113
Laplanche, Jean, 222n
Lévi-Strauss, Claude, 14–19, 36, 45n, 62–65, 161, 186–187, 205–224; The Elementary Structures of Kinship, 175–178; Structural Anthropology, 207–208; Tristes Tropiques, 14–15, 205–207, 209–220
Loy, J. Robert, 79n
Loyola, Ignatius, 144

McDonald, Christie, 125
Mach, Ernst, 42
Malinowski, Bronislaw, 172
Mannoni, Octave, 57, 140n
Marivaux, P. C. de Chamblain de, 25, 27, 31–33, 36, 67; The Virtuous Orphan, 25–27, 30–32, 67–68
Marx, Karl, 206, 209n
Masson, Jeffrey, 201n
Mauss, Marcel, 179
Mead, Margaret, 176
Mehlman, Jeffrey, 216n
Mellor-Picault, Sophie, 187n
Miller, Nancy, 28n
Mirabeau, H. G. R. de, 112n
Montesquieu, Baron de, 14, 17–18, 21, 45–46, 50–55, 58, 62–63, 67–101, 222; Considerations on the Causes of the Greatness of the Romans, 96–97; Observations on Natural

History, 93–95; Persian Letters, 68–91; The Spirit of Laws, 52–55, 72, 95–101

Newton, Isaac, 43–45

Oppenheimer, Robert, 41

Pascal, Blaise, 55, 60
Planck, Max, 42n
Poincaré, Henri, 40–42
Poulet, Georges, 27, 31

Ranum, Orest, 85n
Raynal, Abbé, 45
Repton, Humphry, 121n
Richardson, Samuel, 134–135
Richman, Michèle, 179n
Roger, Philippe, 154n, 164n
Rosbottom, Ronald, 28n
Rosset, Clément, 19, 48, 56, 59n, 221, 224n
Rousseau, Jean-Jacques, 17–18, 36, 45–51, 58, 60, 62–64, 102–132, 217, 222; Emile, 47–50, 102–127; The New Eloise, 121
Roustang, François, 127–132, 188n, 204n

Sade, D. A. F. de, 17–18, 36, 57, 62–65, 133–193, 222; Les Crimes de l'amour, 174–183; "Idée sur les romans," 134–136, 167–169; Juliette, 138–160; Letters, 161–166
Saïd, Edward, 23n
Saint Amand, Pierre, 210n
Sajner, Josef, 195
Sartre, Jean Paul, 28n, 29–30, 33, 36, 56; Being and Nothingness, 28–33
Saussure, Ferdinand de, 208n, 210n
Schlanger, Judith, 44n
Serres, Michel, 223n, 224
Sichère, Bernard, 187n, 188
Singerman, Alan, 89n
Sollers, Philippe, 168n
Spitzer, Leo, 27, 31, 37
Starobinski, Jean, 24, 81n, 88n, 114n, 115n, 125n, 128n
Sterne, Laurence, 136

Tort, Michel, 152n, 167n

Ulmer, Gregory, 121n

Valéry, Paul, 69, 70n, 79
Varney, M., 16
Vartanian, Aram, 92n
Voltaire, 21, 51, 55n

Westermarck, E. A., 172n

Subject Index

Apathy: and nature, 168–169; in Sade's life, 165; in Sade's narrative, 140, 145–147

Bad faith: Marivaudian, 30–32; Sartrian, 28–30. *See also* Good faith; Sincerity
Body: as idol, 83; in Montesquieu's political imaginary, 92, 96–101; as object of faith, 81–84; in seraglio, 72, 74

Castration. *See* Body; Despotism
Critic: as interpreter, 24; as producer of text, 23
Criticism: as academic therapy, 23; traditional versus modern, 21–23

Deconstruction, 21–22
Demand: in Lacanian psychoanalysis, 132; in pedagogy, 109–110. *See also* Desire; Need
Desire: Freud's theory of, 187–188; and libertine discourse, 140–144; and need, 173n; Sade's psychology of, 188–189; in Western ethics, 190–192
Despotism: and authority, 71; and castration, 99–101; imaginary of, 86–89; and reality principle, 81
Discipleship: in Lacanian psychoanalysis, 130–132; in pedagogy, 127–128

Endogamy: Sadian, 177–181
Eroticism: and *jouissance*, 145; of the mind, 145–148, 150–155; and perversion, 147–148
Exogamy: Lévi-Straussian, 176–178

Gift: Mauss's theory of, 179; Sade's theory of, 180–183
Good faith: Marivaudian, 26–27, 31–33, 67. *See also* Bad faith; Sincerity

Image: loss of life as loss of, 69; virtual versus real, 68–69
Imaginary: as countercode of reality, 57–62; in despotism, 86–89; difference from imagination, 60; dreamlike, 60–61, 124–127; and economy of the seraglio, 79–81; eunuch's, 77–78; Freud's, 65, 199–201; of irregular individual, 156–159; Lacan's, 59; Lévi-Strauss's, 65; Montesquieu's, 55, 63, 74, 96–101; of pedagogy, 126–127; as pre-text of theory, 17–19; Rousseau's, 64;

Library of Congress Cataloging-in-Publication Data

Harari, Josué V.
  Scenarios of the imaginary.
  Bibliography: p.
  Includes index.
  1. French literature—18th century—History and criticism—Theory, etc. 2. Enlightenment. 3. France—Intellectual life—18th century. 4. Criticism—France—History—18th century. I. Title.
PQ261.H37 1987   840'.9'005   86-24247
ISBN 0-8014-1842-9 (alk. paper)